THE SKY IS ALWAYS THERE

After their release from captivity Camilla Carr and Jonathan James returned to Britain and married. They now live in Devon. Camilla gives talks and workshops using their story as a focal point for debating the nature of conflict and forgiveness. Jon is following his dream of eco building.

Jon and Camilla both feature in www.theforgivenessproject.com which aims to reframe the debate about how individuals and communities can learn to celebrate difference and overcome division, thereby fostering positive social change.

The Sky is Always There

SURVIVING A KIDNAPPING IN CHECHNYA

Camilla Carr and Jonathan James

CANTERBURY
PRESS

Norwich

© Camilla Carr and Jonathan James 2008

First published in 2008 by the Canterbury Press Norwich
(a publishing imprint of Hymns Ancient & Modern Limited,
a registered charity)
13–17 Long Lane, London EC1A 9PN

www.scm-canterburypress.co.uk

British Library Cataloguing in Publication data

A catalogue record for this book is available
from the British Library

ISBN 978–1–85311–856–2

Typeset by Regent Typesetting, London
Printed and bound in the UK by
CPI William Clowes Ltd, Beccles, NR34 7TL

Being human
our nature is love
our nurture is fear.

For Ben and Ashok
With love

Contents

Acknowledgements

Jon and I would like to thank all our family and friends and those we have never met who prayed for us and supported us throughout our time in captivity and in writing this book. They are too numerous to mention, but they know who they are. However, we would like to make a special mention of Frances Haynes for her initial help and encouragement in writing the book and Margaret Edmonds for all the hours of work helping to edit the final version.

Preface

Ten years on from a meeting in a café that led to 14½ months of captivity in Chechnya, I sit with Jon in our Dartmoor home reflecting on our experience. From the time we were held in the 'Pink Crystal Room', I knew I wanted to write about it and, when our captors were not disturbing us, I balanced some paper on our Russian/English dictionary and wrote in tiny pencilled letters about our first days in the cellar.

We were in deep shock from the kidnap but thankfully had many tools to help us cope and survive – mainly tools of the mind such as yogic and tai chi practices, meditation and belief in the power of prayer and love. Neither of us follows a particular religion but we believe in love, understanding and compassion, the essence of all religions.

After we were released many people were interested in our story but I wanted to use the writing as a form of cathartic healing and not be stressed by deadlines so we decided not to publish until we were ready, however long it took. Over the years, we have experienced how the shock of being held on a knife edge of life or death has given us a greater understanding of the strengths that come out of suffering while also adversely affecting our physical well-being. This is our story of surviving and living with conflict and trauma within ourselves and on the outer world stage, our struggle to connect with the source of love while facing fear. A work in progress . . .

Anyone interested in having a copy of the exercises and meditations we used to survive, please contact us through office@scm-canterburypress.co.uk.

1

The Kidnap

About midnight, 2 July 1997

Jon – A bright purple beam of light shines out of the crystal hanging in front of the window above our heads. 'I wonder if it's a message? If I go back to sleep I might get it.'

Approximately two hours later we wake up hearing angry muffled voices through the thick brick wall. We lie in the darkness, still, alert, tension mounting.

Jon thinks, 'This sounds ominous and there's no escape, the bars on the window protecting us from thieves stop us jumping to safety. Perhaps that purple light was a warning.'

Suddenly a boot kicks open our door and a bit of burning paper is thrown onto the floor. We sit up with a jerk watching the flame. At first I think it's some kind of grenade and is going to explode. Strangely we are both very calm. A head peers around the door, two brown eyes are visible through holes cut out of a black knitted balaclava helmet. He comes in pointing the barrel of a Kalashnikov at Jon shouting, 'Chris? Chris?' 'Niet,' we reply. 'French?' 'Niet, Niet.' He sees my knapsack lying on the floor and turns it upside down. Everything cascades out over the bed. He grabs my camera, pulling out the film, shouting 'Documenti! Documenti!!' No documents are in the bag and he turns to Jon who has managed to struggle into a pair of thin black cotton trousers and has turned on the light. As Jon gets his passport the masked man says something in Russian and indicates that we should get dressed and be ready to go. I am menstruating and so am concerned about taking sanitary towels and gesture to the man with a packet in my hand whether I can pack it in my knapsack, saying 'OK? OK?' He nods. There is a washing line along one side of the room with all my dresses hanging on it. I'm wondering what to wear, I deliberately choose something the most Chechen, the least alluring. I pull down a rather ancient Laura Ashley dress with three-quarter sleeves and buttons all down the front. It hangs to my ankles.

By this time one of the other intruders has discovered a safe in the next room and is shouting triumphantly.

I'm asked for the key, 'Kluchi, Kluchi!', and am directed into the next room with the muzzle of an automatic rifle. I turn to Camilla and whisper, 'Camils, I think this is it, we're being kidnapped.' As I walk towards the safe I smile to myself in this bizarre situation because I know it contains nothing but coloured soft foam balls. I open the safe and they roll out over the floor. I can only guess the masked man's thoughts as he makes no comment. He gestures me into the kitchen by pointing his gun.

This gives me time to pack our wash-bag – toothbrushes, toothpaste, a small pink plastic compact mirror, a comb, soap, two loo rolls, a mountain of sanitary towels and tampons and Jon's razor. I also grab our mini English-Russian dictionary knowing that our sparse Russian won't be enough, an orange polo neck jumper and a cotton sarong. I see my money belt on the floor, I know it has $800 in it left over from buying toys in Moscow for the Chechen children, plus my documents. I don't want the kidnappers to have it so I stuff it under a pillow on the floor. Jon manages to shove some of the dollars he has in his money belt into a drawer as he goes through into the next room. There are still no feelings of panic, our minds crystal clear, accepting and knowing.

I put my knapsack on my back and follow Jon into the next room where Anya has been sleeping. She's a psychology student who has been working with us at The Little Star rehabilitation centre for war-traumatized children in Grozny. She isn't there now. The safe is open, half full of brightly coloured soft balls with more on the floor, I smile inwardly. We had arrived back in Grozny that afternoon from Moscow where we had renewed our visas. We had bought some second-hand office furniture, toys and art equipment for the children, hence the balls in the safe. We had two armed bodyguards with us; Ruslan, who had been a fighter in the war, loved to tell me of his dream to be trained by the British Army. When we had gone to bed he and Hassan were sitting in the bed/sitting room next to the kitchen.

I walk into the kitchen; Jon has already been taken outside. In the room next to the kitchen the computer is still on the table. Our tape recorder is on the floor, surrounded by plates covered in crumbs. The voices beyond the wall and these crumbs make me think there had been much discussion before they discovered us. There are a couple of other masked men. I look into the brown, intelligent eyes of the one who is shouting instructions, the eyes of a young man, showing some fear and urgency. I put on my sandals and turn back to look through to the room beyond. I want to find out what has happened to the others.

There they are. Hassan, sideways on, sitting on the bed with his head bowed and arms tied behind his back. On the same bed is Anya, head bowed, knees drawn up to her chin and arms also tied. Sitting facing me is Ruslan, hands tied behind his back, a lit cigarette shoved into his mouth. It glows very red. He stares at me and I smile. I want him to know that we are OK and it's not his fault. I lift my hand in a gesture of farewell.

One masked man takes me by the arm through the courtyard door into the mud street where there's a waiting white Lada. He pushes me into the back next to Jon and gets in beside me. There is another man the other side of Jon. Our heads are pushed down to our knees. One of them realizes we are not blindfolded and there is a scramble to find something to cover our eyes. A woollen mask is shoved over Jon's head and the sarong sticking out of the top of my bag is tied over my eyes. The man sitting next to me asks us our names and giggles, saying his name is Akhmed. We later came to know him as GA, Guardian Angel – the black joker – fantasy man.

Judging from the motion in the car we turn left on to a tarmacked road, then right on to a dirt potholed road. We stop, are pulled out and guided into another vehicle, this time some kind of Jeep. Again we are pushed on to the back seat, heads bowed, squashed between two tense men, with guns between their knees. After five or ten minutes we stop again, and are led out silently, stealthily. I hold on to a thick muscled forearm with the words 'all I can do is trust' in my mind. We go up a couple of steps through a door, walk across a room, then he lets me go. I take one step forward into the void of an open trapdoor, falling half way down a wooden ladder, hitting my neck on the side of the opening and my shins on the wooden rungs. I cry out, see lots of stars but remain conscious.

As I hear Camilla yelp I call out, 'Camils', and take a step forward. A gun is cocked and pressed into my chest, a sure sign to keep quiet.

I whisper 'I'm OK' and limp down into the black hole.

The sound of the gun being cocked smothers Camilla's reply, I don't know what has happened to her. My hands are untied and placed on a rough wooden ladder leading down into a cellar. After the lid is shut I ask Camilla how she is and she says her neck is hurt. There is not the merest hint of light as we take our blindfolds off. I touch the damp earth floor with my hands and start feeling around for something to sit on. I find two bits of wood.

The black hole of Calcutta, I think. We sit in silence, listening to the heavy booted tread of the Chechen fighters above us, my neck aching in the dark. The trapdoor opens and a small stub of a lit candle and a couple of blankets are handed down. An arm gestures to a hole in the wall that leads to another room. We have our first flickering view of the cellar. Fortunately we're not tall, the wooden ceiling hangs low above our heads with many sharp nails sticking through. There are about three centimetres to spare above Jon's head. The room is about three and a half metres long and three metres wide, with wooden shelves full of empty glass preserving jars along one wall and a stack of wooden window frames along another. Behind the ladder one brick has been taken out of the wall for ventilation; a metal sheet on the outside blocks any view. There is a large grey chest, probably once a dowry chest, with faded and peeling flowers painted on it. On the chest stands a large wooden barrel. The rest of the room appears to be empty. The end wall, opposite the ventilation hole, is bedrock. The earth floor is embedded with small stones. The wall with the opening is a mixture of cement, stones and earth.

Stepping through the hole it is impossible to stand upright, the wooden ceiling only a metre and a half above the floor. To our right there is a sagging sun bed with faded psychedelic 1960s style material fraying along the edges and, in the far corner to our left, three wooden packing cases. This is obviously our bedroom. The bottom of the walls are thick concrete and stones, becoming brick about half way up. This cellar is about a metre longer than the other room and has two thick wooden poles in the middle supporting the floor above. The floor is covered by bigger stones like those you find on a railtrack. Luckily we are not barefoot! There is no ventilation.

We lay a grey blanket on the sunbed and somehow manage to curl up side by side, using my jumper and scarf as a pillow and the other blanket over us. It smells of urine. My mind is in turmoil and my neck throbs with pain. I see the faces of my family in my mind. Ashok, my 11-year-old son, with his neat oval light brown face and expressive blue grey eyes, lives with Marcel, his father who, I know, will give him all the support he can. I comfort myself knowing that Ashok knows I love him and always will whatever happens. That love has always sustained us in the times when we have been physically apart. I see Ben, Jon's son with his curly black hair and sparkling brown eyes. He's 17 and with Jon's parents. I remember him helping me run some drama workshops on a play scheme last summer; he was so full of bright ideas and brilliant with the kids. I'm sure he'll be well supported by Ken and Doris and his large group of friends. Also there's Debbie, his mum, with whom he has been recently re-united after 13 years apart. All the family faces flow past. A thought flashes in that our parents will think of selling their houses to raise money for a ransom. 'Don't do it!' I scream silently into the blackness, hoping I will be heard. I need to let go now and trust that all of them will cope; I need to concentrate on surviving, which means using my mind to relieve the pain and calm myself. So I ask all the universal powers of love and light to give Jon and me the strength to cope with whatever we have to face and suddenly in the deep darkness my mind is filled with white light that helps me let go of enough tension, jumping thought and pain, to sink into sleep.

I do not sleep. My mind a whirl of questions none of which I can answer running like a tape loop round and round. How long before the news will be out? How long before we will be out? What is our fate? How long are we going to be in this place? All the time listening to the sounds upstairs, clues to any movement in our direction. Lying awake staring into the black.

A few hours later the trauma hits my stomach. It starts churning and I need the loo. There is no form of toilet and I am desperate. We light the candle stub and I get out the dictionary. 'Toilet' is a similar word, 'menstruation' is 'menstruatie' and 'water' is 'voda', so it should not be too difficult to make them understand. I'm wrong. With dictionary and sanitary towel packet in hand I timidly knock on the trapdoor. There is absolute silence. I knock louder and there is a scramble of movement with heavy footfalls and guns clicking. The trap door opens and I am looking down a barrel of a gun with three masked faces behind it. 'Toiliette, pajalsta,' I say. They look blank. 'Mye menstruatie is' and I hold up the sanitary towels. They whisper urgently, perhaps one of them is explaining what STs are for, but they still have not comprehended that we have no toilet. The one holding the gun is getting impatient, thinking this is some kind of escape ruse. His eyes are blank, the eyes of one who would think nothing of pulling that trigger. One of the others, realizing the danger, snatches the dictionary from my hand, frantically studying the words. 'Menstruartie, voda, voda (menstruation, water, water),' I whisper. The one with the dictionary speaks hurriedly to a man in the background. A couple of tense minutes pass then a dark pink plastic jug of water is handed down and the trapdoor closed. Be thankful for small mercies, I think, though it doesn't solve our problem.

I search for something that can be used as a temporary loo and find a plastic bag and a cardboard box. Just the job!

2

The Kiva

Day one, Thursday

I wake to darkness and pain. The trapdoor opens, a loaf of bread appears and a loop of salami sausage, 'manna from heaven'. We pour some of the water into the cleanest glass jar we can find and nibble a bit of bread, but we are in shock so we're not very hungry. Luckily when my bag had been tipped upside down some of the small side pockets were zipped up and in one of these are two bottles of Bach Flower remedies, Walnut for change and Rescue Remedy for shock or trauma. We administer large doses to ourselves; the brandy fire warms us.

I spend the next few hours drifting in and out of sleep, jagged thoughts still tumbling in and out of my mind mingling with the gnawing pain in my neck. I pour healing love and light into my neck, knowing there will be no doctors to turn to. All we have are ourselves and our prayers.

I suggest to Camilla that we call the cellar a 'Kiva'. In the Native American Indian tradition a Kiva is a room dug into the earth with a ladder leading to it from ground level. It is a place of inner reflection, prayer and ceremony. It's nicer to think of our new home as a place of contemplation, a place to let our minds roam free rather than a place of captivity.

The trapdoor opens, daylight floods into the first room and seeps into the bedroom. What a joy to see natural light again. We stand under the ladder looking up at two faces, masked by black knitted balaclava helmets, the uniform for this group it seems, along with black tee shirts and trousers. We try to tell them that we are friends and have come to Chechnya to help the children. We know instinctively that the only way to survive is to build up a rapport with our captors so they see us as human beings and not just commodities to be exchanged for money.

7

Fortunately the men want to communicate as well. They laugh saying they're bandits so how can we be friends. We explain about the lack of a toilet and GA, who had organized the water in the middle of the night, ducks his head down through the opening and expresses surprise. He immediately goes off and comes back with a red plastic bucket with a lid. Then he produces an English-Russian phrase book and starts asking questions such as 'What is your name?' 'What is your job?' 'Do you like the theatre?' The conversation is light hearted, there is no malice in their eyes. They're not so traumatized as to have lost all feeling. With a help of the dictionary I ask for a pillow and GA brings a large, square feather one with a faded and unwashed forget-me-not blue flowery cover. I'm having trouble holding my focus because of the pain in my neck and so return to bed with my beautiful pillow.

At least we're talking with each other, that feels good. Soon our conversation runs out due to the limitations of language, hand gestures and possibly our different world views. I sense they are getting tired of the effort, I know I am. The trapdoor closes and the darkness returns.

A little later Jon lights the candle stub and pushes the three packing cases together, covering them with bits of cardboard and the grey blanket to make a second bed. The sunbed is so old and damaged it will not bear the weight of both of us for very long. We talk about our situation, the length of time we may be captive – one month, one year, two? I don't want to think beyond two. We know we have to be ready for anything and not dwell on negative possibilities. We look back over the day, thankful for the few hours of dim light, conversation, laughter and the big red bucket.

I settle down on the sunbed with the pillow and urine-scented blanket while Jon lies on the packing cases. We both fall into a light sleep until the trapdoor is quietly opened and someone comes down the ladder. We are silent, alert. There's the whirr of a generator torch being pumped and a dark figure enters the bedroom. As Jon lights the candle I notice the man has the phrase book in his hand and that he is not one of the men we were speaking to earlier. He squats on the floor and starts asking us questions out of the phrase book. He is younger, slow speaking, his dull brown eyes are not eager to make contact. I'm watching the candle, wishing he would go away as our only source of light is diminishing rapidly. The light goes out and I hear him moving towards me. He sits beside me, putting his hand on my knee. Jon stands up and takes a step towards me and the man forcefully pushes him back. I try to move away but he grabs my arm and pulls me towards the door. 'Jon mye mooge!' 'Jon's my husband!' I whisper sharply. Even though we are not married I know the Muslim law preaches strongly against adultery and I'm hoping this will deter him. I manage to pull away, negotiating the darkness to the packing cases where Jon is sitting. Silence. The torch whirrs and he says something that I interpret as 'What now?' I reply 'Spit, spit', 'Sleep, sleep.' Thankfully he gets up and leaves the cellar.

The first battle won.

Day two, Friday

Sitting on the packing cases in the pitch black, Jon with his back to the wall and me nestled against him, we gain strength from our combined warmth and love. We're shaken by the experience of last night. I think Jon was wise to remain silent; if he had retaliated the men above would have heard and it could have been much worse for us.

'I wanted to hit him. If he had started to rape you I would have done.'

'But if you hit out there'll be more violence and we'll both be hurt. If it happens again and they use force I'll have to go with it.'

I understand Jon's reaction and it disturbs me. I feel hypocritical telling him to hold back as I would also want to retaliate if he was being hurt. We decide it will be better for our survival to follow the line of least resistance.

The trapdoor opens and we hesitantly go towards the light, two bone china cups and saucers appear followed by a plastic bottle full of sweet tea and a newspaper parcel containing hot hard boiled eggs. We ask for another candle and they provide another stub. More manna from heaven.

Back in the darkness, my mind becoming more lively as the pain in my neck recedes, the hours begin to drag. What do I see in the darkness? Pin pricks of light and colour, swirling shapes conjured up by my mind. How am I going to remain sane in this perpetual black, coloured only by my thoughts? Thank God there are two of us and we can whisper, but the fear of insanity doesn't go away.

The tears flow.

I'm numbed out. A mishmash of thoughts come and go about freedom, family, how long we'll have to endure this. I quickly get to a point where I am here and now . . . accepting. This is my logic protecting me from my scrambled emotions. I sense Camilla's panic and suggest a game of imaginary I Spy in the dark; it calms her down for a while until we both get bored.

Boredom is dangerous. My mind turns to thoughts of Ben, my son. He's in the middle of his A levels. I think he'll cope well – he has a strong out-going personality, a stable base living with my parents and a close group of friends. But it will still be hard, my parents and he will be in shock. The trapdoor opens, stemming the flow of my painful thoughts.

'How are you?' chorus the two friendly masked faces of the previous day. Our night visitor is nowhere to be seen. Again we talk about ourselves, our work and our families. They talk about their boss being a barbarian, ready to commit all kinds of atrocities. GA giggles and I do not believe him. We ask if we can have a bit of paper to write to his boss and tell him why we came to Chechnya, it may help. He goes away and returns with a piece of paper and a Biro and tells us that it's OK to write.

With lots of gesturing we complain about the lack of ventilation and talk about going mad in the dark. They say they'll fix up a light, then they pass down two child-sized plywood chairs. We ask if we can have some fruit and one of them disappears and comes back with a branch laden with apricots. Though slightly green and spotty they taste delicious. The daylight is fading fast and the trapdoor comes down. We stay in the darkness, conserving our candlelight for visits to the bucket. Not much sleep this night. Ears alert, listening, listening, to heavy boot treads, the scrape and grating sound of moving chairs, the bounce of bedsprings. Waiting to hear the thud of the weight being removed from the trapdoor and the rasp of the wood as it is opened. It doesn't happen.

Day three, Saturday

We hear morning sounds: the dawn chorus, the thudding of cows' hooves as they are led along the road by the house, the shouts of children, laughing and crying, the yells of their mothers and grandmothers trying to keep order. It's calming to hear the sounds of the day dawning, the sounds of humanity setting about the day's business. And also strange and incongruous hearing this normality happening all around us while we sit in darkened captivity. Only a few yards separate us, but it is as if we have ceased to exist in that world.

The trapdoor opens and once again we are greeted by our friendly hosts. They organize a light bulb to illuminate our darkness by splicing bits of wire together and attaching a socket and bulb. They drop the swinging wire through the trapdoor, leaving Jon to hook it over a couple of bent nails in the ceiling. A plastic bottle of tea (without sugar this time, on request) is lowered, followed by bread, eggs and freshly picked earthy smelling tomatoes, with a small saucer of salt for our eggs and a bowl of sugar lumps because they can't believe we really don't like sugar, a rarity in Chechnya. They tell us that we will probably be moving to a 'haroshi miassa, better place', on Monday. Today they have brought with them a Chechen backgammon board to alleviate their own boredom and they leave us in peace, keen to get on with their game.

Light at last! Such luxury. I immediately set about the task of composing a letter to 'The Boss' retelling our reasons for coming to Chechnya and our work with the war-traumatized children. I explain that neither of our families have much money and that our organization 'Centre for Peacemaking and Community Development' is a small charity with no spare cash at all. I also point out that the British government has a policy of not paying ransoms for hostages. Then I appeal to the goodness in his heart to set us free. This is a painstaking task as I have to translate everything into Russian using our tiny dictionary. Many words have multiple meanings and I have no knowledge of Russian grammar or sentence structure. However it feels very good to do something constructive that might help our situation. The trapdoor opens and I hand up my letter into the fading evening light with many prayers. This has been a good day.

Day four, Sunday

We move the sunbed next to the packing cases; it's nicer to lie side by side and feels safer. During the night we heard a scraping sound in the wall behind our heads and outside the brick hole in the other room. This morning our bedroom is flooded with a soft orange light: someone has removed a brick in the end wall of our bedroom. In the hole lies a solitary ripe apricot. We feel blessed and full of gratitude. They've also moved the metal sheet from the other hole and we smell fresh air tainted by paint and corroding metal. If we squint through the hole at an acute angle we can see the rusting top of a metal paint pot with some green gunge oozing out of the lid. The view from the 'apricot window' is much more appealing – sunlit green grasses with a tall chicken wire fence a few yards away. Occasionally we see the top half of a person walking along the dirt road just the other side of the fence. This is a real treat.

Breakfast arrives. GA is on his own today and a little more jumpy because of that. We thank him for the apricot. He is not in the mood to talk, keen to get back to his solo backgammon. We don't mind, it's very tiring communicating through a dictionary and phrase book and besides, we have a window to look out of, even if it means a bent back and cricked neck.

I am sure I can make something to improve our view of the outside world so I look around our den and find all sorts of string, broken glass and an iron bar that could make a very nasty weapon if needed. I slot two pieces of lath together to make a long thin arm, into which I slot the small pink compact mirror. I push this homemade periscope through the small holes we call windows, being very careful to avoid detection. Wow! Life is a little more colourful. Out of the bedroom 'window', which is half a metre above ground level, I can see clearly some sweetcorn growing near the wire fence, the other side of which is an untarmacked crossroads. There is a road sign nailed to a wooden fence, but no matter how hard I try I cannot make out all of the Russian letters, let alone guess the name. I twist the periscope and see the red brick wall of our house and a corner of asbestos corrugated roof.

Even the view from the 'stinky window' expands. By tilting the periscope through it at an angle, the space between the wall and the metal sheet reveals a triangular opening of sky with the branches of a cherry plum tree spreadeagled across it. We use the periscope to bathe our eyes in natural light, being aware that living in darkness will affect our sight. On a piece of newspaper that had contained our breakfast eggs we find a holographic sticker reflecting all the colours of the rainbow. We already feel starved of colour and use the sticker to absorb the rainbow colours through our eyes, knowing that all colours radiate different frequencies that can be used to heal energy imbalance in the body, keeping disease at bay.

There is only so much meditation, sleeping and peering through small windows one can do. With the sound of the dice rolling overhead, I decide to

12

make some sort of board game. I have to look deep in to my memory banks to find a game. I come up with 'Ludo'. Using the biro I mark out the 'board' onto a sheet of newspaper. The counters are small coloured stones from our prison floor, and the die is a sugar cube. How bizarre. Here we are, sitting in a dimly lit cellar rolling our die, while just feet away our captors are doing the same, playing backgammon in the full daylight.

We spend a lot of this day thinking about the letter we have sent, calling on all the forces of love and light to act and somehow enlighten the mind of 'The Boss' to see that no good will come out of holding us. We feel waves of love coursing through our bodies as we pray, giving us strength to relax, stay calm and accept our captivity without anger or frustration. We have a positive frame of mind; after all, we've not been beaten, chained or tortured in any way, in fact we have been shown some kindness. Today we have a glimpse of blue sky and can smell gusts of warm summer air fragrant with hot grasses and cow pats.

Day five, Monday

I find it difficult to sleep, with the possibility that we might be moved at any time, and the fear of another unwanted night visitor. I lie awake listening to all the sounds of our guards, the continuous rolling of the dice (how much backgammon can you play?). They fall silent when any late night vehicle passes, and I hear them walking to a window to observe. I hear when they lie on a bed as the springs squeak, especially when they roll over. They speak to each other in Chechen; I cannot understand a word. An hour before dawn there's the first call to prayer 'Allah oo akhbar.' Then I know we aren't going anywhere and slip into deep sleep.

As Jon relaxes into unconsciousness I wake up watching the square of daylight growing brighter on the crooked cement walls. I muse on our first few days of captivity and the strange paradoxical relationship we have with our captors. They hold us in this place, prevent our freedom and yet want to be friends and make life as pleasant as possible within the hostage limitations they set.

GA on duty again, alone. Our bucket is getting pretty full so we tell GA and he agrees to empty it. Jon hands it up through the trapdoor and as he closes the lid we look at each other, he has not placed the heavy weight over it and has left the house, probably to a 'dunny' at the end of the garden. The urge to push open the trapdoor and run is very great, but the risks of recapture are far too high. Jon is a good runner, I'm not, GA is probably very fit, we have sparse knowledge of Chechen and Russian and no idea of our location in Grozny. We hear running footsteps. The speed at which he returns and the worried look in his eyes tells us he has realized the danger. He wiggles an admonishing finger, 'Niet problemi. Sta noche haroshi miassa. (No problems, tonight a better place.)'

We talk of other hostage situations we have heard about, remembering John McCarthy, Terry Waite and Brian Keenan held hostage in Beirut in the 1980s. I know they were held a long time, about two years I thought. (In fact it was five, I'm glad I didn't remember that!) They all found ways to survive: John and Brian used humour and story telling, Terry, who spent four years by himself, used his memory of hymns, psalms and poems to keep him sane. We talk about the tools we have to help us keep sane: tai chi, yoga, meditation, visualization and prayer. We have to be prepared to be here a long time.

Every afternoon we hear the drone of an aeroplane overhead. We think it must be the 2.30 p.m. flight to Moscow. It comforts us to hear it, a link with the world beyond Chechnya. We also use it as a timepiece, signalling that half the day has passed and we have managed to fill the time without going 'cuckoo'.

I'm surprised at Camilla's ability to take all that's happening to us in her stride. I guess in many ways she's just like me, accepting things happening in the moment and dealing with it the best way she can. She speaks out her grief, her loss, her fears, I abate my own. But in many ways, by being a listener and reinforcing the positives, my own thoughts of grief and loss are dissipated. The thoughts of loss of contact with those we love and just the simple freedoms of daylight and fresh air and the ability to walk out underneath the sky, sun, stars. All these simple pleasures seem like beautiful treasures in this dark place.

In the late afternoon GA asks for the Biro and a while later hands us a scrap of paper with the words 'I'm sorry, I cannot help you' written on it. We know this is an answer to our letter and become very despondent and uneasy in anticipation of the projected move tonight. I search the dictionary for words such as 'take care' and 'be gentle' and try to memorize them. I don't want another neck injury. All night we lie awake, tense, listening, waiting for the move that never comes.

Day six, Tuesday

A tired morning. Breakfast comes and they tell us the move will be to-night. I practise asking them to be careful in my dictionary Russian.

There's a dip in the floor at one end of the room and Jon has placed a couple of short planks over it. This is our ablutions corner. We have a litre of water to wash with every day, our washbag that I had grabbed with soap, toothbrushes and paste and also a grubby towel that GA had given to us. How our values have changed: now these are some of our most precious possessions, with them we can maintain some form of cleanliness by descaling our teeth, enjoying fresh fennel-scented mouths and soaped armpits. Washing gives us a sense of self-esteem. We always wait until after breakfast so we can strip off without being disturbed. Jon stands naked with his hands cupped as I pour a thin stream of water into them from a glass jar. But his long, tightly-curled hair is beginning to fuzz into dreadlocks.

I think of the first time we met in the swimming pool at Ross-on-Wye. A friend pointed out this figure pounding up and down the pool like a sleek, long-haired, bearded seal. We were introduced outside, I was thinking 'what a nice, friendly guy' when something happened that I wasn't expecting: a tingle of energy passed through my body like a wave from my feet to my head making my scalp prickle. I didn't leap into his arms or even hunt for his telephone number but I remembered the feeling. We met briefly a couple of times in the following months; then, in July 1995, the telephone rang and it was Jon James asking me to come over. I had time so I drove from my home just north of Ross-on-Wye through the Forest of Dean to Lydney by the river Severn. Jon was sitting in his garden under a makeshift canopy, loud music blaring through the window, the sun blazing down. We sat and talked about life, the universe and everything; the words flowed but what I was most aware of was the energy static between us, an almost audible buzz. We walked down to the river arm in arm, I liked the smell of his sweat, a mixture of sun-warmed mash, sweet briars and musk. Now the sweat that we wash from our arm-pits with this dribble of water is soured with the scent of fear.

3

The Pink Crystal Room

Departure and arrival

I settle down to sleep on the sunbed, feeling thankful that we have survived one week in captivity. I don't think there's much point in staying
awake for a move that might not happen.

*I cannot sleep. Our guards are unusually quiet. At some hour after mid-
night I hear the sound of the weight being taken off the trapdoor and see two
of our guards coming down the ladder. I nudge Camilla awake and tell her
we are on the move.*

One of the men is GA but the other is a smaller man, new to us. He is
carrying a pair of handcuffs and is very businesslike in his movements
– no messing. I put my knapsack on my back, packed with our possessions, and just before my head is covered by a black woollen mask I see
GA take the towel off a nail, obviously intending to bring it. I had left it
there thinking it belonged to this house. As I'm guided to the ladder I
hear the handcuffs being put on Jon's wrists.

*I'm cuffed, hands behind my back, and thinking, 'This is going to make
getting up the ladder interesting'. There's some whispered exchange and the
handcuffs are removed. My head is held down as soon as I ascend the ladder
and covered with a balaclava, no eye-holes. My hands are re-cuffed and I
am led out of the building and up into a waiting jeep. Even in my wakeful-
ness I did not hear this vehicle arrive.*

I am guided (gently!) out of the house to the waiting jeep. We are put
in the back seat, wedged between two men. Thankfully (for my neck is
still painful) they don't push our heads to our knees this time.

We bump along a rutted road for about ten minutes then turn onto a
tarmacked street. I can see the flicker of streetlights through my mask.
We stop and there's silence. A lighter clicks and there is a flash of flame

and smell of cigarette smoke followed by a noise of tearing paper and the smell of mint. Chewing gum strips are pressed into our hands. My heart is racing, knocking against my ribs. All sound, smell and movement are magnified in the quiet tension. I take a deep breath and tell myself everything will be all right and my thumping heart begins to slow down. The front passenger gets out: an 'all clear' signal must have been given. One man leads me by the arm. I'm nervous of stepping out and am going too slowly for them and so another man comes round to my other side, links his arm through mine and they hoist me along the pavement. I feel branches brushing my head. We go up a couple of steep steps, turn left and up another step into a house or flat, along a corridor then right into a room. Jon is led in after me and they take off our masks.

What a sight! A large rectangular room with a high ceiling and polished herringbone parquet floor. The walls are pink and decorated with airbrushed geometric designs like facets of a crystal. There's a large wardrobe pushed against the window with a red and green patterned Persian rug stuffed on top of it. In one corner there's a green plastic Christmas tree and a 1920s style telephone, cream with gold trimmings, its flex ripped out of the wall. The 'pièce de résistance' is two beds pushed together and covered with a startling pink ruched nylon bedspread. Coming from our Kiva, devoid of any amenities, we are full of disbelief and inner chuckles. We have been transported to a cheap hotel in a 'B' movie.

They tell us to sit on the bed and the smaller man unlocks Jon's handcuffs. We nickname him 'Handcuffs' or HC. I ask to go to the loo and am led to a proper flushing lavatory, the height of luxury. Then they tell us we will have to be handcuffed together – 'Only for one night if you are good.' HC is definitely the handcuff expert: he takes particular care over the tightness of mine, indicating that it's much easier for a woman with small wrists to slip them off. So here we are, manacled together under our beautiful pink bedcover, in our beautiful pink room.

Wednesday 9 July

We have gone from the ridiculous to the sublime, from a cellar to this brightly coloured room with real beds. My mind churns and spins with endless thoughts and the handcuff chafes my wrist. I hope this is not going to be the way in this new abode, handcuffed for weeks or months. But I know I would get used to it just as the slaves did in British colonial times when they travelled thousands of miles on the ocean chained to each other and the boat. That is, the ones that survived.

I dream we're in one of the abandoned red brick mansions I have seen on the edge of Grozny, the ones with vast holes carved through their innards by tank shells. My sleep is light and I hear the clanging of dishes in another room, then smell fried eggs. There's much laughter and relaxed talk as they celebrate a successful relocation.

Natural light seeps out from the edges of the blanket and newspaper covering our window. There's a knock on the door and HC comes in swinging the handcuff key. He removes the handcuffs and invites us to use the bathroom. We're in an apartment. The bathroom has a bath with taps and a broken shower attachment but there's no hot water or plug, only a couple of enamel wash bowls. We have a quick wash and shake ourselves dry. GA tells me he left the towel in the jeep by mistake; I don't forget his kind thought.

We're called into the kitchen for breakfast. A feast meets our eyes. There's a table laid for two; on the flowery plastic table cloth are a couple of boiled eggs each, fresh bread, two tomatoes, a tin of peas and a freshly brewed pot of tea. The scene is so incongruous, being captive yet waited upon by two masked men in a 'normal' kitchen, that I burst out laughing and am hushed sharply. 'Spion! (Spies!)' they whisper harshly, gesturing to the window, afraid my laughter will arouse the suspicion of the neighbours. My laugh is struck dumb and I sit down opposite Jon. There's a small sink and a gas cooker, a glass-doored dresser with a mirror backing, its shelves full of cut glass dishes and glasses and a tall fridge. The windows are covered with baking paper except for a strip at the top, through which I take surreptitious glances. I see a myriad of leaves, dappled green in the bright sunlight, rustling in the breeze.

Back in the bedroom we lie on the bed, tired from last night's escapade. There's an electric lamp in the corner on top of a desk so we're not in darkness. A sound of dragging comes from the corridor, HC pulls a mattress into our room which he lays in front of the door, he sits on it with his back against the wall, facing us. Stern hazel eyes gaze at us, his mask has a hole revealing his mouth set in a thin, grim, line.

We're both feeling nervous having him in the room. Jon decides to do some yoga mantras in his mind, so he sits crosslegged holding my feet, giving me comfort while I lie, trying to relax. HC's very curious, he says 'Yoga?' Jon replies 'Da'. HC gets up and struts around the room, all in black with pointed leather shoes, his back held rigidly straight, a large knife in a sheath hanging from his belt; he's nervous too. We meditate and stop focusing on fearful thoughts; even if they enter our minds we don't give them attention and focus instead on breathing deeply and slowly, radiating calm harmonious energy out into the room so we can all relax. HC sits down again and gently nods off.

Later he goes out to get a backgammon board and teaches us to play. After the game he disappears and comes back with two cups of instant coffee. We both glance up as he comes in and quickly avert our eyes – he's forgotten to put on his mask. We keep our heads bowed until he leaves the room. This could be dangerous.

HC returns with his mask back on carrying the phrase book and a pencil. With the dictionary and gesture he asks us if we have seen his face and points out two words, 'Danger' and 'Death'. His eyes have taken on the quality of polished moss agate, and we deny seeing his face even though we did glimpse a flat face profile and black hair cut close to his head, and luckily he believes us. Relaxing a little, he tells us that he isn't a bandit at all but a businessman and that before the war he had a business with his brother buying cars in Moscow and selling them in Chechnya. In 1995 the Russians confiscated his flat in Moscow. His brother, father and wife were killed in the first few months of war. 'She was very young, very young,' he said bitterly, 'and my son only three years old, he survived.' Later his house in Grozny was ransacked by the Russians. He describes the senselessness of their actions – a fridge full of bullet holes, his large collection of old historical books burnt and the shelves taken back to sell in Russia. In 1996 the house was bombed. The war has reduced his whole way of life to rubble. He now lives in lodgings in Grozny. Somewhere else his mother, aged 65, looks after her four orphaned grandchildren all under the age of five. 'It is very difficult, very difficult, you won't, you can't understand,' he says wearily. I get a strong feeling from this conversation that he doesn't see his son very often; perhaps the associated memories are too painful.

Just by talking of his troubles, HC is sharing some of his grief. I remember a North American Indian teaching practice I took part in many years ago. We were a group of 14 people from different backgrounds and cultures. We sat in two circles, one inside the other, women on the inside, men on the outside. The men were silent observers while the women discussed what it meant to them to be a woman, each talking in turn. There was a time limit then the men talked about what it meant to be a man. Finally one large circle was made and the discussion was on what it was to be human. We all had the same basic needs and desires. Pain and anger feel the same whatever the differences in race, colour or gender.

There's a knock on the front door and HC disappears swiftly, silently, tying our door shut with wire and rope. Changing of the guard. Time for bed.

I lie awake, thinking of what HC has told us. His wife was only 19 when they married. I think of the Chechen wedding we were invited to. We had come home from an exhausting day working with the children, gasping for cool drinks, when somebody mentioned ice cream. Searching our bags to find some money, knowing we hadn't got enough, we heard a volley of gunshots. Our guards ran outside and saw a wedding party approaching, Kalashnikovs poking out of the car windows pumping the sky with bullets. Quickly they reversed the school bus to block three quarters of the road and we made a human chain to block the rest. Jon and I had no idea why we were doing this and only afterwards learnt that in Chechnya it is a tradition that if the bridegroom is blocked from reaching his bride he has to pay to be allowed through. Thus we got our ice cream money and an invitation to the wedding party just down the road.

The guards knew the family came from a good clan, the father of the groom being a policeman, so we headed off down the road and were invited to 'view' the bride, who stood all in white in a little room by herself while everyone else joined in the music making, dancing and feasting on decorated salads and meat. I could imagine HC leaping around within a circle of clapping friends and accordion players, performing the traditional male Chechen dance that reminds me of a proud strutting cock, all angular and intricate footwork, happy in his conquest.

Thursday 10 July

There's a scrabbling noise of untying and a different masked face appears. My first impression is of wide open innocent blue eyes; later I realize I have been looking into a glass eye. This man is about 1.70

metres high, just taller than HC but much broader with bigger biceps and a large belly so we kindly call him Paunch rather than Glasseye! In the kitchen is another man, taller and well-muscled; he has large, brown, 'puppy dog' eyes and shuffles around the room in his slippers as if they're oversized paws, so we give him the nickname 'Puppydog'. Breakfast is help yourself buffet style. Puppydog stays to guard us. Paunch seems to want as little contact with us as possible. Then we are sent back to our room.

Sensing that we won't be disturbed for a while I decide to investigate the contents of the large wardrobe. I find two large pieces of material that we use as sheets and four new hankies, useful for drying ourselves with. There are two large bottom drawers that are heavily laden with all manner of goodies. I start exploring. One is full of medicines, including needles and glass phials – we hope they don't discover these and start experimenting on us! In the other drawer is an old photo album, a Biro and pencil. So strange having a glimpse of the ex-owner's life. We assume she's the small brown-eyed woman with a bun that appears in a lot of the photos. Most of them date back to the 1960s and '70s judging from the clothes.

I discover some black, high-heeled pointed shoes under the bed; she had tiny feet. Also there's one page of a letter written in Russian and bits of a newspaper dating back to August 1996. The paper has photos of horrific scenes taken in Grozny at that time. There had been a major Russian offensive, flattening most of the city. One photo shows a dead Russian soldier lying amongst the rubble, being eaten by a cat. Perhaps this prompted her to flee, or she may have been banished for collaborating with the Russian army. It's very likely that she had been one of the few thousand Russians living in Grozny.

They call us out and show us some pasta we can cook. Then Puppydog takes down the phrase book from on top of the fridge and asks us to give him an English lesson. It's slow and laborious and I can see he's not that interested. After a while he gives up. We talk about food and I ask for some vegetables and honey to keep us healthy.

Back in our room I find about 30 round pieces of white paper in my knapsack that we had cut out to use as name badges for the children. I begin writing a diary in tiny letters using the dictionary as a support that also acts as a decoy if they enter our room without warning. Later I hide the Biro and pencil in a slit in one of the mattresses and the writing in a plastic sanitary towel wrapper, knowing that menstruation is a taboo subject for Chechen men and it will be the last place they'll look.

I need to move and at least there is more space here than in the Kiva. The room is spacious with a high ceiling not touchable even when I jump. I decide to do some tai chi. Twice when I was a builder I had suffered a slipped disc. The second time I was so afraid of not having enough money I carried on working after the injury until the pain forced me to stop. Six months later the doctor and physiotherapists said they could do no more for me and no amount of painkillers could relieve the agony. Not being able to work brought on depression and huge feelings of inadequacy and lack of self worth. It was then I discovered the benefits of yoga and tai chi. They helped me gain strength physically and mentally, dispelling anxiety.

The essential teachings that I learnt then I can use now; how softness overcomes hardness as flowing water will eventually wear away solid rock, and how energy follows thought. Good lessons to remember as we sit in our captive state.

Friday 11 July

GA comes bounding in, going straight to the window to check if we've looked out or written something on the newspaper pinned to the window frames behind the blanket. We're allowed our morning toilette and breakfast. GA and HC are both weary this morning and have no mind to converse. I notice a scrap of paper and a pencil on top of the fridge and ask if we can use them to mark out a game board. Fine, under supervision, and as long as the pencil doesn't come back to the bedroom with us. HC gives us a mimed lecture about the importance of silence, 'Spies everywhere!' We really don't need telling, we've almost forgotten what our normal voices sound like.

We have a new 'board' yet no dice. Camilla finds some Blu-Tack in her bag, so I mould a cube and mark the numbers as dents with a used matchstick. Booty from the bottom drawers in the form of shiny baubles become counters and we spend a gentle morning playing ludo then practising some tai chi. I muse on the twists and turns my life has taken in its flow towards this place, this pink crystal cell. The little four-year-old Jon happily dashing about outside, climbing trees, running and playing fantasy games then hiding under a table looking out at a forest of legs. Being told that he was spelling his name wrong and having to get Doris to come and tell the teacher that his name was Jonathan with an 'a' and he was spelling it correctly. It was an inauspicious start to my school days. I could spell my name right but found it difficult to remember the shapes of words and the sounds that they were meant to make. English is not a logical language and it confused me. Today I would be classed as dyslexic but then I was a 'slow learner'. Although I spoke up in class on topics I was interested in, I wrote little. My interests lay outside school, cycling and canoeing and making things, like building fibreglass canoes with my father at the age of 10. So, at the age of 17 I left school and worked in a factory. The money gave me freedom to buy a motorbike and take my girlfriend Debbie to gigs. But working long hours within a toxic environment with no fresh air became a torment and I decided to train as a bricklayer. At least I would be outside. Outside mmm . . . now I don't even have the freedom to breathe fresh air. The tai chi helps to control my frustration. Slowly I let go of the yearning to walk in a forest, knowing I can walk there in my mind and feel that I will walk there again one day. I still have that freedom.

Lunch hour. HC is in a talkative mood. Using the dictionary he tells us about the vicious war: 50,000 Russian troops against a few thousand Chechen fighters, the odds against them enormous. He's very angry that the western world turned a blind eye and that Russia has given no compensation for the damage caused by the war, which is why they have resorted to kidnapping as a form of income. He takes a scrap of paper and a pencil and carefully draws a gun, then underneath a tank and below that a hospital. The heading is $1,000,000, beside the gun and tank he writes $500,000 and beside the hospital $500,000. This is the money they are asking for us and how they will use it. Then he burns the paper.

We have a conversation about age. HC says he is 23; judging by the crows feet around his eyes he's either had a very hard life or it's a lie. Much later he confesses to being 32. GA tells us he's 29 and will be 30 in October. He says he will invite us back for his party, gesturing mountains of food and rivers of champagne. They are convinced we will be free by then.

I glance up at the high window open for ventilation watching loops of audio tape caught around branches, brown trails weaving knots in the wind, glinting in the sunlight; a vision of freedom.

Saturday 12 July

A small pot of dark mountain honey and butter for breakfast – thank you, Puppydog!

Paunch and Puppydog are not interested in communicating with us so we are left alone. A day of writing, exercising, meditating and relaxing. I look across at Jon sitting crosslegged with his back against the wall, his eyes closed, in deep contemplation, remembering how I had given him a lift to London the day after we had walked in the burning sun by the river Severn. London was hot and steamy that night; there was no point in trying to sleep so we walked and talked by the Camden canal avoiding the copulating couples, their pale skin illuminated in the leaf blotched shadows by the light of a cricket sung yellow moon. The next morning when Jon leapt out of the car to catch a train he turned to me and said, 'Shall we dance the road of life together for a while?' I smiled, it felt good to me.

A year later, in August 1996, we were still dancing together, this time on stage in a huge marquee set up for the Ross-on-Wye festival. It was the culminating performance of Carmina Burana in which Ashok was given a solo part. The performance was electric. I discovered the director also ran a project teaching the street children of Ethiopia to dance. My whole body zinged: this sounded like the kind of project I wanted to be involved in. A seed was sown.

Now my smile has an ironic twist as I contemplate this road we are dancing along.

What luck that we had time to talk in the two years we knew each other before being kidnapped! We can only whisper now. They are paranoid that our English voices will be heard by neighbours and our presence discovered. Our ceiling is high and noises echo so we spend much time in silence. Before coming to Chechnya we hadn't lived together, only dashed to each other's homes in the times between Jon doing building work and me working as part-time assistant manager at a community centre or teaching tai chi. Sometimes we would sit and meditate together; we knew the power of silence, the power to calm, heal and restore, and we use that knowledge now. We are comfortable with each other in our silence which is set to the distant accompaniment of the clinking backgammon counters, hour after hour.

Evening arrives, our stomachs are grumbling, we hear knocking at

24

the door. GA bounces in and asks if we would like to come out into the kitchen. He lets us cook up some pasta. HC arrives in a jovial mood and produces a tin of instant coffee. 'Nescafé Classic' he says in a reverent tone. The light in the kitchen is turned off – they do not want to draw attention to us from the outside. So we sit, masked kidnappers and naked-faced captives in the half-light from a bulb in the hallway, joking and tittering in whispers around the plastic tablecloth with cups of steaming black coffee – a coffee party!! Could it ever be captured, this 'Theatre of the Absurd', in a play, sculpture, painting, or even believed? I wonder.

Our joviality is interrupted by Paunch, who was sleeping in the other room. 'Problemi, problemi?' he enquires, bemused by the intimate scene. HC and GA calm his fears and tell him he can go home. The 'party' carries on in more hushed tones until weariness sets in.

Sunday 13 July

GA's in a story-telling mood. He tells us about his two years in the Russian army. Chechens suffered a lot of ridicule. Many of them built up a resistance to this by becoming proficient in kickboxing, karate and boxing. They have represented the former USSR and the current Russian Federation in many international events. At one point during GA's national service he and his fellow soldiers were suffering because they didn't have adequate clothing or footwear. All their requests were being refused so he got hold of the storeroom key and distributed new kit amongst his comrades. The authorities suspected GA and put him in the 'lockup', a tiny box room with not enough space to sit or lie and no windows. He relaxed, took off his boots, using one as a pillow, curled up and went to sleep. The officer who opened the door was so angry that GA wasn't quaking with fear that he sent him home and demanded a fine from his family.

HC walks in, bleary eyed from a few hours sleep after a night on watch. He makes a cup of strong, black coffee, lights a cigarette and gives us a history lesson on Chechnya.

'For four hundred years,' he says, 'the Russians have tried to gain supremacy over Chechen territory. We always fight back courageously. Since the coming of the industrial age it has been harder; machines have taken over from horses. In 1944 Stalin exiled our whole population to Kazakhstan.

He said the Chechens had collaborated with the Germans, although the Germans never got as far as Chechnya. Thousands of Chechens were herded onto cattle trucks and thousands died. Only in 1957 did Brezhnev relent and allow us back to our homeland. We have to keep account of our history as the Russians have erased it from all the history books. Many can relate their family tree back through seven generations.' HC gets very animated at this point, his eyes flashing with defiance as he remembers himself as a 17-year-old stomping up to his history teacher's home with a pile of ancient books kept by his family. The books related Chechen history without the propaganda deletions. 'This is our history!' he shouted as he shoved the books under his teacher's nose. And now, in this war, the Russians have bombed the Chechen libraries once more and burnt all of HC's archives.

Monday 14 July

We are let out for a wash, breakfast and later some lunch. Thankfully the lack of interest of Puppydog and Paunch in engaging with us gives us time to rest and recharge our batteries after the intense sessions with GA and HC. In the afternoon Paunch throws us a carrot. This is in response to our demand for vegetables!

I decide to practise some yoga. It's so good to stretch up and not feel a sky of nails and to have my feet firmly planted on a shiny wooden floor rather than on uneven pebbles and earth. Then I ease out all the aches and tightness caused by nights lying on the sagging camp bed and the hard packing cases. Stretching and flexing all the parts of my body my muscles feel more toned and supple and my mind more alert.

Later I find some squared paper under the beds and we play Battleship. This makes me think of Ben and all the games we used to play when he was young, and the mad weekend camping expeditions, driving home with soaked clothes and chattering teeth in the steamed-up car, heater on full blast. I was only 19 when Ben was born, and his mum 18. The responsibility felt huge and I was determined to be a good husband and Dad so I worked hard in the day and looked after Ben at night, changing his nappy and feeding him. Debbie was also finding the strain of being a young mother too much and just after Ben's second birthday she said if she stayed she would have a nervous breakdown, and left. I hoped we would get back together again but it didn't happen. Very quickly I learnt that I couldn't work and look after Ben so we moved back to my parents' house where my mum be-came a surrogate mother. I slipped into grief, crying myself to sleep, not wanting to believe Debbie didn't want to come back. I remember being so hurt that I didn't contemplate another relationship for four years. In my non-working hours I turned to sport: running, squash, swimming. Often I ran 14 miles just for fun on a Sunday morning. One day a guy said, 'Who are you running from?' Then it hit me, and I realized that he was in the same position and had taken up running because of a failed relationship. I thought, 'Wow, maybe so, maybe I am running away from the pain.' For a long time after that I remember thinking to myself that when I went run-ning I wasn't running away from anything but reclaiming parts of myself, running back to myself.

Tuesday 15 July

GA and HC say they are not good at cooking because in their culture the men don't cook. We explain that in our culture many of us work on a 50–50 basis. They find it very amusing when I say I'll do the cooking today, a simple delicacy of pasta and fried onion.

Wednesday 16 July

I wake in the darkness. A babe is crying and a voice singing, sweet tones high and clear, a mother's lullaby. I'd like to join her but my voice is muted by captivity. As the day dawns I walk silently across the shiny floor and wedge myself tightly up against the wall by the wardrobe. With one finger I ease the blanket away, above the paper pinned to the lower panes I see branches and leaves of trees lining a road and the sky beyond. A brown bird alights on a branch.

We hear the children, running, tripping, dawdling on their way to school; sometimes they stop and chat outside our window. Perhaps we know them? They may have been to the Little Star centre. So easy to catch their attention, a quick knock on the window, a shout. The conse-quences are too grave.

I wake to music in my ears, the sounds of people living their lives, keeping me in touch with life. Camilla's urge to get a glimpse of the outside world makes me nervous, as we never know when our captors may enter the room or if we'll be seen from the outside by them or someone they know. During GA's 'inspections' he checks the coverings for signs that we've been looking out of the window. I'm afraid of what will happen if Camilla is caught.

Hearing the children makes me think of my own childhood. Early memories of eating half-rotten apples fallen from a tree or sitting in tall grasses watching a bee settle on my knee and feeling the sharp pain of the sting. A childhood that felt safe but not tightly cocooned. Running naked in the garden in warm summers, no sense of freedom or constraint, just existing and absorbing minute by minute, being part of the landscape.

When my Dad was retraining after coming out of the RAF we lived with my grandparents in Somerset for two years. My parents spent the working week in London so that Dad could retrain and look for work. I remember the freedom of exploring the large vicarage and garden, building dens and finding secret hiding places. I loved singing in the little church and thought it was quite normal for my grandfather to wear his pyjamas under his cassock! I became aware of a figure called 'God' and his son Jesus who loved little children and animals.

Around the age of nine I began to wonder: who is this God? Apparently not human but somehow equated with love, which I experienced as a human emotion. Looking back I can see that I was beginning to question the nature of reality. Around the same time I was also questioning language – words seemed so finite, such a crude form of communication that was often open to misinterpretation. There were ways, I felt, to communicate without words. Sometimes I would close my eyes and create a space around the swirling shapes I saw there. Was the space behind my eyelids as real as the space I saw when I opened my eyes?

Mum introduced me to the idea of meditation when I was ten. She had just started doing yoga. One day I sat on her bed and focused intently on a mandala that she had put on the wall. As I did so I had an odd feeling that my body was separate from me. I felt so quiet and so still. I looked down at my left arm. Whose was it? It seemed to exist as a separate entity.

'Who are we?' 'How do we see ourselves?' 'What is a human being?' These questions began forming in my 12-year-old mind. At this time I was introduced to the work of Douglas Harding and explored some of his perceptual exercises.

We would sit in a circle and count the number of bodies, then the number of heads we saw. What a joke, the numbers didn't correlate! This is something you have to experience to understand. Get a paper tube and look through one end while a friend looks through the other. Are there two faces or do you find face to no face? Point a finger towards your body and describe what the finger is pointing at; then move your finger higher in front of your face, try and describe it, you will only see a finger. Focus on your body and imagine yourself looking through a microscope going beneath the layers of skin and flesh to the cell structure, DNA and beyond. Space within. Point a finger out into the solar system, the galaxy and beyond, space without; all part of our awareness, part of our being. I began to understand that our awareness comes from this no-face space, not boxed into a head. Of course we do have a head, we see it in the mirror, we feel sensations, other people tell us how we look, but it doesn't define our whole being.

Being aware of the space I was looking out of gave me such a sense of release and laughter. And the best thing was the realization that everybody was looking out of the same space too – maybe the only thing that we can all share. We have different feelings, thoughts, bodies, experiences, but they exist in that infinite space. I began to understand that human beings are energy bodies, not just fleshy solid bodies with a space called a mind housed in a solid head that creates thoughts and feelings. We exist in a paradox; the 'I' is different from the Camilla that is presented to the world. The art is to work from that 'I' space and not identify solely with the Camilla who fears looking a fool and being misinterpreted.

Of course I did not think in those terms when I was 12; I just revelled in the sensation of looking out from an infinite space where the creative potential had no boundaries. All my feelings and thoughts about that which is beyond our concrete reality now had a physical, experiential reference. It was OK. There was, paradoxically, a form to the formlessness that I sensed. I remember buying a copy of the *I Ching* where the words 'All is Nothing and Nothing is All' made sense and helped me relax and cope with being in a seemingly mad world; the madness of war and injustice became apparent to my teenage mind.

It helps me cope now as I open my eyes and look out into our pink walled world, no natural light, no open door, but I feel the infinite space out of which I look. They cannot capture that.

29

Thursday 17 July

The day begins as usual, GA beckoning us to come out for a wash and breakfast. HC eventually walks in, sleepy eyed and grumpy, decides he'd prefer not to have our company in the kitchen and shoos us back to our room. The front door closes; one of them has left the apartment. GA pokes his head around the door and calls us out again, we're glad it's him and not HC.

Out comes the dictionary and we talk. He comes from a large family living in four houses built around a courtyard. He is one of 13 brothers and sisters; luckily none of them were killed in the war. He tells the story of how his father had been in a café in his youth when a group of Russian soldiers began taunting him so he pulled out his knife and fatally injured four of them before being injured himself – he survived. The depth of rancour between the two nations is very great. Yet GA mentions visiting Russian friends in Grozny and distinguishes them from the ones that order the bombing by calling them 'Chechen Russians'. For a while there is humour and quiet laughter.

Jon decides to lie down. GA and I continue talking in whispers across the table, then I decide it's time to leave. But as I get up GA moves like a cat around the table to my side, a large kitchen knife in his hand. He catches hold of me, hugging me to his chest with the knife at my back, and tries to kiss me. I struggle, turning my head away and whisper 'Jon, mye mooge, Jon mye mooge, (Jon's my husband),' and he backs off, angrily handing me a reed brush to sweep the floor. I try to keep as much distance as possible between us, wishing that Jon would sense something and come in. My whole body is in shock, shaking, but I know the situation will be worse if I cry out. GA orders me to sweep the corridor and their bedroom. He picks up the gun in the hallway and keeps the barrel trained on me, but luckily doesn't try to touch me, in fact he seems scared to come close. He's angry at the rejection and I can sense some guilt too. Eventually he calms down and I feel safe enough to suggest tea.

We sit as we sat before, but the atmosphere is not as before, it's charged with tension. I tell him I'm his sister and nothing more, he listens and makes no reply. I calm myself, silently asking all the angels of peace and reconciliation to be with us. 'Sorry,' he says quietly.

I sense something is happening that makes me uncomfortable. When Camilla comes in and tells me what has occurred I realize that I am now going to have to be extra vigilant on her behalf as well as my own. I decide that to the best of my ability I must ensure that she and I are always together when we are with our captors. I'm starting to get a glimpse into the trauma that these men live with that has made them unstable; the trauma of war and the vacuum it left, filled with rubbishy American movies full of violence and rape and the concept that the western woman is easy going – sex given if asked. The films have much to answer for and I wish the creators of them have more thoughts of the consequences of the garbage they pump out. All those things we are relaxed about in our country, such as the freedom of speech between the sexes, can be seen as an invitation. We'll just have to be more wary in our dealings with these men; so much is open to misinterpretation.

Friday 18 July

Puppydog and Paunch don't trouble us so we have time to lick our wounds and reassess our friendship with our captors. They are much more unstable than we thought. HC's sharp mood swings are becoming apparent, the walls are cracking around his well of grief and anger. The incident with GA shocks us greatly because he's always been the most constant in his friendship. Now we see it's a friendship built on the quicksand of war.

We had seen the effects of the war on the children and now we are beginning to see the trauma in the men. They've spent two years fighting, coping with the blood, guts and death of friends and family, surviving on little sleep and often little or no food. They have not had the time or the means to deal with their anger and sadness.

The rollercoaster has begun.

Saturday 19 July

GA bursts through our door. Instead of calling us out as usual he closes the door behind him and squats in front of it. This puts us on the alert; we sit up, silently pleading with our swollen bladders to hold on.

'Why did you come to Chechnya?' he says gruffly. 'I don't believe you drove all the way from England to Chechnya.' 'Who do you work for? KGB, CIA?' 'There have been big floods in England, a huge tidal wave. England doesn't exist any more, there's nothing for you to go back to.' The latter was accompanied by expansive gestures.

It doesn't matter how we answer, his mind is set on mental torture. I have the feeling this all relates to the incident two days ago; he knows I won that battle and he's still feeling angry about it. Oddly enough the only thing that really gets under my skin is the vision of England being no more. Of course I know he's telling lies but it brings it home that we have no idea what's going on with our families and friends and no way of getting any information.

With my bladder full to bursting I find it difficult to respond to GA's inquisition. As for England being flooded, well, that was a possibility. But as for it not existing any more, I think they would be more concerned about where the ransom money would now come from for our release. After about half an hour of this torture, the sleepy figure of HC pushes open the door, wondering what is going on. GA abruptly stops talking and in the ensuing silence I ask if we can go to the toilet. Much to my relief HC waves us through without a thought.

The rest of the day passes uneventfully; they let us out to eat then send us back to our room. Here we discuss our situation in hushed tones. We're going to have to be much more cautious about showing our friendship and about the information we give. In the confused state of their minds we know they can turn anything we say against us.

Sunday 20 July

Another breather and a good eating day. Puppydog and Paunch bring a bag full of vegetables – onions, courgettes, tomatoes, aubergines, and a bottle of home-pressed sunflower oil.

Yes! We can make a ratatouille. Camilla chops as I stir it all together on the gas cooker. Luckily there's gas because there's no electricity today, which will affect the water pumps. We fill all the pans we can find with water before it stops running from the taps. Puppydog and Paunch are very slack about doing these things. Thankfully they don't stop us.

Monday 21 July

GA opens the fridge and discovers a white plastic bag full of fatty chunks of beef. The scent of fried beef had wafted into our room the night before but Puppydog and Paunch had declined to offer us any.

This time GA asks me to cook it for all of us, calling me 'the Chef'. I think he still feels disturbed by the earlier 'scene' with Camilla and has decided to focus his attention on me. As a man he can relate to me in a totally different way. I'm glad to have something to do, it takes my attention away from thoughts of escape. Our bedroom window has no bars.

So there's a nice homely scene in the kitchen, Jon chopping the fat off the meat, me slicing vegetables, the smell of frying onions; only there is a masked man sitting with us. GA even finds some peppercorns in the cupboard which I chop up on a board. A nice culinary touch. The chopping helps to calm my frayed nerves. I don't eat any meat, I haven't eaten meat for some years and I'm not prepared to start now.

HC joins us from his smoking den, the fragrant scent of marijuana clinging to his clothes. Fortunately he is the only full-time smoker and none of them seems to drink alcohol, a great blessing in the circumstances. HC has been ruminating on our 50–50 style of living and, as we eat, decides to enlighten us on the correct role of women in society and how to deal with one's wife if she is not doing her duty. First, a woman's place is in the home, cooking, cleaning, tending to the children and to her husband's every need. 'When they disobey,' he slams his fist into the palm of his other hand, 'they must be punished.' He married his wife when she was only 19 and said that he'd had to train her. Two years later, at the tender age of 21, she was killed by a bomb.

I'm so glad I'm not a Chechen wife!

Tuesday 22 July

Time to think. Ashok's face is clear in my mind's eye. How will he be feeling? He will be very stoical, I know; the tears will fall silently. I cannot think of him for too long, my muscles tense with the sad thoughts, it is time to move. I stretch up, then bend towards the ground, legs straight, knees unlocked and head as floppy as a rag doll's. Easing out the tension knots, letting go all my anxious thoughts. I rise up slowly and smile into myself.

33

'Let's play Ludo,' says Jon. 'Good idea,' I reply, knowing it's better to play this mindless game in the present than dwell too long on thoughts of loved ones who are not with us.

Wednesday 23 July

A day of war talk.

GA describes how he carried a mortar on his shoulder and the various ways of taking out a tank. He mimes superbly. This is man's talk and Camilla is ignored. He tells us about the time when he and his fighting comrades were in the middle of Grozny in daylight; they hadn't eaten for several days and had been fighting a snipers' battle non-stop. GA remembered a flat in one of the tower blocks where he had seen jars of pickled vegetables so he asked his friends to cover him and ran to the building, up six flights, quiet as a cat so as not to disturb the Russian snipers on the eighth floor, grabbed three large jars and managed to return to his friends, undetected. They feasted.

Another time he was with some fighters in a bedroom and a grenade came sailing through the window, they somersaulted out of the way and it failed to explode so one of them picked it up and threw it back out; there was a loud bang. On another occasion he had to run the gauntlet when his group of fighters were surrounded by Russians. They decided half would stay and half would run. He mimed the run, feeling the breath of a flying bullet, aware of friends falling, knowing those left behind had no escape.

Many times he helped women and children to escape from the line of fire. His voice cracks, the sadness and despair show in his eyes when he describes the ones that didn't make it. The tiny bodies, mutilated and covered with blood, that he carried away to be buried. The irony was that many of these children were Russian. There were a few thousand Russians living in the centre of Grozny when the war began who hadn't left because they didn't believe their own countrymen would fire on them.

One week GA hadn't slept or eaten and his friends took him to a hospital that was still working. He laughs at how, even in his diminished state, he refused an intake of vitamins because it meant the young nurse would see his bottom as she injected them.

HC joins in and tells us how he and his fighting group slept in the hills during the day and ran the 30 kilometres into Grozny at night, fought until dawn and returned to the hills. At one time there was a Russian column of

tanks advancing up one of the main boulevards in Grozny. The Chechens'
only defence was a group of 15 men armed with machine guns and shoulder-
launch mortars. They managed to hold the column back, and destroy much
of it. Each time one of them got wounded he would be taken to a doctor,
patched up and continue fighting. HC had met this doctor who was in awe
of the courage of these Chechen men. Friends of HC had intercepted the
Russian military radio and fed in false information so the Russians thought
they were surrounded by hundreds of Chechen fighters.

HC shows us his scars, deep indents in his right arm and neck: a grenade
had exploded near him, killing two of his friends. He also has a white scar
spot in his right eye. He only sees light and dark with that eye, no images.
'But it has its uses,' he says, with a wry smile. 'I can tell when it is going to
rain hours in advance by the pain.'

Friday 25 July

HC is determined that we should be educated on the 1994–96 war so he
brings a video and television and sets them up in their bedroom. After
breakfast they invite us for a five-hour video show. Once again we have
a bizarre cameo, four figures sitting side by side on two beds pushed
together, backs leaning against the wall, legs stretched out, two masked
faces and two naked faces. I make sure Jon sits between me and the other
two. No contact please.

The first video clips show the trial and execution of a Chechen collab-
orator. The court is set in a forest clearing where a line of soldiers dressed
in camouflage stand behind their commander, Shamil Basaev, who is
sitting at a rickety table. The prisoner is brought into view, a thin, pale
figure with a gaunt face, a shaved head and a plaster above one eye. The
trial is conducted in Chechen. We see him being blindfolded and stood
in front of a tree; shots ring out and he slumps to the ground.

The video continues with scenes from the war in Grozny, showing
burning tower blocks and artillery fire. HC gets very excited, explaining that the Chechens intercepted Russian military radio and gave them
co-ordinates (in Russian) of the position of other Russian units so the
Russians ended up firing on their own men.

High on a hillside overlooking a valley leading into the mountains we
see a vast column of Russian tanks. Whoever was in command didn't

have much of a brain – even to my untrained eye it was obvious the column was a sitting duck. The Chechens took out the first tank and the
last, using shoulder-launched anti-tank rockets. There was no escape.
There were very few Chechens up in the hills, hundreds of Russians in
the ravine. The man who was taking the video was shot in the leg; he
videoed the bullet hole in his trousers before handing the camera to
someone else. It was April 1996, scant cover, the trees not yet clothed.

Another clip shows three Chechens beneath a road bridge, knee deep
in a gushing mountain stream. One of them has been wounded in the
head and they're trying to keep him conscious by guiding his hands to
wash away the blood in the icy water. They bandage the wound and half
walk, half drag him between them up the hillside to safety.

There follow scenes of carnage, the aftermath of the battle. Tanks
reduced to melted blobs of metal, most of the soldiers incinerated. One
wildly exultant Chechen holds up a long pole with a bit of smoking meat
hooked on the end. We don't need to understand the language to know
this is not a piece of barbecued lamb or beef. How can human beings call
themselves civilized when they still try and solve conflicts in this insane,
barbaric manner?

There's footage from the BBC. Good old Ben Brown reporting from
a road in Grozny in early 1995. At one point he and his cameraman
dive into a ditch to evade a shell that wipes out seven civilians close by.
Another Englishman is reporting from an alleyway between buildings
when there's a large explosion and the man next to him collapses with
his legs soaking in blood. He helps to drag him away saying 'Let's get the
hell out of here.' It's comforting seeing these English reporters, it makes
us feel closer to home.

After two hours of Chechen war video we're subjected to the viewing
of two hideously trashy American films set in Vietnam. The first one is
about five American convicts either lost in the jungle or on some sort of
mission. They miraculously evaded capture and death by various forms
of torture, such as a sack with a cobra inside dropped over a head and
strategically placed tarantulas. The second one is about an American
nurse being taken hostage by a Vietcong warlord. I don't think our captors realize the irony of the situation.

Later, as I lie in bed, I'm full of unease and feel very tearful. The execution scene keeps playing through my head. I know that in their confused,

traumatized state of mind if our captors decide we are spies, anything we say will be turned against us and this could be our fate too.

The video of the execution is too amateur to be fake and I experience a strange feeling of hyperreality – the presence of a table in a forest clearing is surreal. The video is interspersed with American and British news footage of the war and also strange statistics about how long it takes to die from various forms of execution. They seem to want to let us know just how far they are prepared to go. After two hours of their home movies we are not in the mood for watching trashy American war movies.

Saturday 26 July

We have been asking Puppydog for washing powder for some days. Today he presents us with a small plastic packet of Tide – yippee! This act of kindness stops me dwelling on nerve-stretching anxious thoughts of our uncertain future. GA has given me a nylon flowery dress that belongs to his sister, still smelling of her sweat. I have a change of clothing, Jon makes do with a sheet. I wonder if GA's sister will ever find out where her dress has disappeared to.

We have a long splashy session in the bathroom (no shortage of water today). We hang the clothes to dry on the wardrobe above the lamp – fortunately it's hot outside and our room is warm.

Sunday 27 July

Another hot day. We lie on the cool wooden floor, too hot to exercise.

We are asked out to dine in the early evening. As we chop onions and peel potatoes we are plunged into darkness. HC lights a candle on top of the dresser. The silence outside is pierced by children's laughter, the noise growing as more and more children are sent out from darkened apartments to play in the eerie dusk half light. It must be a square as their voices echo off the sides of buildings. We hear the sounds of games being organized, of younger children crying for attention abandoned by their siblings, and wild boyish laughter. And here we sit with our masked companions a few feet away from this semblance of normality.

As the sky darkens the sounds diminish and are replaced by the giggles of teenage girls. GA stiffens and pours out a stream of invective in

Russian. The meaning is clear: 'These are not true Chechen women, they should not be roaming the streets after dark, giggling so irreverently and secretively.' He obviously feels it is an affront to the whole male population of Chechnya. He looks up two words in the dictionary – 'betrayal' and 'treachery' – and swings a large knife above his head bringing it down into the breadboard with a dull thud. It quivers and glitters in the candle light, the sharp tip deep in the wood. HC joins in the tirade with more lectures about the proper place of women in society. It seems clear to me that they have both been emotionally wounded by women in the past and even clearer that I have to watch every word I say and every move I make so as not to offend them and re-awaken angry passions.

Monday 28 July

Alongside the bread on the table for breakfast there's a dark blue washing up bowl half full of squashy bruised apricots. Thank you, Puppydog. Unbeknown to them Jon had washed the bowl in salt after cleaning the meat in it so we have an unusual breakfast of ripe salted apricots.

Paunch decides he is going to be our friend today and brings the backgammon board into our room to play with Jon. It wouldn't do to play with me because I'm a woman.

This is a nice change. It feels like we are being treated as human beings. Such a simple act yet it has a profound effect on how we relate to each other. Paunch tries to teach me the rules of the game. I have played this before many years ago, but I am not very good at retaining that sort of infomation. He soon gets bored of teaching and we move quickly into playing the game. I am still slow, having to add the sum of two dice together and move my pieces tactically, blocking my opponent, and gaining ground for myself. We seem to move to a different space just playing this simple game, two human beings engaging. Even though it's competitive it is much less intense than our captive/captor relationship. A peace descends and the stresses of this bizarre environment melt away as we maintain a single point of focus on the outcome of the roll of the dice and where to move our pieces. Time just slips by as we play one game after another.

I sit and muse on the bed watching Paunch hunched over the board, small and muscular like an alert bull terrier, his concentration momentarily blotting out his anger and grief. The lines of worry and stress on

Jon's face become less deep as he allows his mind to be absorbed in the game. A welcome few hours free from thought of our situation.

Tuesday 29 July

GA and HC are more relaxed today, they joke with each other while we have our breakfast and there's an underlying sense of excitement. We may be moving tonight, they tell us; their boss has said we will be free by the end of the month. GA reminds us of his 30th birthday in October and that he will invite us back for a champagne feast. I enjoy his exuberance but have a hollow feeling inside, perhaps a premonition that we will not be free and GA will have no champagne.

Back in our room I dismiss the hollow feeling and do a little dance of elation, revelling in hope and expectancy. Dance has been one of my passions since the age of 14 when I started learning 'Revived Greek Dance' with its technique derived from the study of painted friezes on Greek pottery. The breadth of the technique was great: lyrical, athletic, warlike and dramatic. Ballet seemed insipid and rigid compared to this. Using a combination of the Greek and creative dance drama, my teacher created a choreography called 'The New Spring' which was performed in Westminster Abbey. I was 15 and the atmosphere was so ecstatic I was overcome by emotion. It was one of the most inspiring experiences of my youth.

Being able to express myself through dance and being shown a Zen way of looking at the world stopped me stepping into teenage neuroses. Somehow I seemed to flow through those years without hitting boulders. My school was all girls and fairly academic, the career options heavily weighted towards professional jobs such as teaching. I was offered a place to study to teach art on a B.Ed. course at Cambridge. As I twirl around on silent toes inside our pink walls I think of those passionate, life-embracing four years in Cambridge. Acting, dancing, singing, falling in and out of love. The all-night last-minute essay writing. Discussing bright ideas for changing the world into a more inspiring place. Believing anything was possible.

After completing my degree I returned to Shropshire where I got a job as a part-time art teacher in a prep school. But I was not ready to settle down into a career, so after a couple of years I moved to Amsterdam where life stook on a magic, fairytale quality. I joined various groups for acting, singing and dancing and started learning tai chi.

Tai chi – what a precious tool to carry with me into captivity! I realized how calm I felt by just watching the grace and beauty of the slow movement. Practising this meditation in movement regularly helps to keep me strong both physically and mentally.

I finish my dance of elation. Anything is possible. Maybe, by some miracle, one of the Russian oligarchs has got involved and will pay our ransom.

4

Flashback

To avoid dwelling on the impending move I reflect back over the time I have known Chris Hunter since I met him through friends in 1990 and became interested in some of the work he was doing. Coming from a Quaker background he and Patricia Cockrell were given the job of running Quaker Peace and Service in Moscow in early 1994. During the autumn they travelled down to the Caucasus and witnessed the machinations of a war about to happen. They knew that soon the civilian population would need a lot of help and managed to get a European Union grant to form 'The Centre for Peacemaking and Community Development' (CPCD).

In mid-December 1994 the Russian tanks rolled into Chechnya. The military expected to conquer Chechnya within two weeks so the country could be presented to Yeltsin as a New Year's gift. After all, they had a population of 250 million from which to choose an army of 50,000 men and the Chechens had a population of one million to scrape a fighting force of 10,000. However, they didn't account for the fighting prowess of the Chechens, who had been defending themselves against the Russians intermittently for about three hundred years.

The onslaught was chaotic. The Russian generals sent in thousands of new recruits in their late teens who had had minimal training. The Russian army itself was in a state of decay, funds being creamed off for those in high command, leaving little money to feed and clothe and train the new recruits, thousands of whom were killed in those first two weeks. This led to the organization of the 'Committee of Soldiers' Mothers of Russia'. Many Russian families didn't know their sons were posted to Chechnya until well after the event and heard no word of whether they were alive or dead, so hundreds of mothers decided to go to Chechnya themselves to discover what had happened. The Chechens were so

41

impressed by the courage of these women that in most cases where they held their sons prisoner they handed them over to their mothers. The Committee organized a Peace March from Moscow to Grozny. Chris became the co-ordinator, inviting Buddhist monks and Russian Orthodox priests to join the 'Mothers' March for Life and Compassion' that took place in the Spring of 1995. As they crossed the border into Chechnya and entered the village of Sernovodsk they were greeted joyfully. For many people in Chechnya, this was the first sign of any interest from the outside world in their plight, a symbol of hope.

A young Chechen man called Shaman Adaev ran out to video the march and started talking to Chris. Before Sernovodsk was bombed, Shaman used to fill his car with loaves of bread and take devious routes to Grozny avoiding Russian checkpoints, to feed civilians trapped in the basements without food, water or light. Many were Russians who had no family to flee to in the villages. Later on, the whole Adaev family became involved in helping to set up and run projects initiated by CPCD.

Chris and Patricia made many journeys into Chechnya during the war to monitor the situation and organize help such as truckloads of blankets, clothes and food as the harsh winter approached. They also held talks and seminars with students in what was left of the university, discussing non-conflict resolution. Patricia used to disguise herself as a peasant, growing her hair long and wearing a headscarf and travelling on the local buses with a plastic bag full of bread covering up a video camera. They wanted to record the atrocities that were happening and not being shown in Russia or anywhere else. The attitude of most of the world was to turn a blind eye.

From Lydney to Moscow

I reflect back through the weave of events that carried us to this place. Back to September 1996 and a meeting with Chris in a café in Glastonbury. He showed us photos of events during the war; lines of dead bodies, tortured and burnt, a dead pregnant woman with a wooden pole thrust into her body from between her legs, Chechen fighters carrying the small limp bodies of children, eyes glazed with grief, faces set grimly masking the volcanic anger and revenge that would later fuel their fighting. A sharp contrast to that peaceful café with its luxurious banoffee pie and frothy cappuccinos. Chris had just come back from the Caucasus having organized for a group of 60 children to be taken out of Chechnya in a lull in the fighting for a month's recuperation and psychological help to overcome their traumas. The trip was very successful, however Chris felt great sadness when taking the children back; the bombing had stopped but the devastation and horror remained. Out of this sadness grew the idea of setting up a centre in Grozny for the psychological rehabilitation of the war-traumatized children in Chechnya.

Chris turned to Jon and me and said with a piercing look, 'Will you both come and help set it up?' I felt a tingle pass through my body and an expansive feeling in my heart, a feeling saying 'Yes' very loudly. I turned to Jon and he nodded.

The feeling in response to this question felt like a very strong 'Yes' even though the logic was a little crazy. I could not speak Russian and there were many unknowns. To set up a centre for the children felt a good thing to do. But there was much to do at home first, and we had to discuss the idea with our families.

Immediately I started scanning the future, knowing that we both needed to honour our work commitments for the next six months. Also we needed that time to save money for the journey and raise money for toys and games for the children. My first thought was April, and Chris said he would need that amount of time to find a suitable building and raise at least $40,000 to renovate and run the centre.

'There is something else you need to consider,' Chris said. 'There is a risk of kidnap. Although no westerner is kidnapped at the moment there were some people kidnapped in the war. You will have to have two armed guards with you all the time.' We said we would certainly take this into consideration.

We heard nothing until after Christmas, but somehow the idea had lodged in our minds and I couldn't sense a continuation of my current jobs. After April my future was a blank, waiting to be lived in a way I could not perceive.

In February we knew for certain that a building had been found, and funding for the renovation and running costs would be given by the Quakers, Mothers for Peace (a German organization), and Norwegian Church Aid. Chris had already arranged for a group of six women to go into the villages and into schools in Grozny to assess the type and depth of the trauma experienced.

'They need a car for the children's centre, do you mind driving to Chechnya?' Chris said. Gulp! 'Er, yes OK' was my hesitant response. If I had been going by myself it would have been a big No, but with Jon it was a different matter. He had all the practical skills I lacked and was brilliant at finding solutions to unexpected problems. At that time CPCD was still a very small, newly formed organization with a tiny budget, so any extra vehicle would be a great help. That is how we came to drive a £500 white Lada Riva laden with clay, paints, toys, footballs, a parachute plus clothing and bedding all the way from Lydney, Gloucestershire to Grozny, Chechnya. On Wednesday 16 April at 5 a.m. we set off, mud flaps scraping the tarmac.

After a night in Amsterdam and a day wallowing in the lorry ruts on the German motorways we approached Berlin in a blood red sunset. We stayed with Chris's friend Ekehardt who had spent much time in the Caucasus. He welcomed us, his piercing light blue eyes glittering behind round glasses beneath a cloth peaked cap. We sat on benches around a long table discussing our forthcoming journey with Ekehardt and three Georgians: his wife, an elderly writer and Zora, a student of politics. The writer spoke the most English and told us we were mad to contemplate crossing the Russian border and driving to Chechnya without knowing any Russian. I knew he was right but I felt it was our destiny; we were following our hearts not our heads. Ekehardt realized we were set on going and started to persuade Zora, who was travelling to Moscow the next day by bus, to go with us instead and help us cross the border. Zora's brown eyes narrowed and his face muscles tensed. He was not keen, and we were not sure it was a good idea considering the extra weight the Lada would have to carry. No decision was made.

The next morning Zora had resigned himself to coming with us. The persuasive Ekehardt enthusiastically re-arranged the boxes on the back seat to make space for Zora and his enormous suitcase. Our journey to the Polish border was grey, rainy and full of diversions. Zora sat in an unhappy huddle in the back seat. We had no problems at the border. On we drove through dank fir-tree forests, the only splash of colour being women leaning against the tree bark in shiny high heeled boots, wearing red mini skirts beneath fur coats and fluffy white hats. They looked ready for a night out in Berlin with their heavily made up faces but this was lunchtime and there was no sign of habitation except for the odd lorry pulled up on the verge.

Warsaw at midnight: wet, wet, wet. Vast shiny roads, no cats-eyes and tyre ruts that caused the Lada to sway like a hippo. One hour on and the car started kangarooing so we stopped at a petrol station and decided to sleep. Zora, however, became very agitated and said we could sleep at the border. We arrived at 4 a.m.; the queue looked endless. Almost immediately a car came alongside us and the driver offered to get us a place near the front if we paid $100. We declined and settled down to sleep.

Our sleep was interrupted as we inched forward into the daylight. There were three queues, one for lorries, one for buses and one for cars. I looked with interest at the queue of laden buses packed with clothing and other goods to sell in Russia. The drivers were all large Russian women with dyed blond hair. They were heavily built and shrouded in massive coats and scarves with glassy-eyed blank expressions that seemed to convey a message of 'Don't mess with me!' Zora told us that it is virtually always the women who do the trading while their menfolk sit at home drinking vodka. I wove my way through the cars and buses to the Portakabin loos along the verge and queued amongst these statuesque, unsmiling women carrying their toiletries in colourful plastic bags. Later Jon brought out our little gas cooker and a saucepan and boiled up some noodles on the car bonnet. We found we could communicate with Zora quite well in broken German and gestures. He was in Berlin to learn about the prison system so that when he returned to Georgia he could improve the system there. He had also fought in the army; his face looked strained and he didn't go into any detail. He told us about his wife and child who were staying in Moscow; he showed us photographs. Finally he relaxed and even managed to smile.

Fifteen hours later we reached the front. An officious looking guard came over and told us we were in the wrong queue and would have to go back. Whaat! Zora's face took on the look of an irate terrier, and he leapt out of the car and started gesticulating to all the cars around and, somehow, despite angry shouts and some fist shaking managed to part the sea of cars like Moses so we could turn in a circle and come back into the right queue. A different guard came over and waved us through. With Zora's help it took less than an hour to complete all the formalities. If he hadn't been with us we would have had to wait for an interpreter and who knows how long that would have taken.

We crossed the border into Belarus as the sun was setting. Camilla explained to Zora in her scanty German that Chris had advised us not to travel at night but to stop by a police check point and sleep. Zora disagreed, gesturing wildly he said the country was full of bandits and we should just drive and drive until we reached Moscow. After fuelling up and changing some money we head for Moskva, only 1,050 kilometres away!

Our journey began along the M1 of Belarus, a rather different type of road to our M1 north of London. The surface was pitted concrete a bit like an abandoned airport runway, no cats-eyes, no white lines and no kerbs. We had to swerve round huge potholes and try not to be distracted by the numerous wrecks of cars and lorries dotted along the verges. As my night vision is not good I was designated navigator for most of the journey.

I was puzzled by oncoming cars driving straight at me then swerving at the last minute. I discovered the road was only surfaced for half of its width. Ten kilometres one side then all change to the other side. I learnt to drive on the wrong side of the road, only moving to the rough side when forced to by oncoming vehicles. I wouldn't want to break down or crash – you have to sort yourself out and rely on help from passing vehicles, no AA or RAC here!

There were police (Gaaii) check-points at every town. Fortunately we were only stopped twice. Our lights were too high, the policeman told us, not surprising I thought considering the load we were carrying. This was my first taste of driving through a police state. Zora said we were lucky we were not stopped more often as they usually found some excuse to take money.

The night continued and the petrol gauge was dropping. Zora was driving and we started looking out for a petrol station. I was not prepared for the swerve off the road into a dimly lit track leading to a wooden house with a decorative barge board around the gutter and one petrol pump. Deep-throated dog barks came from a yard beside the house. It all looked a bit sinister but a man appeared from the house and started up the pump.

Slowly the sky lightened revealing a grey dawn. The road carved its way through endless birch and fir-tree forests. The trunks of the birches glimmered cold silver-beige in regimented lines, scrambled branches criss-crossed against the bleak sky. People were waking. We were joined by more cars, mostly mud-spattered Ladas, many leaning awkwardly to the right or left, bouncing on squeaky springs looking in need of a hip replacement. Figures appeared through the trees, all roundly wrapped in layers of coats and scarves, squatting on upturned plastic buckets with trays of potatoes and onions laid out in front of them, hoping for a sale with a passing motorist. Their faces were cold, pinched and grim – not an easy life.

The trees started thinning out, replaced by rows of grey stucco blocks of flats, varying in height from two storeys to ten; we were entering the suburbs of Moscow. Chris had told us to stop at the first hotel we saw and call him. I scoured the buildings seeing no sign that I could decipher as 'Hotel' so we kept on driving. Moscow sprawls across miles of concrete landscape, and it seemed an age before we reached shops with neon signs and tall official-looking buildings. We looked around for somewhere to stop and phone Chris. Ah! a Macdonalds, that would do. We sidled into an empty parking space and stopped, our bodies still vibrating from seventeen hours' car drone and pothole lurching. Zora woke up and looked bewildered. A car attendant strolled over and we paid for a ticket. By the look on Zora's face it was expensive – we were in Moscow's hub. The cars around us were well washed and sleek as were various high heeled, fur-coated ladies tripping into McDonalds. It was obviously a fashionable place to go. Zora and Jon went in search of a phone and I stayed with the car and luggage. Jon came back beaming: Chris lived only ten minutes away. He arrived shortly, big hugs all round, amazed that we had made it so quickly. Zora was keen to get home so we thanked our guardian angel and offered to take him home but he declined saying the metro was easier. We knew it could have been a very different journey without him. The last we saw of him was his slight body heaving a massive suitcase towards the metro entrance.

We entered McDonalds and ordered a coffee and apple pie, Chris helping us with our first attempt at Russian. Then he drove us to his flat, which was situated near the Kievskaya market. We were greeted at the door by Shaman and Adlan Adaev who had come up from Chechnya to discuss the organization of the children's centre. They looked very smart, in great contrast to our bedraggled, musty, travel-wrinkled state. We crammed into a small 'cat pee' lift that took us to Chris's tiny flat. After a meal and a shower we fell asleep, leaden bodied and dreamless.

Birth of Little Star

We started preparing for a two-day conference that would include people involved in setting up the centre in Grozny. The conference would take place in a sanatorium in the outer suburbs. About five o'clock the crew started arriving: Sasha, a psychologist from Krasnodar, Olya, another psychologist from Stavropol, Elmira and Zarema, nurses from Grozny, Lyoma, a teacher from a small village near Grozny, Natasha, a teacher from Grozny, and Anya, a trainee psychologist from Moscow. There wasn't enough sugar or biscuits so Olya and I rushed out to the market. She was a bubbly person and spoke a little English, so it was fun to shop with her.

Later we drove out with Chris and arrived at a large square building in a leafy suburb full of holiday dachas. We were greeted by a woman in a white coat sitting at the desk in the entrance hall. The dining room looked like it hadn't been used for a while. Chris told us that it had been a rest centre for factory workers in the time of the former Soviet Union. Now there was a problem, how and where could we cook. The kitchen had vast sinks with the odd, unwashed plate smelling of fermented meat, a huge sterilizing unit for glass jars but no cookers. Chris talked to the caretaker and she brought in two electric rings and a selection of flimsy aluminium forks and spoons. Luckily we had brought a saucepan and kettle and Jon had his trusty penknife.

A kitchen with no cooker, unbelievable! Everyone arrived apart from Olya and Sasha who seemed to be lost. Chris discovered there were two train stations with the same name so he rushed off to find them. I started to feel hungry and it stunned me how everyone just hung around waiting for something to happen, waiting and waiting. Was this Soviet thinking, waiting for someone to give an order, or war trauma? So I took the initiative, boiled up some pasta and made a tomato sauce.

Eventually Sasha and Olya managed to find a working phone and left a message that they were at the station. By the time Chris found them, after going to both stations, it was three in the morning. When Chris had come before they had heard his voice but thought they were hallucinating! Totally bizarre. Ever since we had arrived we had noticed little crises popping up out of thin air. I had the feeling the country operated on a thin layer of organized solid ice and if your toe accidently cracked through the surface there would be chaos.

The weekend was spent discussing Zviozdochka (Little Star). This was the name given to the building when it was used as a sanatorium for children with TB. Ironically the building was built by an English company in the 1930s when they were oil prospecting in Grozny. We were joined by Eric and Milla from Médicin du Monde who would act as advisers. We discussed various topics, such as the ethos, creating a safe and caring space for the children, allowing the trauma to be released through use of movement, art, drama, music, games, sport, individual and group counselling. We also discussed daily structure, equipment, food and water, and finally security.

On Sunday we were joined by a group of women from the Quaker centre in Moscow who brought Easter sweetmeats: balls of homemade cream cheese full of raisins and bits of crystallized fruit. They had been working with refugee Chechen children and their families, meeting them each week, helping rehabilitate them through counselling, art work and play. We finished the discussions by sitting in a circle with our eyes closed, holding hands and projecting thoughts of inspiration, healing, smooth organization, love and compassion into the birth of Little Star. Energy follows thought.

Back in the centre of Moscow on Monday morning, Lyoma and I took a trip to buy paper and crayons for Little Star while Jon and Adlan spent a few hours in a garage waiting for Hippolada to have a 'refit'.

Adlan and I found the garage where we could get a new exhaust and the suspension jacked up. This took a couple of hours as they had to remove most of the springs from under the car to insert a rubber block to give us the extra height we needed. As I sat and waited I meditated and felt myself being re-wired. It took some time and I could physically feel my nervous system getting stronger. When the newly fitted Lada rolled off the ramps I felt ready to go.

After a week of non-stop activity I was feeling a bit tired and tearful. Luckily I managed to speak to Mum and Ashok on the telephone and that cheered me up no end, giving me renewed energy to face the next stage of our journey.

Moscow to Grozny

Adlan and Sasha were going to be our travelling companions down to the Caucasus. It was a good job Hippolada now had strong shock absorbers (two new hips) – she would never have coped with the extra weight. She looked very buoyant and perky which is more than I could say for myself, I was still in that gritty-eyeball, 5 a.m, half-awake state. After a few trips up and down the cat pee lift carrying boxes to load into Hippolada we were ready for take-off.

We drove through the grey Moscow dawn, out on the open road towards Volgagrad, long and straight, passing through large expanses of flat cultivated land, the wheat belt. Jon and Adlan shared the driving, which required a lot of concentration, avoiding potholes, overtaking lines of ponderous lorries belching black smoke and avoiding being mesmerized by the mirage shimmer on the horizon. I asked Sasha to teach me Russian words for various parts of the body as I would be doing some movement with the children. Eventually our stomachs began to rumble and we started looking out for a roadside shack selling food. Adlan swung the car off the road in front of a man cooking 'shashlik' (bits of skewered meat) over hot coals in half a rusty oil drum. Behind him was a hut selling soup, homemade cake and chai poured from the everpresent samovar. Jon and I sat inside at a rickety wooden table supping thin borsch amongst the plastic flowers while Sasha and Adlan stretched their legs and ate meat. The trees were budding in the expectant pale spring sunlight.

Onward, straight mile after straight mile, I took over the driving. We stopped at another shack with a dunny, to relieve ourselves. My menstruation had started – what excellent timing! The 'dunnies' were more filthy than anything I saw in India, piled high with paper, nappies and human dung. If I could I found a discreet tree to squat behind. It was easier for the others, all being men. We were stopped by the Gaaii who were curious about the foreign number plate. One time they said I was not wearing a seat belt (when I was!) and insisted on a 10,000 rouble fine; £1 was worth 1,000 roubles. Adlan drove us into Volgagrad at dusk, the air heavily scented by hundreds of white May blossom trees on the surrounding hills, luminescent in the half-light. He was getting tired so Jon took over and Adlan navigated us through the enormous city looking for the road to Elistar, the capital of the province Kalmyk. We were stopped by the Gaaii, and questioned by a very pompous and aggressive officer who said we needed special clearance to travel through Volgagrad. Sasha solved it in the usual way, by paying a fine. The plan was to get to

Stavropol to stay with Olya's parents, but we had been over-optimistic with our timing and were still miles from Stavropol. I took over the driving. A lonely, dark black night road, no white lines or catseyes. It was approaching 1 a.m. and I saw a café at the side of the road with lots of cars and lorries pulled up to rest for the night, so decided to do the same. This was in the middle of Kalmyk province where most of the people have eastern-shaped eyes and the religion is Buddhism. Adlan and Jon slept in the back of the car while Sasha and I explored the café. Quite a surreal atmosphere, a tinny radio playing instrumental music, a few travel-weary figures hunched over cups of sweet chai and plates of steaming meat stew and rice. We bought some homemade doughnuts and chai and slouched over a yellow Formica-topped table like the rest. I felt we had entered another country with all these unexpectedly eastern faces around us. Later I curled up on the front seat, tying a vest around my head for warmth; bright stars twinkled in the cold night.

Woken at 5 a.m. by the rumble, cough and splutter of the trucks, I turned and woke Sasha who was still asleep curled up in the sheepskin car seat cover, sensible man! I felt alert and well rested. We took our own picnic into the café and ordered tea. There was a small sink in the corner which was kept very busy with a line of shaving men. We drove on over high plateaux of grassland with a few still lakes in scooped out hollows, empty except for herds of grazing horses. The Gaaii stopped us a few times, always intrigued by our car documents because they were written in English. Sasha didn't tell them we were going to Chechnya, this would have created many problems, so he gave the name of the next large town as our destination. We had decided not to go to Stavropol because it was not directly on our route and so from Elistar we took the road in the direction of Pyatigorsk that took us through rolling hills with orchards and pretty little villages. Groups of children with brightly coloured satchels bouncing on their backs, the girls with neat plaits and patterned tights, were coming home from school for lunch. We stopped for a picnic near a village called Alexandraskaya and sat in a field overlooking a valley of orchards and grazing horses. Jon cooked noodles and boiled tea on his little stove. The air was soft, the sun was warm and all the trees dressed in bright green spring leaves, birds chirping on their branches. I felt nourished by the beauty and peace.

After our picnic we continued driving for a few miles until we reached a small village. Suddenly the driver's seat came adrift and I lost contact with the pedals. We had to stop, it was dangerous. I was glad I had packed some tools and after a little fiddling we were ready to roll again. Out on the open road I wound up the Lada's elastic band. The landscape opened out – we could see for miles. 'Bang!' A big jolt shook the car and I pulled over. I'd driven through one of the biggest potholes I had ever seen. The hole was at least 12 cm deep and 70 cm in diameter. Adlan and I inspected the wheel. The rim had a dent that we managed to hammer out using a wheelbrace; it was amazing that we didn't have a blow out.

Unbeknown to us, a bomb had exploded at the train station in Pyatigorsk the night before; two people were killed and two Chechen girls were being blamed, so the whole town had been put on security alert and all the roads leading to the town had high security check points. Thus we found ourselves at the back of a long queue. Sasha got out to investigate and advised us to drive past the queue right to the front. We were all nervous, particularly Adlan. At the border Sasha explained that we were carrying humanitarian goods and the guard opened the boot and prodded a few footballs then let us through without even looking at our passports! We silently sent a prayer of thanks. Suddenly Sasha cried out. He had seen a bus in the opposite queue going back to his home in Krasnodar. He told Jon to stop the car and said he was going home for a few days, gathered his bags, ran across the road and jumped on the bus. I was gobsmacked, having no idea that he wasn't coming with us all the way and because of the swiftness of his exit. We never saw Sasha again; his wife objected to him coming to work for Little Star because of the danger of working with unmarried women in Chechnya.

We were stopped as we entered the town of Nalchik; the Gaaii asked us if we had a transit visa. Adlan said we were staying there overnight and they let us through. But as we were leaving the town we were stopped again. Two policemen got out of their blue and white Lada, their eyes dark rimmed and empty and their breath smelling of vodka. Adlan had a nervous sweat on his brow. He got out to talk to them, and they told him to get into the back of their car. We were praying hard, this being the only thing we could do. After about 20 minutes, which seemed like hours, they allowed Adlan to get out and he came over saying they wanted 150,000 roubles but he talked them down to 100,000. We rummaged in our socks and produced the notes. They let us drive on. We felt blessed –

they could easily have taken Adlan away and locked him up. Now Adlan drove harder than ever, determined to reach Nazran the same day.

Northern Ossetia was very beautiful, with fields of yellow flowers, more horse-and-carts than cars on the road and a few stray cattle. We were stopped by a militiaman in khaki uniform; I think he noticed our English number plate and he spent some time perusing our papers. He had quite a sensitive, intelligent face, very unlike the last two policemen. He was concerned that we did not have all the right permits but allowed us to continue on our journey. Adlan drove as fast as the road allowed until we came to the Ossetian/Ingush border.

We drove through an avenue of trees dodging shell holes. It was coming up to sunset and the colours were beautiful. The avenue led to a roundabout of black-and-white concrete blocks, with barbed wire decorating the top and machine-gun placements – our first taste of entering a war zone. Adlan got out and showed our papers to the policeman at the barrier and he waved us through into Ingushetia. The sky darkened and within minutes we passed Russian tanks going in the opposite direction: Adlan swerved off the road and we heard this sinister low noise and saw tiny specks of light within a huge mass of rumbling metal that made the car shake as they passed.

It gave me a strange hollow feeling in my stomach as these vehicles, built for war, passed us. We entered Nazran, the only light coming from swinging electric bulbs lighting up the wares of roadside stalls. Adlan drove to one of the more wealthy neighbourhoods that had rows of large houses behind huge walls and gates. Patterned friezes stamped out of thin silver metal decorated the tops of the walls. We stopped outside the house rented by Médicin du Monde.

Adlan shouted and a man opened the gates, we drove into a courtyard that had a white blossom tree in the middle, a peaceful oasis after the continual drone and drama of the journey. We were greeted by the Médicin du Monde team. They fried up some eggs and sausages which we ate before collapsing between cool white sheets surrounded by walls stencilled with flowers and trompe l'oeil columns.

May 1st was a day of rest for Jon and me and also a holiday for Médicin du Monde. So nice doing tai chi on the balcony and simply sitting watching the blossom tree. In the afternoon Anya arrived with Madina, a teacher from Ingushetia, who will be working with us. They gave me a tour of Nazran, the capital of Ingushetia. A group of lads overheard

Anya talking in English with me and we ended up with quite a large entourage shouting out, 'Hello, how are you? What is your name?' Most of the men were small with dark hair and brown eyes, many wearing trilby style hats. The women wore long, flowery dresses; nearly all of them had a headband or scarf. The roads in the centre of Nazran were wide and dusty, some like boulevards with small parks along the centre where there were vast statues of young communist men and women sculpted in the 1920s and '30s. There was an empty man-made lake with cows wandering about in its bed, overlooked by the most expensive hotel in Ingushetia, the hotel Assa.

The girls told me about the last six months when they, Madina, Anya, Olga, Natasha, Elmira and Zarema had been going into the villages and working with the most traumatized children helping them to release their trauma through counselling, play and art therapy. Chris had met Natasha at a 'Peace in Caucasia' conference run by the United Nations of Youth (UNOY) in Yalta 1996. Through Natasha he met the others who would make up the core team.

5

The Kiva Revisited

I am jolted back to 'now' by Jon knocking on the door to be let out for our nightly teeth brushing session in the kitchen sink and last pee of the day. No response. He knocks again and we hear the heavy thud thud of Paunch's fairy feet approaching. He opens the door with a jerk, one eye glaring. This is not usually his job, Puppydog is out. We clean our teeth with him sitting watching us, playing with a carving knife, a nervous, fearful man. Jon gives him a small bow of thanks and I say 'Spaseba'; we are both very calm, we feel no fear. He glares at us, slicing the knife through the air, snarling like a cornered bull terrier.

I only feel his fear, so strong that he has to hold this large knife to protect himself. He surely is a wounded being.

Later we hear their code tapping on the front door, many quiet footfalls and whispering voices in rapid Chechen. Our possessions are packed and we sit in quiet anticipation, my heart flutters as I hear the scrabble of ropes being untied and the creak of our door opening. GA and HC come in, they are relaxed and smiling. 'Only two days then you will be free,' they say. HC apologizes as he locks handcuffs around Jon's wrists, 'It is necessary, you understand, yes?' They pull black balaclavas over our heads, the eyeholes at the back. I hear the voice of our driver, a deep rich whisper. We had heard his distinctive baritone before when he had visited the flat, just right for a voice-over on an advertisement for smooth velvety 'dark chocolate', so that's what we call him. We are gently guided out of the flat into the night air.

They have parked the Jeep in the square, much closer than before. The silence is resonant with intent, I sense their taut muscles, jaws clenched, stealth in every footfall. We are pushed into the back seat between HC and GA. This time they don't ask us to bow our heads and I can see a glimmer of streetlights through the wool of the balaclava. We turn off on a rough dirt track, bouncing through the potholes until we creep to a halt. I hear a gate being opened and the jeep rolls quietly into a driveway. I am helped out, up some steps and left into a small room where they take off my mask. I keep my eyes facing the floor and notice a patterned red carpet, half of it rolled back revealing an open trapdoor leading to our Kiva.

I am led briskly from the Jeep. I am not warned of some steps I have to climb, trip and almost fall – my guide is not taking much care. Has our value dropped? A deal collapsed? Into the building, mask removed, handcuffs off, it looks a little familiar, I am led to a ladder and allowed to make a gentle, careful descent. Oh shit, I was hoping we wouldn't see this place again.

My heart feels heavy and I can feel my face putting on a 'stoic' mask, a 'grin and bear it' without the grin. Someone has cleared away all evidence of our previous existence here. The campbed is turned on its side, no Ludo 'board', no little chairs, only a patch of white sugar crystals stamped into the earth floor, the end of our sugar cube dice. Later I suspected from a chance remark by HC that the sugar was crushed in great anger, food is seen as sacred especially after the hunger suffered in the war. We had committed an act of sacrilege and were lucky not to be punished for it.

This time they hand down a bucket straight away and the same two blankets and pillow. We settle down to the first night back in our old home.

Thursday 31 July

I open my eyes to dim, brick orange light. They have built a brick wall outside the hole in our bedroom a couple of inches from the house wall so we can't see out but some light and air can get in. I sniff the warm, slightly musty earth and pebble air, slip into my sandals, no barefoot walking here, and stoop back into our eating and washing chamber. I sit on a pile of wooden window-frames; the light is very dim in here. Jon sleeps soundly, our guards dream, cockerels crow and the thudding of cows' hooves shakes the earth. A good time to do my tai chi, and quite a challenge on this uneven earth floor in near blackness. The soft flowing moves calm my mind and I sense the wooden prop holding up the roof so I don't bump into it. I focus on my quiet breath and radiate love out into this place, into Jon and into our sleeping guards.

A loud yawn, squeak of bedsprings and heavy footfalls wake me out of my reverie. I hear the scrape of the weight being removed from the trapdoor and a flush of daylight brightens the Kiva. Jon moves swiftly through the hole in the wall to be with me. The masked face of GA peers down, 'Dobrie Oodra,' we chorus, and he hands down a litre jar of tea followed by a loaf of bread and two small cups. We ask for water and another litre jar appears. Jon wisely makes a 'tea cosy' out of one of the masks: this may be the only hot drink we will get all day. The tea is hot and very sweet, the bread definitely yesterday's, dry with a sharp tang of soda. GA switches the electric light on; what a difference it makes!

I rearrange the pile of window frames so we have two seats, one high and one low and on top of the high pile a plank of wood to serve as a table. The air is pleasantly warm and I douse my head in water and comb out a few nits. The itching began a couple of weeks ago. My thick, long, curly hair is becoming unmanageable. With no shampoo or strong enough comb to disentangle the knots it makes a beautiful nesting habitat for lice!

Our stomachs are rumbling, it must be late afternoon. GA opens the trapdoor and invites us to come up into the room above to eat. The two windows are covered in polythene. The walls are painted pale blue; one has a spray of plastic flowers hung against it. A doorway leads to another room curtained off with some frilly pink nylon material. There is a large glass dresser with delicate china cups and saucers and dainty glasses and a door next to it leading to a passageway. On the floor is a huge dumbbell, the weight that is used to stop us pushing up the trapdoor. Opposite the windows there's a white-painted brick stove in the corner with a sofa next to it. The room is like an oven, stifling. I keep looking across at the fireplace thinking it's alight as the heat is so intense and oppressive after the pleasant cool of our Kiva. No, it is not, this is pure solar heating. We have been the lucky ones today.

They motion us to sit on the carpet next to the brick stove with our backs against the wall. GA goes out to the kitchen to cook something to eat, joking about having to be the cook now. From the clanking saucepans I guess the kitchen is outside under a veranda as in many Chechen houses. HC has a pile of Russian passports. 'This was the home of spies, Russian collaborators,' he tells us. He shows us the passports, making a sign of slitting his throat. 'Traitors,' he says with a sly smile.

GA reappears with some small new potatoes boiled in their skins wrapped in newspaper, a pile of corn on the cob and a small dish of salt. The taste is indescribably wonderful. Freshly dug and picked, straight into the pan. The Chechens never eat potato skins but we explain as we munch them that most of the vitamins are in the skins and as long as they are not sprayed with insecticide they are fine to eat. They are not convinced.

We continue to sit while they talk amongst themselves and read a newspaper. I take a furtive look up at the windows and can just make out the fuzzy forms of leafy branches. We begin to feel uncomfortable, wishing to be back in our cool Kiva, away from talk of traitors and death. As the light dims we climb back down into the 'safety' of our earth and rock home.

Friday 1 August

I wake up early and sit on my window-frame seat of contemplation. I am sad today, it's my mother's birthday and I was hoping that by some miracle we would be released on this day. I cry many tears; the flow of pent-up grief is so strong I cannot cry silently. Jon comforts me while Paunch grumbles angrily above our heads, he cannot bear to hear tears, he has too many of his own, an ocean of grief hidden beneath his anger.

I think about my relationship with Mum with our similar interests in the arts and spiritual matters emerging as I grew into a teenager, and the many trips we made together visiting various countries, especially India with its vast rainbow spectrum of beauty through to poverty, all on display from the most exotic colourful clothes, architecture, wise spiritual teachings, heavenly incense and healthy smiling open faces, to the rigid caste system and the putrid smells of rotting vegetables and decaying human flesh. The Indians seem to accept death as part of life. I think about our shared experience of my father's death.

Memories of the summer of 1977, sitting on a beach in Italy, Dad showing me a mole on his chest, it looks very strange, pink, in an island of white skin. 'You need to let a doctor look at it as soon as you go home,' I say. He does, they take a biopsy and find it's a melanoma cancer. After a further operation when they took out his lymph glands the doctors are 90% sure he will be fine. 'Beaten the Big C,' he tells everybody.

Three years later, in the summer of 1980, he started having stomach pains but is determined to go on holiday with Mum and me to Germany to stay with friends in Bavaria. In the chalet bedroom I find him shaking all over, in a rigor. At hospital they diagnose a gall bladder infection but there is something wrong with his blood. Mum drives him back to England, feeling she's entering a tunnel and can't quite see the light at the end. Dad goes to hospital for an exploratory operation. Mum and I have a meeting with the specialist. Dad has malignant polyps in his stomach and there are shadows in his lungs and liver; there is nothing they can do. We leave the hospital and stop the car in a lane and breathe the scent of swaying scots pines in the afternoon sun, crying to the strains of Joan Baez singing 'L'amour' and 'We will overcome'. I decided to take a term off college and help Mum look after him.

I watched his world getting smaller and smaller until it became bedroom size. I watched his body shrinking and the silent grace with which he accepted the challenges of each day. I was thankful for the cheerful nurse who came daily. November 10 arrived; I and my brother came back from shopping. The nurse told us that he had cried out, 'Mum help me, the pain's coming.' So she gave him morphine to help him sleep. Mum came back and we sat with him as he slept. We were all tired with nerves fraying and had arranged for a night nurse to come. At 11 o'clock she called out, 'His breathing's changed.' We sat with him in candlelight and felt his spirit leave his body and look down on us from above.

My reverie is broken by Puppydog handing down a litre jar of tea and one of water, followed by a loaf of bread and some hot boiled eggs wrapped up in newspaper with a little dish of salt. Nothing like a good hot sweet cup of tea to calm emotional seas.

A short while after our breakfast the light goes off. Someone has brought a television into the house and we are serenaded in our darkness by the excited commentary cheers and shouts of a boxing match. At first it brings back happy memories of Dad watching the heavyweight championships when Muhammad Ali was at the height of his career. Then the incessant noise becomes oppressive, especially in the near black, only a shimmer of light coming through the brick window. I am still feeling a weight of sadness around my heart. Jon sits with his back against the wall on the boxes and I snuggle into his chest needing the warmth and comfort of his body and soothing words in my ears.

Remember to breathe slow and deep, release, let go of the panic. How long in this darkness? How long do we have to put up with the mental torture of listening to a loud television and heavy boots above our heads?

Hours pass and I've had enough. I hear Puppydog's voice and knock on the trapdoor, 'Light, light, please,' I whisper in Russian. ' Niet sviet, trudni, (no light, difficult).' He seems surprised to find we haven't got any and turns to talk to Paunch who replies in a rumbling grumble. Thankfully they find another socket for the television and we have light. It was not a power cut as we had originally thought, just a touch of Paunch meanness.

Living
Second by second
Minute by minute
Hour by hour
Day by day

That night our lullaby is the rattling of dice and the smack and slide of plastic counters interspersed with animated Chechen discussion. Our guards are joined by voices of other men who arrive with quiet purring engines squeaking through the potholes. One soft husky voice we assume belongs to a much older man (later we get to know him as 'Batman'), not more than in his forties. He seems to be the bringer of tidings; tonight they are not so fair, there's a bitter sharp edge to the conversation.

Saturday 2 August

GA is our breakfast angel, bringer of tea, bread and boiled eggs. He is subdued, not so chatty as usual. We set about our morning wash and exercise, some tai chi for me and some yoga for Jon. The trapdoor opens and he calls us, asking us to bring the dictionary. We stand beneath the opening behind the ladder looking up at GA flicking through the book, enjoying the reflected natural light on the pale blue walls and the splash of plastic flower colour. 'I want truth,' he says. This puts us on the alert. 'You spies, who do you work for, MOSSAD, CIA? What is your organization? Who is your boss? Why did you come here? Truth, Truth!!' We repeat all that we have told him before – how we came to help the children, that we work for a very small organization, that our boss is Chris Hunter. He scrabbles through the dictionary, 'Lies, lies!!' He gives us a piece of paper and ballpoint pen, 'You have half an hour to write the truth, I want address and telephone.'

He leaves us for a while, we know we will have to write as much truth as possible without putting Chris in danger. Thank God neither of us can remember Chris's address or phone number in Moscow. But I do know Chris's father's address in Devon, so I write that. Maybe it can be used positively as a contact for negotiations.

It seems as though they haven't made any form of contact yet, with any-one, and already one month has passed. GA returns and asks us to trans-late what we have written into Russian. 'All lies!!' He whispers angrily. He takes a pair of handcuffs off the dresser and chains my right wrist to the ladder, then brandishing a large kitchen knife and a small digital clock he says we have half an hour to tell the truth before he cuts off my fingers, one at a time. He mimes slicing one off and pokes the tip of the knife into my hand, then he brings the knife down hard between each finger making notches in the wood; fortunately he has a good eye and is accurate in his aim. I feel calm and strong, I look him straight in the eye, not believing he will carry out the threat. His eyes slide off my face, unable to hold my gaze.

Half an hour becomes an hour, I'm getting tired of this game. I can only tell the truth, as the fabrication of lies will only confuse the issue. Truth I tell, over and over. Even if he cuts my fingers off it will not change the truth of our being here. So I call his bluff and spread out my fingers, offering them to GA. I am prepared to take the pain. GA changes his tack and starts telling us that we will be separated tonight, I will be sent to their base in the mountains, tied up and tortured. His methods of torture bear a distinct resemblance to those used in the Vietnam films, such as putting a sack over my head and before tying it up dropping in a viper, or covering my body with enormous tarantulas. Fantastical though they are, he has talent as a mental torturer. I am feeling weary, worn down with standing for so long and craning my neck. My arm has gone numb and the idea that we could be separated is worrying. Our fate is in their hands.

All this time I stand next to Jon looking intently into GA's eyes, sur-rounding him in golden light and appealing to that part of himself that knows the truth. I talk to him in my mind: 'You don't have to belittle yourself by doing this, you know.' His gaze flickers towards my eyes, he cannot look at me for more than a second – he knows. Fortunately he grows weary and unlocks the handcuffs and replaces the trapdoor, leaving us to recover in solitude and peace.

Alas, the peace does not last. We hear the sweet strains of HC's voice mingling with those of GA, relating his morning's 'joke' with a stream of witty invective. The trapdoor opens and I am told to come up with the dictionary, but not Jon. This is where I begin to shake, I am fearful. Then I see HC reclining on the sofa, looking distinctly stoned and sleepy, his eyes are bloodshot and there's a whiff of marijuana hanging in the humid, 40-degree heat. He motions me to massage his calves. This I can handle but GA is determined to carry on his game. The same old questions come pouring out and I reply with the same truthful answers. HC sits up and decides to join in, adding his own rather gruesome tortures, such as being chained up against the wall with a knife inflicting small but painful cuts. I can see HC is laughing and I try and appeal to his logic, pleading my innocence, I grab his hand talking about the children we had been helping. It makes him angry, he thrusts my hand away and snatches the dictionary. 'You not Muslim. How can you help them, you don't know Chechen culture, you teach them western ways, bad bad!' I see I have made a big mistake and decide to stay silent.

GA senses the real anger in HC's voice and is obviously in this game more for the sport than actual violence so he turns the conversation back to tarantulas and snake pits. HC loses interest and eventually silence prevails. So I sidle towards the trapdoor, 'Pajalsta (please)?' I enquire as I start opening the trapdoor, and they nod. I hug Jon as I reach the ground. 'I'm OK, I'm OK,' I whisper. Then a voice comes from above with a distinct American psycho-thriller twang: 'Johnny, Johnny, come here.' Jon disappears through the trapdoor and I am left alone with the electric lightbulb.

I am lucky that I have never seen the horror film that GA is referring to (later Camilla remembers it is The Shining*), so 'Johnny' used as a psychological weapon is meaningless to me. As soon as I enter into the upper world of natural light and heat, I am told to sit on the sofa next to stoned HC; his eyes bloodshot and a little far away, he handcuffs my hands behind my back.*

GA is standing in front of me holding a large hunting knife. I am already soaked with sweat, then the questioning starts:

'Why are you here?' 'Who do you work for?' 'What is your mission?' 'What is your target?' I answer with the truth, that we came to help the children and I say I do not understand the question about target. HC even though he is stoned picks up on the word 'understand' and starts using it. 'You understand, you understand?' Implying the harm I will come to if I do not answer the questions. 'Boofff!!' He punches me in the chest. I stagger but manage to hold my balance.'Understand?' he snarls.

HC conjures up all sorts of wonderful tortures I could experience if I do not answer the questions; separated from Camilla, taken to the camp in the mountains where many Russian soldiers are held. I am very scared as I don't know how far they will go with these threats or actual physical harm. The hunting knife placed at my throat has a very sharp point.

'Who do you work for?' 'What is your mission?' 'What is your target?' On and on!

I answer with the truth. As time goes by the thought of saying I work for some government organization like MI5 does come to mind so they will stop asking me mind-numbing questions. But I also know the consequence of saying a lie when I have nothing to back it up with. I think they know why I'm in their country, but they do not want to believe it as they feel guilty about kidnapping us with no good reason. So HC is trying to find some other covert meaning as to why we came here to make them feel better about abducting us.

'Why are you here?' 'Who do you work for? CIA? MI5?'

I am bored of this game. My silence does nothing to improve the situation so I continue to answer the questions with the truth, even though I detect that they are don't like the answers I am giving. My mind is both my ally and my foe. My meditation practice gives me inner strength. Whilst engaging in mundane conversation with GA I can also have a conversation with myself and ask for help from our guardian angels. After what feels like an eternity they tire. I am uncuffed and allowed back to the safety of the Kiva.

I hear the slightly muffled voices above me, recognizing the same threats and the innocent denials, I hear a muffled thump, I know Jon is being hit. What can I do, what can I do? Then I know I have to shake, shake out all the fear, fear paralyses, you can do nothing when you are paralysed. I jump up and down, shiver and shake all over. Then I go and

sit on the boxes in our bedroom, close my eyes and go into deep contemplation, praying for all the powers of universal love, all our guardian
angels to be with us now, particularly with Jon. I feel healing energies
pouring through me, helping me to remain calm and focused.

Some time later, one hour or two or three, I don't know, Jon is allowed
back down. He is shaky, his chest bruised from the punch but otherwise
OK physically. Mentally his confidence has been worn down. He tells
me of the threats to separate us and we promise each other that we'll
be strong and hold onto our sanity for as long as possible. We know
we'll never be apart in our love, we believe love is eternal, it crosses all
physical boundaries. Of course we know it will be hard and that one or
other of us may not survive. Love is eternal, love is eternal; focus on that
thought.

The light goes out, it is the changing of the guard. Paunch always puts
the light out at night. We can't sleep and decide to light our emergency
candle stub, we need its warmth, its fire, its light. We hold hands as we lie
side by side, listening to the voices above, the crickets outside.

*It's in times of great hardship when I find my inner strengths and also
where I find what really matters to me. The thought of us being separated
makes me speak my truth. Inside I know we will always be together no matter the time or distance, yet that truth has to be spoken.*

*I turn to Camilla and say, 'I love you.' 'I love you too,' she replies. ' Will
you be my wife?' 'Of course,' and we smile.*

We listen on into the night. There's a low engine rumble and squeak
of brakes, it sounds like a jeep. This could be it, the promised vehicle to
whisk Jon away. There's a lot of movement overhead, heavy steps, creaking chairs and lowered voices in urgent discussion. We continue holding
hands waiting for the sliding rasp of the dumb-bell on the trapdoor.

We listen on into the dawn.

We are still together.

Sunday 3 August

We have just fallen into a light sleep when the trapdoor opens and a litre
of tea appears followed by a litre of water. Puppydog seems so calm and
'normal' that we decide to tell him about yesterday. We are both still
pretty wired and it doesn't take much telling before the tears come.

I tell Puppydog of the tortures of the previous day in a very matter of fact way, unaware of the emotional weight I am bearing, then the dam bursts and I find myself crying, sobbing, unable to continue the tale. Camilla carries on with the story as Puppydog looks down on me in horror.'Jon, Jon!' he says. He is shocked. His reaction shows us that the mental torture of the day before was definitely not a group decision but something concocted out of the confused and frustrated minds of GA and HC.

Puppydog is the most balanced of all four men and it is a great relief to tell our woes from the day before – it helps to release the tension and reach a more balanced state of mind in ourselves. Only later did we realize it was a big mistake.

Paunch is not around today and I think Puppydog feels more free to indulge us with boiled corn on the cob and tomatoes fresh from the garden. He always defers to Paunch when he is around, being the older man. We hear someone else enter the house and realize GA has come on duty early; our hearts sink. We hear Puppydog relating all that we told him this morning, they giggle and GA embellishes upon the theme. The words are incomprehensible to us but the meaning is all too clear. GA sends Puppydog out.

'Johnny, Johnny.' The squeezed American vowels dripping with malicious intent make our skin clammy and hearts race.

We both stand beneath the open trapdoor holding hands discreetly to give each other support. No handcuffs this time, just the same stream of accusations and threats. My neck is creaking, my back is aching and the list of 'fantasy' tortures rolls on. GA focuses on Jon; he knows that we know there is a large element of truth in what he says: all these horrors have been used in the past and probably still are. I start thinking what I can do to change the situation, and realize I can only use my mind. I focus on his third eye chakra and talk to him through my mind, 'Why do you have to treat us like this? Look inside yourself GA, know the love that is in you, that is in all of us, feel the light within you. Feel beneath the trauma, the suffering, know that you are loved and have no need to treat your fellow human beings this way.' I pour golden light into him and around him; his words begin to falter. The electricity goes out and he lights a candle, the day is darkening into evening. We hear footsteps outside going into the kitchen and Puppydog appears with some tea, a plate of biscuits and a small dish of homemade jam – Hallelujah!!

Monday 4 August

Breakfast, a steaming bowl of buckwheat and tea. GA hands it down with a 'Dobri Oodra (Good morning)' and then closes the hatch. What a relief, we'll have the chance to digest without a torture monologue.

A silent start to the morning, only muffled voices in the kitchen and birdsong. Then footsteps overhead, the slide of the weight and the trap-door opens. A foot appears on the top rung of the ladder, 'Oh God, they're coming down,' my heartbeat quickens. First HC appears, then GA; we remain sitting on the window frames. GA carries a Kalashnikov. They motion us to stand with our backs to the wall facing the ladder. GA stands in front of us pointing the gun at Jon's chest and HC sits on the ladder, staring at us, eyes blazing. 'You tell lies, lies! Who your boss, CIA? MI5? MOSSAD?' 'Robotat dieti, cover, your work with the children was a cover, false.' The accusations carry on and on. I am panting, my breath tripping over itself, HC looks at me and seems concerned; I sense that this might just be a sick joke born out of tortured minds.

The barrage of questions continues with the loaded gun pointing at my chest. 'You tell lies.' 'We want truth.' So we tell the truth and they don't like it. The sweat pours off their faces as the tension mounts. I find a place in-side myself that is very calm, I guess it is the place of truth. It gives me great strength, my heart rate slows. My senses heighten, I become acutely aware of my surroundings: the earth and pebble floor, the rough-cast crumbling concrete wall at my back, Camilla by my side. If this is the place I am to die for speaking the truth, so be it. GA draws back the bolt on the gun putting the first round into the firing chamber; there is fire in his eyes. It jams!

As GA releases the safety catch my breath slows down, I feel so clear and calm. I have the same thought as Jon: if we are to die, we will die in our truth, no lies will pass our lips. As the bolt jams HC giggles, GA gig-gles, the tension snaps. They turn away and climb back up the ladder.

We hug each other, chests touching, aware of our breathing. The breath of life.

The rest of the day passes quietly until the late afternoon. The trapdoor opens and GA pokes his head down 'Chai?' he asks innocently. 'Pajalsta,' we reply. He leaves the trapdoor open while he goes and makes the tea. A shaft of natural light and HC is nowhere to be seen – what a blessing. GA returns and says 'Dis oodra shutka, shutka, sorry (this morning joke, joke, sorry),' and giggles in a strangled guilty sort of way.

What a joke Ha Ha! A strange dark sense of humour. I guess it's born of war. Can you see me laughing? More like falling over fainting in fear. I feel angry and swear at him in my mind.

Tuesday 5 August

Yet another breakfast of boiled eggs and tomatoes. At least we have more appetite this morning, Puppydog is in a calm mood and no sight or sound of Paunch. We do some exercises and have a quiet meditation time, sending SOS messages with our prayers as we are living on a fault line of rasping and conflicting emotional energies. So easy for a crack to become a chasm with our lifeline cut for ever. If we feel life becoming too intolerable we know there are ways we could end it; there are plenty of sharp shards of glass lying on the ground. But no, our faith that we will be given the strength to cope with every eventuality is too strong. I feel I could close down my body if there was too much pain and allow my spirit, my soul, to fly free.

The day is warm, even in our Kiva, and we sleep out the tension of the last few days.

Evening. We hope desperately that Puppydog is still on duty as our bucket needs emptying. Every two or three days we have to knock on the trapdoor late at night and hand up the bucket. None of them likes to do the emptying job, but Puppydog makes the least fuss. We are in luck.

Wednesday 6 August

Two bowls of steaming pasta and butter for breakfast plus the usual bread and tea. A welcome change. GA's in a conciliatory mood, still feeling guilty after Monday's performance. 'How are you? Enough water to wash?' he asks, miming a face wash. 'OK,' we answer, 'except for the lice.' Jon shows GA his matted hair. To which GA mimes using a razor to shave Jon's head. 'Niet, niet. Shampoo, da,' Jon replies. GA laughs and says he will try and get some.

Even though the lice have formed a major colony in my dreadlocks I am making a stand on the shaving issue. It took me a bloody long time to grow my hair this long and in a strange way to refuse to have it shaved is the only control I have in this captive situation. They have given me a choice and I am choosing to keep it despite the itchy, sleepless nights.

Late evening lying on our 'comfortable' beds we hear the trapdoor open. Bare feet and calves appear followed by a Paunch body in stripy shirt, black trousers and mask. He looks through the brick window opening behind the ladder, someone is whispering in Chechen through the window and moving things around outside. Then he disappears again not disturbing us at all, most peculiar.

Thursday 7 August

Something's different. I open my eyes and notice the room beyond our bedroom is illuminated, a play of shadow and light that could not be born of one electric bulb. I quietly crunch through into the other room. We have a new window on the world: someone has moved all the objects masking our view through the small brick opening.

My delight is boundless. I look at a framed rectangular piece of the world with the eyes of a newborn, except to me it also represents freedom. To smell the sweet scent of dewy grasses, steaming in the early morning sunlight. To watch the dance of light upon the bark of a tree, a glittering cobweb and a busy spider. So this is my picture: a base of a tree trunk, a wooden slatted fence, brown packed earth with a few curled up drying leaves resting on it, an end of an old rusting sledge and a bright red brick.

I gaze out for some time, ignoring my bent back and crick neck. Suddenly there is movement; a pair of enormously long, thin, crinkled-skin and knobbly-knee legs come into the picture with two clawed feet – a chicken! Its head jerks to the ground just in front of my window, pecking deftly at any scrap of nourishment lurking in the soil. Suddenly its beady eye notices my beady eye; we are caught in a still moment, each part of each other's existence, two eyes, two species, two different pasts and futures but a sharing of the present. Fear of what this enormous eye might belong to shocks the chicken into a scurry of movement. Swiftly it goes out of my picture.

This is a rosy day. We are presented with half a large water melon, fragrant, juicy and pink. Carefully we extract the seeds and spread them out on a newspaper to dry, new counters for our Chechen backgammon game.

Friday 8 August

A large bowl of buckwheat for breakfast. In Russian 'buckwheat' sounds like 'grit' and we joke about our sumptuous meals of grit. Jon is enjoying his morning 'world viewing' when the trapdoor opens unexpectedly. He leaps round the ladder to join me on the window frames and we sit there quivering. The stiff neat legs of HC descend. In his hand he carries a can of spray. Was this some new form of torture? No, this is a spray to fumigate our Kiva. 'Dobri Oodra' he says in a business-like way and proceeds to examine our home for any escape attempts then shows us the spray and mimes the killing of insects. We cover our bread and water with some newspaper and he stoops into our bedroom to spray our pillow and blankets. The smell is very toxic and I start panicking about the effects on us and ask HC to leave the trapdoor open miming the effects of asphyxiation. Fortunately he is in an amenable mood and does as we have asked.

We are enjoying the extra natural light when a galvanized bucket full to the brim with hot water is handed down from 'Heaven' followed by the longer more beefy pair of legs belonging to GA. In his hand is a small yellow plastic bottle of insecticide shampoo; there's a drawing of a magnified louse on the label. He instructs us how to use it in Russian with a splattering of English. Yes, yes, yes, anything to rid us of the incessant itching.

There follows a delicious hour or two of hair washing. We work ceremoniously, slowly and with intent, scooping hot water out of the bucket with glass jars and wetting each other's hair, lathering up, sitting in semi-naked shampoo glory, then rinsing; constantly on the alert to reclothe if there is a noise from above. As a flourishing finale I dunk my head into the bucket. Jon doesn't think this is a good idea and is proved right later that day, but he ends the ceremony by washing his shirt in the opaque shampoo water.

All clean. We sit on the window frames feeling relaxed enough to whisper quietly to each other. Story time. I tell Camilla about some North American Indian workshops and the ceremonies I took part in. The pipe ceremony suddenly seems relevant to use in our present situation. I don't remember all the details but it goes something like this: a special pipe represents the joining together of male and female. The bowl (female) is filled with a mixture of herbs, each small pinch of herbs dedicated to a power — the healing powers of north, east, south and west, followed by the sun, earth and moon. Finally all the ascended masters such as Buddha, Krishna, Christ and Muhammad. By then you more or less have the whole of creation in your pipe! After lighting the pipe you put your thoughts and prayers into the smoke and as it ascends it takes your prayers with it. I was also taught not to get hooked up on dogma; the most important thing is that the prayers are made with wholehearted intent for the best for all.

So we withdraw to our bedchamber and sit crosslegged opposite each other on the boxes. Lighting a candle we invite three special people to join us in our circle. I bring out an imaginary peace pipe from an imaginary pocket and we hail the four directions, the heavens and the earth calling in all the powers of love and healing. Then we pass the peace pipe around, making our own prayers, thanking our families and friends, known and unknown, for all their thoughts and love and efforts towards our release. We ask them to send compassion and love to our captors and feel a wave of loving peaceful energy flow through us and know our prayers are heard.

They keep the trapdoor open until the daylight begins to fade.

Later we hear the voices of Paunch and Puppydog arriving and much scurrying to and fro from the kitchen. The trapdoor opens abruptly and Paunch thrusts his head down saying angrily 'Chai bucket, chai bucket,' pointing at the bucket full of dirty shampoo water with a few dead lice floating on the top. I hand up the bucket and receive a swift punch on the mouth. I stagger back bemused and confused, my lip thickening.

I have, unwittingly, committed the crime of sullying the bucket used to carry fresh drinking water. I can hear Paunch carrying on his tirade to any that will listen and surprisingly hear HC standing up for us – I can tell by the tone of his voice and the fading venom pouring forth from Paunch's mouth. Paunch respects the logic and intellect of HC.

Saturday and Sunday 9 & 10 August

A weekend without electricity. Luckily Saturday is Paunch and Puppydog day and as Paunch is a lazy grunting slob we have no dealings with him. In fact I get the impression that he knows some of the neighbours because he is out a lot.

Puppydog kindly brings us a candle with our breakfast of eggs, bread, fresh tomatoes and tea and a little later a newspaper article about Paul and Linda McCartney. What a treat! I never quite got the exact meaning of the article, it was some sort of deal with McDonalds in Moscow, maybe to sell veggie burgers. Just seeing those smiling, English and American, faces did a lot for our morale. It was our first contact with anything English since the kidnap. I spend hours trying to decipher the article with the dictionary when the electricity comes back on.

Another evening of 'Toilet Terror'. We decide it's better for me to knock and ask as there is less chance of me being punched in the face. There is much spewing forth of loud grumbling but Paunch eventually consents.

The hot week, 11–16 August

We can smell the heat through our window and hear the sighing grunts of sweaty, bored humans up above us. Someone has brought a little cassette machine to alleviate the boredom but they only seem to have one tape. We suffer hours of mind-numbing 'Euro-Disco Crap' (as Jon so eloquently describes it) recorded off a radio. An excellent form of mental torture.

Our daily routine:

I wake early with the earthquake of hooves and call to prayer. Jon has generally just fallen asleep after a night on the alert. I stretch out all the aches and numb spots after a night on the packing cases then tiptoe gleefully to our window to smell the damp morning air and watch the streaks of morning sunlight light up the dewy cobwebs with sparkling rainbows. I think about the beauty of our planet and how blind we are to it, mostly preferring to destroy rather than appreciate, preserve and create. Why are we generally motivated by fear rather than love? I don't know, but I still feel love is intrinsic and sacred to our beings, which gives me hope.

Washing time with the ritual wetting of the hair and checking of any stray lice that have survived the shampoo onslaught. Cleansed, I sit on the window frames, relax, let all the tension drain out of my body. I focus on the universal energy of love within and without and feel it pour through me. I think of my son, Ashok, and both our families and all our friends and radiate love to them and I know they are doing the same. I think of our captors and shower them with love and light; their wounds are very deep. Sometimes the pain of not knowing how my loved ones are, having no communication, hurts so much that tears fall silently down my cheeks.

Exercise time: tai chi on a wobbly floor. I empty my mind of everything apart from the movement so I am fresh to cope with whatever comes our way this day. As soon as I hear the scrape of the dumb-bell I whisper loudly to Jon 'Breakfast', and he appears, tousle-headed and bleary eyed as the hatch opens.

The next hour or so depends on who has brought us breakfast and if they are in the mood to talk. Now we often have fresh sweetcorn and knobbly cucumbers. The latter give me indigestion and soon they become too numerous for Jon so we have to send them back. Then a spate of watermelons; just remember never to eat them with bread unless you want a regurgitating experience. This week's culinary delight arrives in twists of newspaper, the fruits of Puppydog's tree pilfering: cherry-plums. We do go on at him about needing fresh, vitamin filled food because of the lack of sunlight and he has the kindness to act. We also ask him for some nail scissors which he eventually brings reluctantly and with fear. He keeps the hatch open until all our nails are cut then whisks them away. What he fears we could do with a pair of nail scissors I fail to understand.

We while away the hours of the day with exercising, meditating, watching a slice of life through 'the hole' and story telling. The routine of filling the time with different practices helps to stop the mind from too much wandering down unpleasant tracks. But there are always those blank hours in between. Left alone I think about digging a tunnel to freedom. The floor of this prison is just packed earth and I am sure our captors would not notice the disappearance of a spoon, they don't venture down into our world very often. But I have surveyed the outer world through our 'bedroom window'. Beyond the thick wall there are several feet of unkempt garden and cracked concrete, a wire fence, then the road. Out there we would have the problem of not knowing where we are and only a little Russian. I envisage arriving at the Little Star centre, but it is a dream.

In a shaft of late afternoon light we sit, side by side, recounting tales from our childhood, bringing alive all the characters, painting detailed pictures of the scenes, transporting our minds away from the musty cellar with its impenetrable walls of rock, cement and brick. Away from the heavy tread of our captors above our heads and the never ending loop of sickly music.

Memories

I tell Jon about my trip to Australia during the second year of living in Amsterdam. I travelled through the powerful humming land to visit friends and met a long-haired, barefoot Dutchman while picking peaches. We talked for long hours into the night by a campfire, under the stars, then I had to return to Amsterdam to act in the musical *Chicago*. Mid-production I was asked to a dinner party and there, by a queer quirk of fate was Marcel, the Dutchman. At the time I thought he was very interesting but nothing more. Now, I looked across the room, our eyes met and I knew we would be together. Six weeks later Ashok was conceived. A bit of a surprise, but when the pregnancy was confirmed I felt such a surge of joy I knew this being would be born.

And so began another phase in my life, being in a relationship and having a baby. I felt so tired those first weeks of pregnancy; however, I still managed to do some singing and acting. At five months pregnant I was acting in an improvisational piece, sliding along the floor in a strapless dress, belly bulging, saying 'I'm late for the train, late for the train.'

At six months we moved to England, staying with my mother for the birth.

Giving birth – what an experience! Pain like I had never experienced before. How do people have the energy to shout I wondered, it was all I could do to breathe deep and strong. Then I crouched on all fours on the bed and the sweet, calm midwife said she could deliver the babe with me in this position. I felt her moulding the baby's head and easing it out so my skin didn't split and she manoeuvred the slippery being onto my belly as I knelt up. Black wet hair and puckered brow, eyes opening, squinting in the light. 'Hello,' said Marcel, and the baby turned his head – he knew his voice. He had no name as yet, only 'Little Whale' as he was called in my belly. Then he turned back to me and opened his mouth as I took him to my breast. The pain was forgotten leaving feelings of elation and wonder.

On the eleventh day we crammed all our possessions into our little blue minivan and drove to Devon. Little Whale now had a name, 'Ashok'. We arrived at a little stone cottage; it was cold and the wood stove was not eager to light. I remember days swimming in tiredness. Apart from breast-feeding, Marcel took on most of the daily tasks; he was very quick and efficient, a bit of a superman really. What I didn't realize for many

years was that this was the beginning of my disempowerment programme. Nine months previously I had been living alone, spending most
of my time out of the house doing various activities and seeing friends.
Now I had a partner, a young baby and a home-based life. I began to realize I was not as maternal as I had thought. Being with Ashok was wonderful but out went my fanciful teenage ideas of being a good farmer's
wife and having four children.

In many ways Marcel and I were well suited. We had similar ideas
on how to bring up Ashok, on what to eat, the benefits of homeopathic
medicine and living in the countryside with lots of fresh air and walking. On the surface everything was good, but we didn't seem to be able to
communicate on any deep level. So there we were, five years later, both in
love with Ashok and both unhappy with our relationship to each other.
In the end we decided we would give up all our jobs and just travel, find
a smallholding and start again. This seemed like a good idea but deep
inside I couldn't see us staying together and I knew I would not be suited
to life on a smallholding although I felt it would be excellent for Ashok.
Fate intervened a few weeks before the departure date, when a friend of
my brother's came to stay and Marcel fell in love. It didn't last long but it
served as a catalyst for our break up.

We decided that Ashok would live with Marcel. I had thought deeply
on this and although it pained me I knew Ashok needed the qualities
that Marcel could give him such as discipline, a structured life style,
climbing high trees and general rough and tumble. I knew I wouldn't
have been so good on making behavioural boundaries, for I was too
soft and indecisive. I felt very strongly that my love for Ashok would
overcome all obstacles of time and distance, I would cope and he would
cope. It was not easy. Six months later Marcel decided to move to the
Netherlands and I would visit every month. Now I had to face the fact
that although I was still Ashok's mother I had lost my motherhood;
Marcel was his sole carer in all practical matters. I didn't even think
of it in those terms in my emotional rawness but that was what was
happening.

In October 1993 I moved in with a friend and her two children near
Ross-on-Wye. Mentally and emotionally my façade was cracking, that
façade projected out to the world with its coping grin and bounce. The
parting with Ashok after our monthly week together was always sad

although neither of us showed it until after I'd left, then both of us cried silently in quiet corners away from curious eyes.

'It's time to let go,' said an acupuncturist friend while twiddling needles in my flesh. 'Too much grief in your lungs,' and the tears splurged forth. 'It's time to take more risks,' said another friend as I talked about my itchy skin caused by frayed nerves and my feelings of being disassociated from myself. A voice in my mind talking to a voice in my mind talking to a voice in my mind ad infinitum, like the repeated receding image that happens when a mirror faces a mirror. I feared I was becoming schizophrenic. What did he mean, 'Take more risks!' I felt affronted. Hadn't I risked enough already by not following a career path, by valuing time with Ashok above all else? But I knew that he was right. I needed more focus, more direction. What use would I be to Ashok if I became a blubbering wreck? So I gave the idea of 'risk' some thought. What did I fear most? Failure and looking a fool? Maybe I secretly felt I had failed in being a mother, something I couldn't voice to myself. The decision had been made, rightly or wrongly, Marcel was now Ashok's mother and I the absent father. I had to look for something else that I found challenging. 'Yes, I've got it, computers.' There was a free course for the unemployed of Ross-on-Wye. I had felt an abhorrence towards computers, so here was my chance to risk failure and looking a fool. A year later with my newly acquired qualifications and confidence I got the job of part-time assistant manager of the local community centre and began teaching tai chi again. I organized my time so that I could still spend a long weekend with Ashok every four or five weeks. Acting, singing and dancing once again became part of my life. Camilla had found Camilla again.

Although I was happy sharing a house while spending a lot of time by myself, what I really wanted was to share life with a friend, brother, lover all rolled into one. Asking for the impossible? Maybe. I created the thought and then let it go. So when I was introduced to this curly-headed, bearded man in the swimming pool and felt a tingle of energy pass through my body I didn't give it too much thought.

The hot week continues

There is a swish of a brush above us and the low tones of a woman's voice. Paunch has found someone to do the chores. Does she know? How would she feel if she did? Compassion? Resentment? Fear for us or herself or both? We know it is dangerous for us to make a sound but it is so tempting to call out 'Hello, we're here, we exist under the floorboards, under your swishing broom, two innocent human beings.' Later, as I put an eye to the outside world, I see half a grubby naked foot, a woman's foot, small with a neat line of toes. Somewhere above there is a body attached to that foot holding a reed broom, swishing in my ears, out of my sight.

Puppydog hands down a crumpled page of a Russian newspaper and there is a photo of Princess Diana and Dodi on his yacht. I try hard to decipher the article, there is speculation about her being pregnant. I feel sorry for her – not an easy life always being in the public eye.

Ahh, Adam. Paunch has made a friend, and very much a friend of us. I have a mental picture of naked three-year-old Adam carrying his jug of warm soothing oil to pour over the troubled, angry, grief stricken waters of Paunch's heart. He comes into our lives one morning, staccato footsteps above our heads and a high lilting voice of a toddler just discovering the world of language. Out comes the backgammon board, Paunch is determined to teach him all the numbers on the dice in Chechen (Tsa, Shi, Ho, Di, Pri, Auogh); sometimes he sets up a game and then gets so absorbed in it he forgets about Adam, who gets bored and disappears outside to find a more interesting occupation such as chasing chickens. Yes, I manage to see his glorious chubby legs running past my eye in pursuit of some tiny fluffy chicks. Later the chicks come back, pecking right outside the hole. The smallest scrawny moth-eaten one suddenly notices this massive eye gleaming out of the darkness and scuttles away squawking loudly. I often wondered what Adam would have thought if it was he who had discovered the eye: fear, or just curiosity? Maybe he would have regaled us with a peal of high laughter, sweet music to our ears.

Time for our nightly backgammon session. Jon has marked out the gameboard using charcoal from dead matches on a wooden board. I sit crosslegged on a concrete ledge. Jon sits opposite on the lower window frames, the bulb casting eerie shadows around our sleazy gambling den. We hear the rolling dice and swift slide of counters above us as we perform a mousely replica beneath.

The days end with dealing with the dreaded bucket, and sleep (for some).

My sleep has become even more disturbed as my head is alive with lice;

the shampoo can only have killed the adults. The next generation has now hatched, so small as to be almost invisible, yet the amassing army is continually on manoeuvres, looking for food I guess.

The cold week, 17–23 August

The temperature has dropped dramatically, cold air blows through our brick holes, the earth floor has taken on a darker, damper look, my bag smells musty with a hint of white mould where it lies on the concrete shelf. Threads of frayed panic are inching their way into my psyche. No heat to warm up cold, damp bones. No warm food to fuel our bodies.

At breakfast we complain of being cold. In the afternoon we are presented with a plate of hot fluffy buttery omelette, the best I have ever tasted. In the evening Puppydog and Paunch raid the cupboards and hand down two longsleeved check shirts, one purple and one red, and two pairs of nylon holey socks (you can't win them all!). Later GA gives us another blanket, impregnated with exhaust fumes but at least it protects us from the icy draughts.

Monday. Red letter day. 'Your parents are in Grozny, I've seen them on TV.' GA's eyes grin through his mask. He describes Jon's father with his white hair and grey beard and our mothers wearing glasses. Of course we know they are not in Grozny and what he saw must have been a news report from the BBC, but it certainly warms our hearts to know they are OK, the first concrete news we have had. We feel closer to them and to freedom.

Something is happening. I wonder what channel this video came through – was it official? At least we know our folks are OK and believe we are still alive. This raises our morale. There must be communication between the British and Chechen governments, but I am not sure if our captors have any links with the present Chechen government.

Tuesday morning the rain pours down. No electricity. We stuff the holes with plastic. Puppydog brings a long white candle, what a treasure. Again we ask for hot food and he returns with a jar of opaque thin fish soup. As each exquisite mouthful slips down my throat I wonder about the female hand that stirred the pot and her surprise if she knew who was eating it.

Wednesday morning and a bowl of hot 'grit' (buckwheat) from GA, but no time to eat it as HC's legs descend the ladder. He asks for the dictionary and gives us a lecture on how wrong it was for us to come and teach the children our western ways alien to their Muslim culture. I try and explain how we were working with the children but realize there is little point in defending ourselves as he stirs himself up into a fury and throws the dictionary at my head. We sit, mute, on the window frames, waiting for the storm to pass, hoping there will be no more physical violence. It passes, we are alone again and can eat our bowl of cold 'grit'.

I tell Camilla to be more careful when talking with these guys. They, certainly HC, are like tightly wound springs of tension needing to uncoil now and again. Best to keep your distance.

Puppydog gives us a newspaper article about four kidnapped Russian journalists who have been released for a million dollars each. Somehow, seeing them walking across the tarmac with big bunches of flowers makes me feel nearer to freedom or at least the possibility of freedom. There is much discussion upstairs which I sense is related to their release. The anger in HC's voice chills my skin.

Those lucky guys walking across the tarmac of their homeland. One day we will do the same, one day. Difficult to conjure up. Will we ever make it back? Thoughts of home, England, my beloved parents, my son, our friends. All so distant. So close.

Friday – another interrupted breakfast. GA and HC descend in silence, the aura of fury around HC is palpable. He carries a Polaroid camera and GA hangs a plaque around my head that reads $2 million dollars. Oh no! Our price just went up to crazy unreachable heights our families can never reach. I have to stand in front of the cement wall with the grey rock jutting out like a miniature mountain. They fiddle with the camera, make a bad shot and try again. What a fracas, they can't even take a photograph with a Polaroid. I can see it'll take a few miracles to get us out of here. My heart sinks.

Then it's my turn. Luckily they take both photos in front of the same background so that when our parents eventually see them they know that we were still being held together. I stare into the lens trying to convey a sense of strength and calm. When I eventually see the photo I look more like a startled rabbit caught in car headlights. Later we hold another prayer circle to bring peace to our minds and calm our frazzled nerves. It has become a Friday afternoon ritual.

'Freedom week', 24–31 August

Sunday, excitement in the air. We catch glimpses of a car squealing to a halt through gaps in the wooden fence, clouds of dust rising. Urgent voices above, clanking in the kitchen, laughter. And there is much praying and giving gratitude to Allah. We have learnt the call to prayer from Paunch who prays most nights in a loud singsong. It seems he has decided to become an overt Muslim, singing out his prayers for all the neighbourhood to hear and growing a beard to give him a more priestly air. (We know about the beard because he forgot his mask one breakfast.) Actually he reminds me of pirate Cap'n Jake with his stripey jumper, one eye and protruding belly.

All four are here today taking it in turns to use the room above our beds to pray. Puppydog and GA recite in a low, soft drone while HC prays in a carrying voice, peaked by Paunch with his loudly sung oratorio. There is a sense of anticipation and gratitude in all their voices.

Evening, the hatch is lifted, Paunch, taking off his 'I don't want anything to do with you' mask, wishes to speak with us. His tone is that of a conciliatory father. 'Haroshi novi, cveboda, piat, shiest dien (good news, freedom, five, six days).' He counts the days on his fingers, 'If you are good, niet problemi,' he adds. Of course our hearts leap, full of hope. He is so excited he forgets to put the dumb-bell on the hatch and leaves the house. The house is empty, no weight, no guarding of the hatch, an eerie silence. Should we leap into action and make a run for it? So tempting but in our wisdom we do not, there are still voices in the street. Paunch returns and realizes his mistake so to cover his guilt he mimes, with expansive arm gestures, putting a grenade on top of the hatch and the explosion that would occur if we try to escape. Empty threats, Paunch is a man of much bark but no bite, or so we thought.

Wednesday, early evening. Sitting quietly munching cold pasta. Now, because of the colder weather they bring us one big pot of hot food in the morning, either rice, pasta or 'grit', a nice warm start to the day but by evening it's turned to a glutinous, sticky mass of cold stodge. It's food, we can't complain. Outside in the half light, the cows are making their journey home. The highlight of my afternoon is putting my eye to the 'world hole' and catching glimpses of those sleek brown cow hides plodding past the gaps in the fence. If I am very lucky I see a small, bent, headscarfed woman in a black dress with white spots herding the beasts along, slapping their behinds with a stick.

This evening we hear a creaking lorry bouncing on its haunches pass-ing our fence then changing gear as the road goes uphill. It slows down on its growling, laborious journey. There's a screeching of brakes, but instead of the expected silence we hear cascades of rolling stones and the roar of out of control wheels getting louder and louder until the inevit-able crunch. The whole house shudders and shakes and we are plunged into blackness. Is this our angel of freedom in the shape of a runaway lorry?

Paunch and Puppydog scurry outside and there's a crescendo of Chechen voices, suddenly the piercing voice of Adam rises above the rest: 'Isa, Isa,' full of anxiety for the safety of Paunch. An empty house, we're forgotten, time to run? But we don't know if they can see the entrance of the house. My mind races with possibilities of how to avoid being detected. Run as fast as we can? Walk swiftly and just keep going? Hide nearby and see which way they go, then follow discreetly hoping they will lead us to the main highway. But then, how do we make contact with people we know? I wonder if anyone is still at our house or if 'Little Star' is still working?

I move through the darkness to get a candle from the bedroom and listen to the discussions, the sounds of wood and metal debris being cleared away; finally our existence slips back into Puppydog's consciousness and he runs into the house. We look up into his startled eyes, full of concern for our safety or maybe just surprised we're still here! Relieved he explains about the crash in Russian with gestures which we interpret as 'lorry, out of control, careers into fence and corner of house breaking gas mains and electricity lines'. I guess we're lucky there wasn't a big explosion.

In our experience most Chechen men are brilliant 'fixers' when it comes to anything functional and mechanical. Within an hour or two the electric-ity has been reconnected, however they obviously don't have the tools to reconnect the gas and for the next week all the cooking is done on an open fire in the yard.

Thursday. I awake and peer through the hole into our 'living room,' luminous reflections of the morning sun shimmering on the walls. I haul myself out of the sagging campbed and crouch through to the other room. Of course the light had to be coming from the 'world window' but why so much?

The fence has gone, and our world view has extended dramatically. We can now see a large portion of dirt road, and all the people who walk along it: an elegant woman with a headband and high heels walking her daughter to school, a group of small children squatting together on the farthest verge playing with sticks and stones, an old stooped man brown and wrinkled as a walnut. It is not a busy road. I wake Jon so he can enjoy our new, wide-angle cinematic screen.

Breakfast comes in a large saucepan, blackened, and smelling wonderfully of wood smoke. The smells evocative of times camping on Dartmoor, frying spitting eggs on an open fire and singing operatically to a buzzard flying high as we leap naked into an icy gurgling stream. We have stuffed the hole with plastic so they don't wonder about the sudden burst of extra light. As precious to us as a jewel is the dazzling reflection of the sun on the road. I take the pink hand mirror and lodge it at an angle in the hole. I see some broken fence and the cherry-plum tree, then footsteps and I quickly bring the mirror in, my heart pounding. An old man comes with some wood and a rusty saw and begins to mend the fence. I see the feet of GA with his pointed black leather shoes, looking on. He turns and very quietly moves a metal sheet over our hole. The curtain's down, the show's over. Did he notice the pink mirror? I'm shaking and listening, listening for angry whispers, for the scrape of the dumb-bell. Nothing. That was a dangerous game.

Last days in the kiva, 29 August – 2 September

Friday, the weather is colder and the electricity is off. We hear from Puppy-dog that the main power station is outside Chechnya near Stavropol and the Chechen government doesn't have the money to pay the Russians for the electricity it needs. Thankfully someone has moved the metal sheet so it leans at an angle to the building and we can see a triangular slice of brown earth, trunk and fence. Enough light to walk without bumping into the wood props, but not much else.

Hour after hour in dank dimness with cold draughts chilling our skin: sitting, standing, stretching, sitting, chilling, sitting, standing, stretching, sitting, chilling . . . thinking.

We allow ourselves a bit of candlelight in the evening and do some qigong exercises to warm us up, then curl up into small balls under the smelly blankets, me falling into a shivering sleep, Jon awake, alert, listening to voices he doesn't understand.

Saturday darkness, GA opens the hatch and hands down a large steaming pot. We ask for light, hoping for another candle and are presented with a lighted length of fuse wire! I bet there's not many people who have dined on mutton broth by fuse light, followed by a real treat – 'Chechen doughnuts', freshly deep-fried dough, crispy on the outside and gooey in the middle, and we have a bowl of sugar to dip them in, much nicer than the bought ones in England. But the sulphurous fumes became too much after a while and we slip back into darkness.

Sunday early morning. The scrape and scratch of the hatch wakes us and we hustle through in a dishevelled state, Puppydog's eyes are nearly popping out of his head. 'Princess Diana kaputt, Princess Diana kaputt!!!' Is this another game? No, the prickles all over my body tell me it's the truth. 'Car crash in Paris,' he whispers. I feel strange; one part of me is tingling, another part numb and the whole situation feels quite absurd. Jon and I don't cry, our cup is too full, if we tip it and let the torrents flow it'll take all the energy with it that we need to keep strong and survive. Our precious tears flow in silent moments for our families and friends, and then it is always good to end with a smile and feel trust and faith that all is well.

Monday. Digesting our pot of 'grit' we hear movement and tense our muscles as two pairs of legs descend, HC followed by GA. HC sits in fatherly pose on the steps holding the dictionary with GA above him. 'Freedom coming soon,' he says earnestly. 'I don't know when, but most likely the Chechen festival, 6 September, next Saturday, the day the war ended in 1996.' 'Would you like some coffee?' 'Da, Spaseba,' we reply. GA disappears upstairs and brings back four bone china cups, a tin of Turkish instant coffee, and a glass jar full of hot water; we are honoured indeed. 'We move tonight or maybe tomorrow,' continues HC. 'Haroshi miassa (good place), Luche (better).'

We have been in Chechnya four months now and I think back to that grey May dawn when we crossed the border . . .

6

Into Chechnya

Adlan drove Chris, Jon and me to the border, we presented our papers and were waved through the barrier. The roads were pitted with holes as we approached Sernovodsk, a few kilometres from the border. On the edge of the village was a large building punctured by shell holes. For every house on the main street there was a hole where another once stood, now bombed into oblivion. Many stalls lined the street selling loaves of bread, packet goods, plastic bags of sugar, fizzy drinks and cigarettes. Selling goods in the bazaars was one of the few ways of making money as other work was scarce since the war. The houses lining the road were behind huge walls and metal gates. At one of these gates we stopped and Adlan knocked loudly. We were let in by Aslan, his youngest brother, and drove into a courtyard.

The house was single storey, like most houses here except for those owned by the rich. It was Tardis-like with rooms leading to rooms leading to yet more rooms. There were two kitchens, one for summer outside, under a veranda and one for winter in a room by the gate, separate from the house. The women were having a meal in the winter kitchen when we arrived; they always eat after the men. Adlan's parents greeted us, his father small with a nut brown wrinkled face and twinkling brown eyes and his mother a statuesque figure in a long floral dress and head scarf, with a beaming smile. We were led into the winter kitchen through a thick silver door that originally belonged to a walk-in fridge. The walls were cobbled together with bits of plywood and board. All the women moved to seats around the edge of the room. Shaman, Adlan's elder brother had just married – he was 28 and his wife 19 with a beautiful moon-shaped face. She helped to serve us with vegetable soup and hunks of white bread, followed by a grated salad and cubes of cheese tasting like salty mozzarella. The meat eaters ate lamb stew. To end the meal there were bowls of cherries, apricots and plums in thick syrup dunked in black tea poured from a small teapot and topped up with hot water from a samovar.

We were shown around the main house across the tarmacked court-yard. There was a large covered veranda where you left your shoes then took your pick of slippers depending on the size of your feet. This led to the living room and beyond into a corridor, off which branched three bedrooms and a bathroom; no toilet, that was outside in a wooden shed. At the end of the corridor was 'the big room' entered through drapes of white muslin. There were carpets on the walls, large glass cabinets and a shiny wooden table. It looked like the equivalent of the front parlour of Victorian times, only used for special occasions. This would be our bed-room, Jon, mine and Chris's, so we rolled out our mats and bedding.

I had my period so I asked Chris where I could dispose of my sanitary towels. Menstruation is a taboo subject in Chechen society so it can be awkward for foreign female guests. He asked Shaman, who told him I could burn it on a pile of rubbish behind the toilet shed in the garden. So later that night I had a little burning ritual behind the potent smelling toilet, in the spotting rain.

Sunday morning, the first grey day since we left Moscow. We had bread, cheese and slices of beef sausage for breakfast with sweet fruit syrup tea. Mrs Adaev kindly tied my scarf 'Chechen style' around my head so I looked less foreign with my short curly hair. Then off to Grozny, 60 kilo-metres on a flat, straight, potholed road, landscape similar to some parts of England. We passed green fields and beautiful forests, although parts of them had been uprooted and burnt to make space for Russian check-points. We stopped at a large sign made up of seven-metre-high concrete red letters saying 'Grozny' pitted with bullet holes. Then the devastation began: tower blocks blasted by tanks, blackened by fire, shell-holed roads, some gushing with water from burst mains, the above ground gas lines contorted and strangled, little fires burn off escaping gas here and there. But, amazingly amongst all the rubble and chaos women were walking in bright, freshly ironed frocks with high heels and make up, poised and chic, and men in neat shirts and pressed trousers. What courage and dignity these people have.

Not much of the centre was left standing, the presidential palace and all the buildings around it having been razed to the ground. I got the sense that before the war it was rather a beautiful city and had been called the gem of the Caucasus. There were many tree-lined roads; you could see tree stumps and skeletal branches here and there. A river running through the centre was now contaminated, partly, we heard, by the bodies of dead Russian soldiers that had been dropped from helicopters into the mountain streams by the Russian military to keep their dead count down and save face during the conflict. One boulevard reminded me of the centre of Aix-en-Provence, wide, with trees either side of the road and up the centre. The bullet-riddled buildings were yellow ochre and pale pink with ornate Arabic-style wrought iron balcony railings and plasterwork. The few thousand Russians still living there didn't believe their fellow countrymen would bomb them, consequently they suffered greater casualties than the Chechens who moved out to stay with relatives in the villages. But most of the villages didn't escape the brutal embrace of war, especially after the initial bombing and ground force attack on Grozny where the Russian military suffered enormous loss of life. Some villages were told they wouldn't be bombed and then they were, so the women and children did not have time to evacuate, and died. Chemical weapons were also used in the countryside and many trees have not refoliated.

The driving reminded me of India, with much hooting of horns, near crashes and last-minute swerves. We were driven by Shaman at a manic pace, lurching this way and that, avoiding puddles of unknown depth, passing food stalls and gallons of different shades of homemade petrol in glass jars being sold on the road side, lethal for carburettors. The city lived under the threat of pestilence as piles of uncollected garbage grew taller. I noticed people sitting by the roadside with polystyrene boxes – full of ice cream, as we discovered when Shaman stopped to buy us one. We snaked through the city to the outer suburbs, turning off the pot-holed dual carriageway onto a compressed earth track, passing a bombed-out car-parts factory and a ruined brick works before arriving at the ornate iron gates of the former Little Star Sanatorium.

The Little Star centre – a group of one-storey whitewashed buildings surrounded by two cracked tarmac playgrounds and two fields with small fruit trees. Within the playgrounds there were three octagonal open-sided structures, which would be fantastic for group sessions. There were two big rooms and two small rooms that we could use for sessions and a storeroom. The kitchen and dining room building was light and airy; a large square cooker sat in the middle of the room with vast, round rusty electric plates. It looked like it hadn't been used for years. I wondered if everything would be ready in a week. There were no tables or chairs, but Chris wasn't worried, we had been promised a lorry load from another aid organization and I was getting used to the idea of trusting that by the eleventh hour we would have all we needed. Although the weather was grey and rather dismal, Little Star had a peaceful feel; there were many trees and the lilac was just coming into bloom.

Before we could open the centre we would have to collect plates, cutlery and plastic stools from a state called Adagey, Chris explained, where he had taken 60 children for a break from the war in 1996. The organization didn't have money to buy new ones. This meant a 12-hour drive to the other end of the Caucasus!

Two days later we arrived back in Sernovodsk, exhausted. A huge meal awaited us but, as we were about to tuck in, a message arrived that Sasha and Olya had been expected at the bus station in Grozny one hour ago and we were meant to be there to pick them up. So, tired and hungry, into the car again driving to Grozny and our new home.

No. 197, our Grozny home

At the bus station we screeched to a halt. There was no sign of Sasha or Olya. We were all worried but could do nothing except continue to the house where we'll be living, number 197.

The sun was setting as we climbed over the metal spiked fence and threw our baggage over the high gate – no keys. While Chris and Adlan went back to Sernovodsk to pick them up Jon and I camped out in the courtyard making ourselves comfortable. We sat on the stools and I fumbled around in various bags until I found a candle. Jon made some tea on his stove and I brought out what was left of the cardboard swiss roll and some bananas. After the long sweaty journey and the huge rush in Sernovodsk this was so peaceful, supping tea and quietly chatting while the birds gave us a bedtime concert and the candlelight flickered.

Our peace was interrupted by a gaggle of young men climbing over the fence and introducing themselves as 'Voice of the Mountains (Lamman Ass)'. They were young students whom Chris had met when he organized a youth conference about 'alternatives to using violence in conflict' and were interested in helping with mine location and clearance. Following on their heels came Chris and Adlan with a key, news that Sasha won't be coming to work for us as his wife had objected but Olya will arrive soon. We entered our new home; it smelt airless and musty, with damp blankets. Later we heard the owner had disappeared during the last war and his sister had kindly lent us his house; she still hoped he may turn up one day. Off the kitchen there was a bathroom with a bath, western-style toilet with no seat and a large geyser on the wall. We never used this loo because there was no mains water so we used the wooden 'dunny' shed at the end of the garden. The walls of our room were covered in dark brown, patterned wallpaper with brown lino on the floor and pale blue bars over the windows. At least there were circles in the metal designs making them a little less prison-like. The next morning we discovered the garden, lush and green, with one cherry-plum tree and the wooden dunny. Near the house there was a standpipe that we used to pump water for cooking and washing. This then, was our new home.

Friday 9 May. Happy Birthday Jon. An auspicious day to meet the whole team at Little Star. Shaman arrived with the women, wearing a smart green shirt, a Kalashnikov slung over his shoulder.

On hearing that it's my birthday Shaman fired six or seven rounds into the air. I pleaded with him to stop, but he didn't understand why I did not want firearms used on my behalf. He then unclipped the magazine and offered me a round of live ammunition. A very strange birthday gift!

The sound was raw and loud, scaring the birds into silence. Jon protested, but apparently it was a normal custom here, an honour.

We met our translator Fatima and talked about which rooms we would use and what we will teach without having to use tables and chairs because none had arrived yet! I presented my idea of working towards a performance at the end of the week and suggest creating a kind of carnival. They were all very enthusiastic about it. Luba arrived, a Chechen doctor who was also helping children. She had set up an organization called the 'Agency for Rehabilitation and Development' with the help of Dutch funding. They worked in the villages in much the same way as had the team from CPCD. She felt we were being too ambitious in the range of activities we wanted to do with the children but I felt it was important to shake the fear out of the body using various forms of creative expression. Also the trauma will have affected their concentration and some ways will work better for some children than others.

I felt sorry for Chris, for apart from the teaching he was expected to solve every little problem. There seemed to be a lack of forethought and the taking of individual responsibility that may be a legacy from the Soviet era. I could see the stress showing in his face.

Olya arrived that evening from Stavropol and we spent the next day talking about the daily structure. She had worked a lot with children as a psychologist and thought all our ideas were sound and workable – phew!

Little Star, beginnings

Sunday 11 May. The big day. We got up at six and did some Sufi breathing exercises outside, to calm ourselves, had some bread and honey and were driven to Little Star, stereo blaring. Luckily a few tables and chairs had arrived. The children were welcomed, registered and given decorated name badges. I ran through a movement sequence that helped me calm my nerves and feel more prepared. Jon had gone with Adlan to find a lock for the storeroom and buy cheap wallpaper to use for painting. I discovered an electrician had re-wound and taken my tape out of the recorder that I had set to play at a particular piece so I had a rant, jumped up and down and flung my arms around before resetting it. Luckily no one was watching my dance of rage release, but it certainly helped relieve my tension! Then I heard the bus arriving and ran outside to welcome the children. Chris was watching a manifestation of a dream; I saw tears in his eyes and felt pretty emotional myself.

Twenty-five children piled out of the bus, ages ranging from 8 to 14, all looking rather numb and scared, not knowing what to expect. We split the group into two according to age. While one group was being shown around the site, the other group came to me to do some movement. The older group were understandably more inhibited than the younger and there were only three boys. I was wishing Jon was with me because he had no problem with leaping around the room and I think he could have helped the boys unwind. The general feedback was good, and they began to loosen up and relax. Later the other members of the team gave the children tests to assess the depth of their trauma. A power cut meant lunch would be over an hour late, a long wait for hot and thirsty children. Luckily we could give them water from a tank on stilts that had been filled by Merlin, another British aid agency, and the team were brilliant at keeping all the children occupied with games aimed at building self confidence. Lunch at last – a vegetable soup, a piece of chicken and pasta. This could have been the most nourishing meal the children had had for sometime.

Food was not cheap, as I had discovered the evening before when I went to the bazaar with Anya and a guard to buy food for supper. When we got back the two guards had a discussion and decided neither Jon nor I could go to the bazaar again as we looked too foreign and it was a security risk. I was sad about this as I loved the hustle and bustle of the market place and the wide gold grins of the sellers popping up behind the colourful pyramids of fruit and vegetables.

After lunch there were parachute games, which everybody enjoyed. Then we got on the bus and Olya organized some chanting with hand clapping and foot stamping. The children loved it, especially when there was a competition between the boys and the girls to see who could chant the loudest. The bus was full of bright chatter and grins, very different from the mute, scared silence of their arrival. All the children were dropped off and we arrived back at number 197 feeling a mixture of exhilaration and exhaustion.

But the day was not over yet. Our household had grown, Anya, Olya and Madina shared one room, Jon and I in another, Chris and Adlan in another and the guards in the room nearest the kitchen. All the 'Mountain Boys' arrived and so we were 17 for supper. The tape recorder we brought from England was greatly appreciated – music blasted through the house while meat sizzled in the pan.

The rest of the week went past in a blur of movement. Up at six to have a strip wash at the standpipe before the others arose – Jon filled a bucket of cold water and threw it over his head, I'm not quite so cavalier! We then spent time mixing powder paint ready for the painting sessions. Sometimes we got frustrated because there were changes in the schedule that we were not told about until they happened. I think they just forgot we didn't speak the language and didn't ask Fatima to tell us. We certainly learnt to be adaptable and live in the moment.

Adlan and I teamed up to solve any practical problems that arose. The use

of sign language in my previous work with severely disabled adults helped
me to communicate with him. Camilla wanted some clay to make models
with the children so Adlan and I scoured the city for brick works. The third
one we came across was still functioning, the others having been bombed out
of existence, and the site manager told us to help ourselves so we filled sev-
eral plastic bags with clay. Camilla and I had to soak and pummel it before
it could be used for model making.

One of the rooms at the centre was locked and we discovered the key was
held by Merlin, the British aid organization that helped with the renovation
work. As Adlan and I zigzagged across the war-torn city I heard a rattling
sound coming from the glove box, I opened it and there was a hand grenade
trundling around, an unsettling reminder of the recent conflict and the con-
tinuing fear. We drove from home to office to home (no working telephones),
eventually finding the right person in the middle of his birthday celebra-
tions. Out came bottles of vodka and plates of salad. Adlan abstained – he
had to drive back and if a Chechen was caught drunk at a police check-
point the charge was 40 lashes. One bottle downed, I ate more salad, my
head spinning. We tried to make our excuses to leave but another bottle was
produced, and then a third! Eventually we managed to leave gracefully, all
parties happy, very happy. Arriving back home I retired to bed after gulp-
ing as much water as possible and mumbling about birthday celebrations to
Camilla.

The children were separated into groups to work on ideas for the carnival. Our group came up with an idea of a song and dance about knights
and clowns and another small drama piece based on a fairy tale also
involving the knights and clowns and a bad witch. They liked the idea
of the song being in English so I made one up and choreographed some
moves to go with it. Adlan managed to find a stack of old cardboard
boxes that we could cut up, paint and convert into costumes.

The day of the performance arrived. All the parents and guardians
were invited and Eric, Frank and Milla came from Médicin du Monde.
Balloons and sweets were bought to hand out at the end. The gazebos were
decorated with paintings and clay objects that the children had made.
The walls inside the building were covered with life-size self-portraits of
the children, the aim of that project being to increase their sense of self-
identity and confidence, as well as being good fun. I was amazed at the
lack of stage fright and nervousness shown by the children. There were

some wonderful performances of dance, poetry and drama sketches. Jon did a good job being 'Babayaga' the witch, with his long hair flowing and a mask on his face. He hypnotized all the knights into statues, then the clowns came along and used their laughter to break the spell pelting 'Babayaga' with brightly coloured foam balls. Many of the parents came up to thank us for helping the children and saying that they noticed a big difference in their behaviour, they were more relaxed, playing again with toys and had fewer nightmares. Their faces were opening up like flowers coming into bloom, sunlit with smiles.

Little did I think how my training in community care and working with disabled people would come in so useful after all these years. I had started to work voluntarily in a local day care centre after spending a year out of work with a damaged back. Some of the adults could only communicate through head or arm movements, having no recognizable language. I found I could communicate by creating a language with them of sounds or tiny movements so we ended up having reasonable conversations and jokes. It seemed that no one had tried to communicate with them before, beyond the basic 'yes' and 'no'.

A new group of children arrived on the Sunday, and during the day officials from the Health Ministry came and told us we could not continue working with the children until we have all had a full medical examination. A real blow because organizing appointments would take time and the following week all the team were attending a seminar organized by Médicin du Monde. This meant not starting work again until 1 June.

While we were waiting for the medical examinations the women carried out more assessment tests with school children. This was a job that Jon and I are not qualified to do, neither of us having training in diagnostic work, so we used the time in organizing the stockroom and making an assessment of the materials we would need in the future.

Life at home was still busy; with the guards, the women, us, Chris flitting in and out and the eight 'Lamman Ass' boys arriving most evenings to join us for supper. No electricity meant no running water from the standpipe so we made daily trips to Little Star to fetch water from the water tank.

Cooking facilities were poor; the gas cooker only had two rings working, one full blast, the other slow simmer. But then, we only had two pans (little and large) and one amazingly bent frying pan with no handle lent to us by

a neighbour. Our diet consisted of vegetables of the moment, homemade
cheese, rice, buckwheat and eggs. Fruit was rare and expensive. For a few
days we had the luxury of Dutch baked beans, apple purée, sauerkraut,
sweet pickled red cabbage and some washed-out tinned green beans nobody
was interested in.

The day for our medical tests arrived. The school bus drove us through
Grozny, providing us with another chance of seeing some of the city. One
of the most poignant sights was seeing the rusting trams turned on their
sides, sculptures of twisted buckling metal, all the tram lines in disuse,
the land being reclaimed by nature's grassy fingers. In the silence I heard
memories of ringing tram bells, the chatter and laughter of passengers,
the sound of the wheels on the rails and the occasional crackle of electricity from the overhead lines.

The hospital had no electricity so could not X-ray us, but we were
tested for Aids and had swabs taken from various orifices, with some
twittering from the women and indignation from the men. On the road
again to find a hospital with electricity. Two hours later we found one.
Near the main door was a large pile of rubbish with scavenging brown
cows climbing over it. X-rays complete, Adlan gave us our medical passports – little notebooks stamped after every test.

Back home we found we had running water for the first time in days. After
the hot sweaty day touring Grozny and its hospitals there was much bathing
in our dangerous bathroom! Plumbing in this part of the world seemed to
have a different meaning, for example if you found the oldest gas geyser that
just about worked and welded some pipes to it you could call it a hot water
system. Luckily they were rare, but apparently a luxury!

Little Star, full on

Another week, working with a new set of children. The size of the group
had risen to 35 as some mothers were sending younger brothers and sisters. Also some of the most traumatized children had been allowed to
come back again.

Lyoma's wife joined us to work with the children. She was the first
Chechen woman I had seen wearing a Muslim veil, revealing only the
face. Chechens are Sunni Muslims and are considered moderate. During the war shariat law and interest in jihad (holy war) became more

popular, particularly among the fighting men who were influenced by the Wahabi of Saudi Arabia who gave them financial help.

We arrived at Little Star as early as our drivers were willing to take us, to prepare for the day. After we had sorted out the paints and paper and set up the tape machine, Lyoma and I went to the peace room, the only room that had a rug on the floor. We sat in silence together and chanted 'Om', our voices echoing beautifully through the building.

Two seven-year-olds, Akmed and Ali, appeared to be severely traumatized. Akmed talked in short, sharp bursts and had very little concentration span; when the afternoon plane came over he wailed and his whole body became tense and rigid. Ali wouldn't talk at all. They played with the Lego we had brought from England and found comfort in each other's company. At lunchtime I found them crouching under some bushes outside the canteen playing games with a few nuts fallen from a tree. It was nice to see them relaxing together and there was even a glimmer of a smile on Ali's face. Later Akmed's mother told me that their family was caught in the middle of a big bombing raid, which shattered Akmed's confidence and strained his nervous system. The war trauma expresses itself in various ways: some children are over active and nervous like Akmed and some mute like Ali; many of the older boys are angry and they use sport to get rid of their aggression. It is frustrating that, because of the lack of a common language, we cannot talk directly to the children and always have to rely on Fatima, our interpreter. She interprets for us during the times we teach but during meal and break times she has a break as well which means we can't communicate to any depth with the children.

One evening I was having a lie down, stretching my aching calf muscles, when Chris bounded into the room and told us about a dance festival taking place and would we like to see it. Too good to miss so off we went, weaving through the streets to an open-air amphitheatre that had escaped the bombing. We were astounded by the skill and professionalism of these child dancers; the double spins in the air landing on their knees, intricate foot work, mock sword fighting of the boys and the grace of the girls gliding across the floor as though they are just hovering without their feet touching the ground at all.

At the end of the week the children put on a surprise performance for us. We helped them with props, costumes and music. The performance was hilarious with many comic skits, some about the shariat law of 40 lashes for those who drink alcohol, and mimics making fun of the body language and habits of our team. There was also rock and roll, pop and folk dancing, poetry and songs.

A little chap called Rustam attached himself to me. He hardly spoke a word, was very self contained and followed me wherever I went. I played with him, often in a clownish sort of way, and slowly over the week he relaxed and started joining in games with the other children. At the end of the week his mother said he had started to talk and play again and take notice of his surroundings. He gave me a digital watch, and was absolutely adamant I accept it, a gift of friendship.

I felt the children needed something more than we were giving them. They needed tools that they could use to increase their own inner strength so I started thinking of some qigong exercises that I could teach them. I taught them how to ground themselves, imagining themselves as trees and feeling their feet on the ground and their roots growing into the earth; then allowing all the tension and stress in their bodies to flow down through their roots into the earth so they could relax. They played a game in pairs lifting each other up, first with the person being lifted not focusing on any rooting and then being lifted while imagining roots growing into the earth. It was much harder for their partner to lift them up the second time, a good example of mind over matter. I also taught them the 'egg timer', an exercise for balancing the energy flow in the body and releasing stressful thoughts. At the end of the sessions I took them through a visualized journey leading into relaxation.

Many of the children told me how they enjoy the sessions. Jansoor, a 13-year-old boy, gave me a thumb-up sign. He only had one hand, the other blown off when he picked up some live ammunition while playing in a pile of rumble during the war. I had particularly noticed him in the movement session because of his love for dancing – he was brilliant at double spins in the air. One little girl called Aisha came and sat beside me after a session and laid her head on my shoulder; she smiled with such a sweet peaceful expression, no words were necessary. Later on in the week a teenage boy called Aslan told me that his seven-year-old sister Rosa had used the visualized journey to help her get to sleep and it was the first night she hadn't had nightmares since the war.

We arrived home one evening fairly exhausted after holding a sports competition with lots of team games. Chris arrived with three men from Norway to join our merry household. Our guests were here to help with mine clearance. Eric ran a Peace Centre near Lillehammer; he had arranged for Michael and Gaier, who worked for a de-mining operation in Norway, to come with him to Grozny. They were great guys and didn't mind mucking in with our extensive and somewhat disorganized household.

The next morning we all rushed around, trying not to bump into each other, getting ready to leave. The day got hotter and stickier. As we helped the children get ready for their performance, dark clouds rolled across the sky, big drops of rain splashed onto the steaming tarmac and we carried chairs inside into the biggest room. At the end of the show there was some traditional Chechen dancing. Everyone stood or sat in a big circle, clapping or drumming on chairs, while one man took the floor with some intricate foot work and chose the woman he wished to dance with. She glided across the floor like a swan, he danced around her guiding her to a group of his friends where his dance became more frenetic as he showed off his conquest. It reminded me of the wooing prance of a male bird. We all took a turn and even the Norwegians were enticed into the circle where they leapt about bravely!

The storm was tropical in its intensity, crystal rods of warm rain. We ran to the bus. I was sitting opposite Magomed, the seven-year-old brother of Aisha, who was watching the rainfall and the road becoming a raging brown stream. The bus lurched in and out of potholes. I saw a slow smile spread across his face as he watched the dance of the raindrops. This was the first time I'd seen him smile all week, and it made my heart feel warm.

Back at home I was getting fed up with the constant blaring of the tape recorder and asked Ali not to play it early in the morning to give us some peace, he remembered for a day then it was back to 'boom, boom, boom'. So I said to Camilla 'Let's go for a walk around the block'. What a joy to walk without a guard but after a few minutes she noticed Ali and Shamkhan following at a discreet distance and felt guilty because she knew they felt responsible for us. It was only a ten-minute walk, around behind our house, looking out over flat fields but it served to cool our tempers and gave us a touch of independence to keep us happy, and Ali stopped playing the early morning Russian pop.

Being followed everywhere was driving me nuts. One day at Little Star I found myself alone so I took the opportunity to explore outside the boundary fence. How good it felt to walk alone in woodland. I found a small pond and walked around its edge; there did not appear to be anyone around. After 20 minutes I went back to the break in the boundary fence only to see that my guards were waiting for me once again. The guards were furious, saying there were bad 'Tapes' (Chechen word for clans) in the area who would know I was a foreigner because of my long hair, and I could be kidnapped.

Moscow visit

On Sunday 22 June Jon, Anya and I left Little Star to fly to Moscow, us to renew our visas and buy more equipment and toys and Anya to report to the University. The children came to the gate and cheered us off in a cloud of dust.

After a week in steamy, fumy Moscow having renewed our visas and bought extra equipment plus some second-hand office furniture and a safe, we had to find a way of getting back down to Chechnya. A train journey was not appealing with all our luggage and the bureaucratic hassle it would attract, so Anya asked the Red Cross if we could fly on one of their planes. A plane was leaving for Nalchik in Kabardino Balkaria on the following Monday and there was room for us and our luggage. This was the last plane scheduled to fly to the Caucasus because the Red Cross were scaling down their operations in that area. We were very lucky.

We arrived at Nalchik two and a half hours later and were picked up by Mrs Adaev and Shamkhan. They had brought an open-back lorry and hired a taxi to take us back to Sernovodsk. For five hot and sweaty hours, covering just 100 miles, we drove. At every checkpoint we were stopped and had to pay a fine because the lorry had a Chechen number plate. The main border was closed so we went to Sleptsovskaya and crossed at a small border post, driving on dusty, rutted mud tracks, the tower of white plastic chairs swaying precariously on the back of the lorry.

On Wednesday afternoon, 2 July we arrived back in Grozny with our guards Ruslan and Hassan. That evening Ruslan talked of his dream of being trained by the British Army. Eventually Jon and I grew weary and retired to bed leaving them to their computer games.

'*Why is there a purple light shining from the crystal, what does that mean?*'

We hear angry voices beyond the wall.

And here we are ... now ... our stomachs tightening with fear, another move into the unknown but this time we know the fickle nature of our captors; one day they are our friends, the next day our enemy.

7

The Hot House

I hear them coming and nudge Camilla awake. Two black-clothed and masked figures descend with strips of curtain material in their hands. We are blindfolded and guided out of the house into the Jeep. The whispering tones of Dark Chocolate come from the driving seat. A ten-minute bumpy ride then a squeak of a rusty gate and we are helped through slip-sliding mud up some steps into a house. It has a musty, unlived in smell. Later HC tells us it had been used by Chechen fighters during the war as a 'safe' resting house.

Masks off, I see two beds pushed together made up with clean white sheets and bed covers – unbelievable! Outside a window with vertical bars an orange fluorescent streetlight is throwing reflected leaf-patterned shadows onto the glass and into the room. GA quickly throws a bedcover over the curtain rail and they turn on the light; the switch is in the hall. The floor is rust-coloured painted hardboard and there is even a carpet. A doorway with no door leads to a smaller room that is empty except for a wardrobe. It also has a barred window; HC covers the lower half with a white cloth and with an admonishing finger makes it very clear that we are never to set foot in that room. We return to the kitchen that we had walked through to get to our bedroom. It's a large rectangular room with a wooden coffee table and four child-size chairs in the middle. At one end are a gas cooker, boiler and a small cupboard with a plastic drying rack for plates but no sink. At the other end a door leads to the outside world. Opposite a large window covered with opaque plastic is the hall, with our room on the right, another bedroom straight ahead and bathroom to the left with a bath, working shower and child-size loo but no running water.

Muddy footprints cover the linoleum floor and HC asks us to clean it. What with? There's a large green enamel pot with a dribble of water in the bottom and GA finds some rags. Lots of wet mud and no water, this is difficult. Jon does a much better job than me. We're sent to bed. What luxury, nice firm mattresses and soft white linen sheets. GA pinches a bedcover – I don't think they have any bedding. We use our shirts as pillows and stretch out our limbs; no muscle cramps from hard-edged wooden crates or a collapsing sunbed this night. Before I drift into sleep I watch the shadow reflections of leaves swaying on the ceiling.

I wake up with a sinking feeling in my belly; my bladder is full and we have to knock on the door to be allowed out. What will the response be? Fortunately HC opens the door and doesn't bother us while we use the loo. Water is running through the pipes again so we have a session of filling large glass jars and enamel pots. There is a moth-eaten cloth covering the window in the bathroom and as we are on our own, door shut, I dare to peep through a hole and see an overgrown magical garden. Bunches of small black grapes hang from vines strung up on a veranda, and beyond is an old white bathtub enshrined in weeds, dwarfed by a few bowing sunflowers. HC beckons us to the kitchen and allows us to make tea and eat some bread; then we are sent back to our room, the door wedged shut with a shovel, while they try to figure out how to get the boiler working. They manage it but the thermostat is broken and we have to endure steamy hot temperatures. HC comes into our room and seeing our red sweaty faces takes pity on us and opens the window in the adjoining room. We start bringing two glasses of water with us every time we come back from the kitchen but it's not enough – after a few days our pee turns brown.

HC goes out for provisions; we have heard them both having showers and so we ask GA if we can do the same. Yes, Yes, Yes, hot running water for the first time since our capture. I spend half an hour lifting off layers of dirt with some bright green soap and there's shampoo. Pure ecstasy! Then I wash my pants and dress, I rinse and rinse and still the water is grey; anyway, they are certainly cleaner than before. I wrap my hair in a towel that I found on the back of the door and slink out of the bathroom. GA is watching from the kitchen and shakes a finger, whoops! I think I went over the top, but it was well worth it.

It's my turn. I start scrubbing away the layers of grime and old skin. I am shocked by the amount of skin I shed. Washing my hair over and over, the feeling of hot water on my body is divine, being kissed by the water, running hot water! The water comes through a very old gas geyser, no shower nozzle, just a swinging metal pipe with a rubber pipe on the end as an extension. I feel uneasy; GA is timing me, so I quickly finish my ablutions, dry and return to the bedroom.

HC arrives back with a bag of potatoes, a tray of eggs, sunflower oil and some beef scrag ends. They invite us out to eat and allow us to drink hot sweet tea while we prepare the meal. I wash and slice the potatoes and Jon fries enough for a heaped bowlful which we all share. HC fries the meat and he, GA and Jon fork lumps from the pan into their mouths – mostly fat, so I'm glad I declined. The mood is peaceful, they feel sure we are going to be released soon. I value these times in the kitchen where I can steal glances through a high small window above the cooker and gaze at the vine-leafed sky. Also the kitchen is much cooler than our room, the big window having some holes through which the September air sucks and billows the plastic covering.

This meat is like rubber, but it feels good having a good chew. I like cooking – it gives me something to do, and I can use my mind, even if is only a very small part. It gives me a focus and also means I do not have to engage in mundane and potentially dangerous conversations. HC is definitely heady, logical and clever enough to turn anything around. I have to choose my words so carefully not knowing what connotations he will put on them, especially with his strong views coloured by his recent reading of strict shariat law. It's like walking across a minefield: you think you are just walking across a beautiful meadow then Boom! One of your words is an explosive trigger.

Thursday 4 September

I'm in agony, my bladder full to bursting and Puppydog is having a long bath! Finally he comes out and I'm allowed to relieve myself. He redeems himself by bringing some new music. Now we have the Gypsy Kings blasting through the house making a change from the sickly Euro-Pop we had been subjected to in the Kiva. He also brings aubergines, courgettes and onions and asks me to make some chips.

Outside our bedroom window is an enormous walnut tree and through the clear bit of window, above the curtain rail, we see Puppydog climbing up. When we are allowed out for the second meal of the day there's a tin plate piled high with walnuts, a good dollop of protein to add to our diet.

Puppydog teaches me how to crack open a nut by grinding two together in one hand.

Paunch isn't keen to communicate with us. He stumps around angrily, ordering Puppydog to go to the bazaar, give him a massage or deal with us and we sense that Puppydog resents this. When we are in the kitchen Paunch lies on his bed in the room at the end of the corridor, leaning up on one elbow so he can watch us, not a nice feeling. I'm happy to be back in our room laying out a backgammon board on our carpet with pieces of cotton and seeds or doing some tai chi barefoot on the smooth hardboard, a nice change from the earth and pebble floor of the Kiva. Having natural daylight makes such a difference.

Friday 5 September

Our delight in the daylight is short-lived; paranoia raises its ugly head again. GA appears with a thick blanket, a jar of nails and a hammer; soon we are back in the twilight zone. My heart starts racing with the fear of lack of air; we try to smother the radiator with clothes but it doesn't help much. Eventually we summon enough courage to ask if we can have the light on and they consent. It makes a great difference as now we can divert our minds from thinking of the heat to playing backgammon. The sound of cracking walnuts comes from the kitchen but they don't offer us any.

Saturday 6 September

Paunch's bad mood continues – we hear him grumbling to Puppydog. Puppydog lets us out to wash (still running water, a miracle) and to have some breakfast. He asks Jon to make some chips but they refuse to eat them with us. There is one egg left. I place the egg on end in a golden woven plastic bowl with a dip in the centre. It creates a surreal sculptural image in the middle of the empty table. My creative act is not appreciated. Both of them come into our room, Paunch grunting and growling swinging his arm in a threatening gesture towards Jon. Puppydog pulls him back, giggling, saying 'Weiner contusie, weiner contusie (war madness),' pointing at Paunch. It's a bit of an act but I know that using food as art would appear sacrilegious to them.

Then we hear Paunch sending Puppydog out and by the sound of Puppydog's light happy footsteps he's as pleased as we are not. So far he is the only one who has treated us with respect and not played any silly psychological games. Not long after he's left Paunch bursts into our room carrying a big knife that he waves around as he rants in Chechen, his bloodshot eye staring. Then he takes Jon by the arm and hauls him into the small room adjoining ours. He has handcuffs dangling out of a pocket, which he uses to attach Jon's wrists to the radiator. He mimes cutting off Jon's ear and although neither of us thinks he will do it there's a chance that he will, in his heightened, emotional and unbalanced state. Instead he grabs me by the hand and takes me to the kitchen, pulls out a newly opened packet of tea from a ledge under the table and seems to be saying we have made a big mistake by starting to use it before the other one was finished. Is this the reason for his anger? How totally mad and confusing.

I realize it is all a ruse to separate me and Jon. He goes back to our room to check on Jon and I try to squeeze past him but his arm bars my way. He pushes me backward and slams the door, wedging it with the shovel. Then he pushes me into their bedroom and down on a bed, and I understand what his game is. So I start whispering loudly, 'Jon mia mooge, Jon mia mooge (Jon's my husband),' 'Niet, niet (No, no)' and struggle to get up. But he forces me back down, half throttling my neck. I appeal to his religious side, whispering 'Allah oo Akba, Allah oo Akba' and he slaps my face. Then I know I cannot escape. I glance down at his penis – I want to know what's going to be invading my body. Thankfully I see that it's not too big, so I won't be hurt. He still has his mask on and doesn't try to kiss me which means I can close my eyes and take my mind away. I'm thinking: 'You can never touch the essence of me. My body is only a part of who I am. My spirit will always be free.' The act is over fairly quickly – luckily he's not very experienced.

I sense what is happening. A strange energy of realization washes over me, a flush of heat and tingling at the same time. Shock. I glance at the handcuffs, I twist and turn them but they are well secured to the heating pipe which is fixed to the wall. There's no way I can free myself from them. How much trauma can a body and psyche absorb without losing contact with the outside world? I can only guess what is happening in the silence. I make a prayer that there is no violence and that the violation will pass swiftly. I

102

need to be calm for Camilla as she will be in more shock than me. Listen without judgement, just allowing the story to be told.

Afterwards he allows me to go back to the bedroom while he goes to the bathroom. Jon is still tied up and I sit on the side of the bed; I feel numb but tell him that I'm OK. 'He . . . raped me,' I whisper. I hardly want to mouth the word 'rape', it's such a foul violation of a human being. I also can't really believe it has happened to me. I feel sullied. Paunch re-appears and tells me I can use the bathroom and brings the key to untie Jon. Thank God I can wash, and with soap as well. I wash the scent of Paunch off me, which helps me feel cleansed and brings me back into my body. Then Jon and I sit side by side on the edge of the bed and I tell him the whole story. What is so amazing is that he doesn't show his anger and he doesn't smother me with sympathy, he just listens and sits like a warm, comfortable mountain by my side. He gives me all the support and understanding I need.

I see a distant look in Camilla's eyes; grief and horror are painted there. I hold her in my arms, wondering why we ever came to this place and why this is happening to us.

Paunch comes in again and beckons to Jon, saying 'Igre, igre (game)' and turns to me saying 'Chai, OK,' pointing to the kitchen. Jon reluct-antly follows him into the other bedroom while I go into the kitchen and brew some tea. Paunch was obviously feeling guilty, and inviting Jon to play backgammon and have a joint makes everything OK in his eyes. A mini hell for Jon.

What sort of guy is this? First he rapes my partner then invites me out to play a game! I play this game the best I can, my mind full of thoughts of what has just occurred as I look across the gaming board at this one-eyed beast. He calmly plays away, smoking a joint and offering it to me. I decline. My mind is reeling. At least this gives Camilla some space and partial free-dom of the house. I see that Paunch is relaxed, he thinks himself king of the castle, totally in control. And in this small world he is.

As I sit in the kitchen my body begins to shake with delayed shock and the tears begin to flow. 'Why me? Why now?' I talk to my mother in my mind and wonder if somehow she will feel what has happened. The hot sweet black tea soothes me and I appreciate being on my own with my anguish, no one watching and pointing guns or knives. I can look at the swaying vines as much as I like and I find peace.

A few days later, back in England, my mother had a dream. I walked up to her bedside and said, 'I have been raped. I'm all right, but I cannot stay here. I have to go back now' and disappeared.

I'm thinking that we always have a choice how to deal with every situation that we face and as much as possible I choose to find the positive within the negative. This is the toughest situation I have ever had to face. It helps that I believe my eternal essence can never be harmed, that the power of love can overcome all obstacles. But I still have to deal with my emotions, because that's part of being human and in this I ask for help. I ask for guidance and feel powerful waves of energy pouring through my body, rejuvenating and cleansing.

By the time Jon and Paunch finish their game I feel calm again. They come into the kitchen and Paunch allows us to cook some food. He is relaxed and struts around the room like a cock on top of a manure heap in his white-hooded mask, regaling us with Chechen history, totally oblivious to the trauma he has caused. I feel as if we're taking part in a play, laughable in its absurdity if it wasn't so sad and fearful.

Puppydog returns and we keep our emotions hidden. We long to tell him what has happened as we are pretty sure he wouldn't condone the act and would be shocked, but we know he is the youngest of the four and therefore has little authority. If he mentioned it to the other two, anything could happen. The thought of gang rape makes me feel sick.

Sunday 7 September

HC and GA make remarks about Jon's long face and grim set mouth. HC had just offered him some fatty fried meat and they can't understand why we don't look happier, particularly as they keep telling us we will be released very soon. I'm better at acting than Jon but it's a tough part to play.

In the evening they burst into our room, HC leading the way with an air of importance clutching a piece of paper, he's so excited it takes us a few seconds to understand that on the paper are questions sent from England that required answers from us. 'Two million dollars are coming, you will be free!' 'Coming from where?' I reply, 'It doesn't matter' he smiles, and hands us the 'Proof of Life' questions and a piece of paper and a pencil. I have to write the name and address of my secondary school and Jon has to write where he used to go on camping holidays as a child. All the time I'm thinking why didn't this happen a few days ago, just too late, too late.

Monday 8 September

The tension is mounting. I wet one of the hankies that we found in the pink crystal room and tie it around my forehead trying to ease the pressure building up between my brows (the point known as the 'third-eye chakra', a psychic centre). I don't want to know what the near future holds for me. I pray that the rape was a one-off, but it was not to be. We hear Paunch giving Puppydog permission to leave, we hear the jangle of manacles and a belt being unbuckled to the accompaniment of Gypsy Kings. However long this goes on I will do my best not to collapse; with Jon's help I will hold on . . . and on . . .

Paunch, king of his domain and his subjects, directs me to the bathroom where I am chained to the heating pipes. I know what will come next, as I hear him direct Camilla to the other room. I make prayers as there's nothing else I can do to stop this happening. After committing the crime again, I am invited out to play several rounds of backgammon while he smokes his joint. I see he is relaxed and vulnerable. Afterwards I tell Camilla: 'I think I could ease him into a false sense of security and use a pan from the kitchen to knock him out so we can leg it. He always sends Puppydog away for a few hours so we would have at least an hour before he came back.' My mind moves on, into fantasy. 'We could light a candle in the kitchen and leave the gas on, Boom! A big distraction and no one would know how many people were in the house.'

'It's too dangerous,' I reply, 'and I still don't like the idea of using violence however angry we are. Fantasy and revenge is what they're all about.' Of course it appeals to our base human instincts but I know we both have the courage not to act on them. In my mind I know how impotent Jon feels. The rape is just as bad for him as for me: Paunch has raped him of his right to challenge and protect, there is no outlet for his anger and rage so he buries them. Puppydog arrives back with some vegetables and they urge us to cook but we have little appetite. Back in our room we can relax, play our own game of backgammon and do some tai chi and qigong to ease the tension.

After dark we hear lots of gunfire and HC crashes into our room. 'They're shooting the moon, shooting the moon.' He explains that whenever there is a lunar eclipse they follow a tradition of shooting out the light in the moon. I wonder where all the bullets land when they arrive back on earth!

I've learnt much about firearms whilst in captivity. I'm told about the tracer rounds in a magazine. These are the glowing rounds that are fired every ten or twenty rounds so the direction of fire can be seen. Tonight there must be thousands of rounds being fired in the air, looking like fireworks.

9–21 September

The rest of the time in the hot house had its own sweltering routine broken by sharp volcanic eruptions jarring our nerves as we walk the tightrope of existence.

Every other day I wake with the pressure in my head growing. Sometimes I am lucky and either Puppydog arrives back early or HC decides to visit. HC spends most of the days in a marijuana smoke haze, trying to block and suppress his emotions. One time I use my menstruation as an excuse which Paunch accepts, although in fact I am bleeding very little as the stress is affecting my cycle.

As they realize we are not going to be freed as soon as they thought, boredom sets in, bringing with it paranoia and dangerous games. Puppydog finds out that we are locking the bathroom door which makes him very upset and this leads to a game of 'Let's barge in while Jon is on the loo' and 'The pipe tapping nightmare'. Until now it has been a luxury to sit on the loo but Puppydog and Paunch decide I'm a sitting target. One or other taps the heating pipes and when I emerge they accuse me of trying to send a message. However much I deny it they continue with their accusations. It's a pathetic game.

GA and HC crash through our door at about three in the morning, GA insisting that I must have gone through to the small room and tapped on the pipes for a joke; he's been talking to Puppydog and Paunch. He's in one of those moods when he is certain he is right and you know that whatever you say won't make any difference. In fact we were so fast asleep it took us a few seconds to wake which I thought would be proof enough, but no, he continues to interrogate us for at least ten minutes until HC decides to go back to bed, he looks pretty wrecked with heavily lidded, red-slit eyes. Without his

106

back-up GA isn't strong enough to continue – he is not a born tormentor,
just a tormented soul. The next morning he continues to interrogate us in
the kitchen while refusing to let us eat. Strangely, HC stands up for us, say-
ing it's all nonsense. This breaks the torturer's spell. He cracks some walnuts
which he offers to us.

One morning we walk into the kitchen and see HC, sitting, back bent,
watching the ground intently. As we get nearer we see a half-grown
hedgehog with its little snout twitching, lapping up some milk out of a
saucer. The look of wonder and love on HC's face is a beautiful sight. He
buys some out-of-date UHT cartons of milk for his and the hedgehog's
consumption; occasionally we are lucky enough to have some to add to
our sweet black tea, every last mouthful savoured like a good glass of
champagne.

The effect the hedgehog has on the atmosphere of the house is quite
extraordinary, like the presence of a newborn baby. Everyone relaxes
and watches the antics of the hedgehog as it scurries around the kitchen,
nibbling bits of food or sniffing disdainfully. One day it disappears and
we have a massive house search. After a couple of hours GA discovers it
sleeping peacefully behind the radiator in the bathroom, covered in cobwebs. Then HC decides to take it back to its natural environment out in
the garden, in case it starts to hibernate inside the house.

After a week or so the quality and variety of food starts to go downhill
– no meat, no fresh veg, back to eggs and potatoes and often stale bread.
One streak of rusty light in our diet is the arrival of about five kilos of
rice in a well-recycled plastic bag. Wonderful we think, until we find all
the nails! But after much sifting (no sieve) and rinsing (when there is
enough water) we manage to make some delicious meals of scrambled
egg and boiled rice, which change into egg fried rice for the second meal
of the day.

There did come one day when there was no food and no tea which meant
no outings to the kitchen, only hours in our steamy half-lit room handing
each other mythical slices of my Dad's deliciously rich, moist, chocolate
cake. This imaginary eating sustained us until Paunch took pity on us, put
on our light and brought us a handful of walnuts.

The 'no food days' don't last for long as our captors get more fed up and
bored than we do with no meals to break up the day and they manage to
wheedle some money out of their superiors for some rations.

On a few occasions HC and GA invite us to play long sessions of back-gammon with them on the low coffee table, the board gazed at through a mist of tea steam and tobacco smoke. HC talks of his dreams. His family has some land in the mountains and when he has the money he wants to build a ski resort on the slopes. He has a passion for well-designed handmade shoes (preferably Italian). He describes some that he used to own, dark brown soft leather, curving nearly to a point at the tip, a punched paisley swirl pattern on the top, a half-inch square heel. In his enthusiasm he expands his dreams to include a shoe factory. HC likes to use our dictionary to help in his communication; GA, who is less liter-ary, uses mime and drama to illustrate and add humour to his stories. Stories about his exploits with past girlfriends driving on the dirt tracks in the mountains, swerving wildly around the sharp bends, vast craggy rocks overhanging one side and deep ravines on the other, until the girls screamed with fear and exhilaration. One evening when we are in the kitchen the electricity is turned off, but instead of telling us to go back to our room, HC lights a candle and the storytelling continues. What a contrast from a tense day with Paunch (once again I had been violated) to this peaceful storytelling scene illuminated by the soft gentle light of the candle.

Monday 22 September

We are on the move again. HC and GA ask us to help pack up the food, some kitchen utensils, crockery and kettle. I do a good job, wrapping all the breakables in newspaper and neatly stowing them in plastic bags. HC has gone out and we sit in the kitchen, late into the night, chatting to GA. There comes a point when he says 'I've had enough of wearing this mask,' and to our amazement pulls it off. I am stunned by this act of trust and friendship. I say 'thank you' as it truly is a great leap in faith. As my words reach GA's heart he fidgets and giggles. It takes a while for me to get used to this new face. We are both a little shy of looking and being looked upon.

It's a shock to see GA with a naked face, different from what we had imagined. The mask gave the impression he had fat, puffed up rabbit cheeks whereas his face is thin and long with vertical lines of stress scored into his cheeks; dark brown wavy hair covers his ears, and his eyes are light blue-green. His lips are full and one of his front teeth is missing. I'll never forget the tableau of GA and Jon sitting opposite each other across the low table, Jon's clear blue eyes beaming love to GA and saying 'Thank you' and GA laughing uncomfortably, the invisible armour around his heart almost audibly cracking. We talk, laugh and joke for a couple of hours until we hear the squeak of the gate. Swiftly and quietly we go back to our room. GA and HC talk in low tones in the kitchen before knocking on our door to say we won't be moving tonight.

Tuesday 23 September

Breakfast time, HC sitting hunched over the table in a doped stupor. Suddenly he mumbles in a grumbly tone something incomprehensible to us and whips off his mask. We are stunned and look quickly towards the floor; GA chuckles. Gradually we realize HC doesn't actually mind us looking at him. He looks older than I had imagined with a flat sharp face, thin lips and tight jaw and almond-shaped eyes with long straight black eyebrows. There's a large splodge of white scar tissue covering part of the iris of his shrapnel-wounded eye. His black hair is cut close to his skull.

We cook egg fried rice and are given time to sit with our out-of-date milky sweet tea. GA and HC are not in a talking mood so we sit in silence listening to the tinny tones of the Walkman tape machine.

Some time after midnight the gate squeaks and we hear the low rumble of a Jeep. HC says we don't need masks but gestures to us to bow our heads and look to the floor. I hear the deep tones of Dark Chocolate's voice and Puppydog answering. In the Jeep we have to put our heads in our laps. This time they drive into the courtyard outside the main door of a familiar building.

As I am led hurriedly from the Jeep by Puppydog, I trip badly on a step damaging my big toe. 'Ooghww!' I grunt, and am kicked up the bum and shoved forcibly up the rest of the stairs into the building.

We walk, heads bowed, into the pink crystal room. The beds have been moved from the left side of the room to the right. All the belongings of the previous occupant have been taken away. No small elegant shoes under the bed and all the drawers and cupboards empty; only the lamp remains, lying on top of a cupboard.

No masks, no handcuffs – more trust.

8

Pink Crystal Room, Autumn

Wednesday 24 September

Puppydog is there at our wake-up knock so we can wash and use the loo. We are in luck: water in the taps and electricity. Paunch doesn't appear until later in the day and isn't keen to see us. Has the pattern changed, I wonder? Am hoping. GA arrives in the evening and invites us to eat. A feast of grated carrot, cabbage and sweet peppers rolled in cabbage leaves with fresh bread. HC brings a tin of Nescafé. We are all sitting and eating in a relaxed manner when Paunch appears. He had been dozing and heard our whispered chatter. GA and HC are not wearing their masks and Paunch, looking startled, retreats quickly.

25–29 September

Food money has arrived, trays of eggs appear, half a sack of potatoes, homemade cold pressed sunflower oil, bread, tea, and a glittering white mountain of sugar. In the corner lurks a full sack of vermicelli. One morning we come into the kitchen and there's a cut-glass pedestal plate on the table with a pyramid of shiny green apples arranged on it – GA has gathered them from an apple tree in his family's garden. HC and GA are sure we will be freed on 1 October and so they treat us like friends, allowing us to come into the kitchen more often. Always a joy to bathe in the natural light, though we have to be careful not to show too much interest in the window unless it conjures up paranoia, which we know is only snoozing lightly beneath the skin of friendship.

HC has discovered a pile of novels in their room and these occupy him for most of the night, preventing his mind from being engulfed by war-induced nightmares until he's exhausted enough to sleep without dreaming. Of course the marijuana helps too. He rises late (leaving GA to look after us in the first half of the day), has a glass of black coffee and a cigarette and dives into the next romance. It's intriguing watching how his face relaxes, becoming young and boyish. Lines of tension disappear as he absorbs himself in the story, forgetting about his own life of angst. Long may the supply of books last.

They have become so relaxed that one day GA doesn't immediately realize his ID card has fallen out of his pocket and I catch a glimpse of his photo by an emblem of a wolf and a man with a trilby and a moustache. It reminds me of a photo of Dudaev, the Chechen president who was killed by a bomb following the radar signal of a satellite phone. Later HC, on one of his 'stoned' days, shows us a leaflet advertising a meeting of their group of freedom fighters, carefully covering the address with his thumb. It had the same picture of Dudaev and the wolf, but I don't have time to take in any of the Russian words.

Sadly the days in between are not so happy for us: Paunch has decided to continue raping me. With unerring regularity every other afternoon we hear him relieving Puppydog of his gaoler duties and the light happy step of Puppydog leaving the flat. Then a saucepan of water goes on the cooker and he comes to get me, tying up our door so Jon can't escape. At least he's stopped using the handcuffs. Afterwards he washes, then takes the backgammon board into our bedroom to play with Jon leaving me to wash and make a cup of tea. These times being alone in the kitchen are very precious to me. Time to weep, time to find my inner peace. When I feel more composed I sneak glances outside, tweaking back the edge of the baking paper covering the window. Through the crack I watch women gathered together sitting on a bench, chatting under a line of colourful washing fluttering in the wind, children playing around their skirts. There are two young women talking not far from our window, elegantly dressed with headbands and lipstick, city folk. One of them has a paper cone full of sunflower seeds which they are munching, spitting out the husks in between gales of laughter. From another crack I can see a Russian armoured lorry in the middle of the square, children climbing on the bonnet and leaping off with loud sqeals of delight. I watch a father and his son washing the mud off their white Lada, carrying buckets of water, sloshing it over the vehicle, rubbing it with rags, totally absorbed in the enjoyment of their task.

My silent face through the glass watches a celluloid reality.

111

After a couple of weeks Paunch changes his tack and begins taking the backgammon board into the kitchen, demanding that I make tea for them as well. So I retreat to our bedroom and dance out my misery Isadora Duncan style.

Tuesday 30 September

A gentle evening in the kitchen with GA. He's relaxed, in a good mood, enjoying regaling us with anecdotes from his past. Suddenly HC bursts into the room like a furious tornado, jabbering at us with accusatory tones. We don't know what it's all about but manage to stay calm, if somewhat startled. GA laughs. HC slows down enough to use the dictionary to explain that a friend of his has heard us knocking on the wall of our bedroom. Recently we have heard male voices beyond the wall behind our beds talking, laughing, singing to a guitar – other members of their gang, perhaps. HC is convinced that we have been trying to contact other people in the building to help us escape. There is nothing we can say except 'Niet' and 'Niet' again. This does nothing to improve his humour. There is a knock at the door (their special 'rap code') and I hear the voice of Dark Chocolate. HC tells us angrily to stay sitting in the kitchen with GA to guard us and he takes DC into our room. I can hear them searching, turning my bag upside down, all my possessions clattering on the floor. Now I am really worried, my heart beating like a steam engine, I'm so fearful they will find the bits of paper with my tiny pencilled diary. I had hidden some of them in a plastic bag of sanitary towels after hours in the Kiva rolling and placing them on the sticky strips on the underside of the absorbent pads, covered by the shiny rip off paper. The rest I had given to Jon to conceal in the waistband of his trousers. I keep a diary in my head now, it gives me something to focus on and helps me keep track of dates. It also acts as an anchor for my flow of existence as I feel held, captive in a web of suspended time.

The search continues, tension mounting, GA gesticulating with the sharp kitchen knife in front of our faces saying 'Spies, spies'. Suddenly there's a yell of triumph. 'This is it,' I'm thinking. HC runs into the room holding a small lump of peacock ore and a tiny white quartz crystal; inwardly my body slumps with relief. 'Thieves,' he shouts, not attempting to whisper, 'These have come from our mountains, the mountains of

Chechnya. You have been spying on our minerals, gathering information to exploit us.' The tirade goes on and on. 'We are going to take these rocks away to be tested to show they come from our mountains.' I try to explain that they are presents given to me in England for good luck, and that the peacock ore came from Australia, but it's not cutting any ice with him. He turns his attention to Jon.

HC grabs my arm, taking me into the bedroom and pushing me against the wall. I am totally unprepared for the karate blow to my neck; I grunt and flit briefly into unconsciousness and back. GA appears and I pray he hasn't come to join in.

I hear a muffled thud and a yelp from Jon. Even GA looks worried, and he swiftly walks into the bedroom followed by me. HC is holding Jon against the wall, his angry words spraying Jon's face with spit. Jon's massaging his neck. GA starts sifting through the things on the ground and my heart starts thumping again. I squat next to him and start putting things back in the bag, very slowly and without showing too much nervousness, luckily he discards the sanitary-towel bag without opening it as he is more interested in the tampons. His mystified expression indicates that he has never come across them before and he has to ask HC what they are. We are told to go back in the kitchen and Dark Chocolate rejoins HC in our room. In the interim he had stayed in their bedroom so we couldn't identify him. There's hammering and the sound of wood splitting. We wonder what will face us when we're allowed to return.

Initially the room looks the same, then we notice a snaking wire coming from a hole in the wall and rising between the beds with a loop on the end. HC tells us to lie down as he attaches some manacles through the wire and locks Jon's right wrist into one and my left wrist into the other. HC is rough with Jon and I can see the handcuff is too tight, digging into his skin and bone. He's a bit more careful with me. I have enough courage to ask what we will do if we want the loo. He ties a metal pencil sharpener that was in my bag to a string long enough to reach Jon's bed, indicating that Jon can swing the sharpener at the door alerting him or GA. Better than nothing.

They leave us, staring up at the ceiling, willing our bodies to relax into sleep.

Wednesday 1 October

GA unlocks the handcuffs. We are allowed out to wash and have tea and bread, our muscles are stiff from lying in the same position all night and Jon's wrist is sore but otherwise we have survived the night. HC wakes up and hustles us back to our room to be handcuffed again. He is still fuming, and decides to leave our door open so he can keep an eye on us from the kitchen. We lie in silence, the geometric patterns of the pink stencilling on the opposite wall interweaving with my thoughts. There is nothing we can do, there's no mental or physical torture and in a strange sort of way it's relaxing, especially following that evening of heart-thumping terror. Later on GA gets bored and decides to interrogate us further about the rocks and the knocking, pacing up and down at the end of our bed, words interspersed with high kicks and handstands. We tell him that neither of us have been anywhere near the wall with a knock and that's the truth, 'pravda, pravda (truth, truth)'. But the interrogation is wearying and I do begin to wonder whether during our exercises one of us had inadvertently hit the wall. Eventually he gets bored of our monosyllabic answers and leaves us to our silence.

Evening change of guard. I am nervous, wondering what's in store. Puppydog comes in fiddling with the handcuff keys. He asks us about the knocking and seems to believe our denial as he tells us that if we are good we won't have to sleep in handcuffs and takes them off. I could hug him!

Friday 3 October

Bracing ourselves for another evening of accusations, HC walks into our bedroom looking stiff and awkward. He tells us the knocking story was a big joke, not his but his friend's, and would we like to come to the kitchen for some food. This is his way of apologizing; at least he has the courage to tell us the truth. Jon fries a huge pile of potatoes and some eggs by the light of a candle. HC and GA share it with us. It tastes so good.

During the next few days our hostage life goes fairly smoothly, only Paunch's routine is interrupted by visitors which is very good news for me. Electricity is intermittent so other members of the gang bring large metal containers of water to store in the bathroom. GA tells us the water comes from a mountain spring.

The only hiccup (quite a big hiccup) is my right leg. As I exercise I notice a lack of feeling in the sole of my right foot. It feels as though a thin piece of paper has been glued to my foot, deadening sensation. During the next few days the lack of feeling spreads up my leg and also into my left foot. Logically I know that something is pressing on the nerves in the sacral region of my back, probably due to a distortion in my spinal column from five weeks sleeping on the 'luxurious Kiva beds', and that with gentle exercising my back will heal. But it doesn't stop my imagination leaping to conclusions such as multiple sclerosis or some other debilitating disease, causing many tearful nights.

HC notices that I walk with a limp and offers me a massage, saying 'I studied sports massage, you can trust me.' I decide to trust him and lie down on one of our beds. He leaves the door open and Jon and GA are in the kitchen across the hallway, so I feel safe. He gives me a fairly strong massage but I stop him from going into the muscles too deeply because of the pain. He asks me if I know how to massage. Alarm bells begin to ring and I say I don't but Jon does. So he asks Jon to massage his calves and it becomes a late night routine. A knock on the door, a beckoning finger, and Jon disappearing for an hour to massage HC into a relaxed sleep.

I'd prefer no contact with this person, not someone I would choose as a friend back home. Well, I've been volunteered and I think it's safer for me to do this job rather than Camilla. I do the best I can, working away on his calves, hoping it will relax him into sleep, healing sleep. At least he doesn't ask crazy questions. I am very nervous within myself. Over the past few days I have hardly slept. Just to be an ordinary prisoner would feel like luxury. I channel as much love and healing as I can into this wounded being, asking his inner self to go a little more gently on us.

Wednesday 8 October

Black Wednesday. The source of books has dried up, HC is bored and trying to find a logical reason why we have not been freed. His thinking is so warped that he is sure it has something to do with us being spies. The morning begins blandly enough although I'm aware of HC's brooding silence and am glad to get back to our 'haven'. Our reverie is shattered by our door crashing open and HC beckoning Jon into the kitchen; he has a sharp sinister look in his eyes. I begin to follow but HC bars my way. My stomach contracts, I feel sick and queasy and I know that all I can do is pray. HC leaves the door open, but however much I stretch my hearing the words are blurred and indistinct. I sit on the bed with my back against the wall, legs crossed. I still myself, lengthening my breath, reaching that place of inner calm. I ask the universal energies of love and light to surround us all and feel the wonderful energy of their presence filling my being. Time loses all meaning until Jon's footsteps bring me back to the pink crystal room reality.

This is the classic interrogation scene, two chairs facing each other with the table in between. I'm questioned intensely. I was never much good at remembering dates or names so I have to scrabble around in my memory to try and find answers for them, hoping I'm right. I don't remember the detail HC is asking for. HC starts getting irritated with my inability to give precise dates and times. He rips a chunk off the paper sack containing vermicelli and asks for a map. At least I can remember the date we left England, so I slowly chart our almost unbelievable journey across Europe. I am sweating with nervous energy and very scared, hoping the sparse information I give them will get the pressure off. The time drags. Why don't you believe me? Just lock me in the room and leave me alone.

My turn. HC sits with his back to the window, GA opposite me. On a bit of brown paper I can see a map that Jon has drawn of our journey to Chechnya and some dates. I try to read it without appearing to do so but HC is not stupid and he turns it over with a small shake of his head and a mean smile. I am aware that dates do not interest Jon and he may well have come out with different answers to the ones I'll give and am extremely worried about what they'll do if our stories don't tally. The questions flow steadily and incessantly. When did we leave England? Who did we stay with on the way? What did we do in Moscow? HC tries to make me admit we are in collusion with the KGB. 'Niet.' 'MI5?' 'Niet.' 'MOSSAD?' 'Niet.' I'm sticking to the truth and he doesn't like it.

He shifts tack and tells me that my brother is in Odessa and asks me what is our connection with Odessa. Now this throws me for a few seconds until I remember CPCD runs a project to help children with cystic fibrosis in Odessa and I guess he's muddling my brother with Chris. I can't imagine why my brother Raj would be in Odessa, there would be no sense in it.

HC is getting frustrated and his claims become wilder and more transparently fabricated. 'If you tell the truth $2m will come in two days' time and you will be released and I will be able to go to Germany and get my eye healed. If not you will be separated and taken to the mountains, chained up and tortured in our base there.' I become silent as I know he won't believe my truth and I have no other. Finally he gives up and follows me back to our room putting us in handcuffs again. We're exhausted and, apart from making sure we are both OK, remain in silence, still unsure of the outcome of our interrogation.

He leaves us alone for the rest of the day, blasting his brains with marijuana. GA decides it's his turn but he doesn't have interrogator talent. His words are a parody of HC's. He prances in front of us like a court jester. He tells us how we should pray five times a day and we say we do, all the time. We sit up and close our eyes, glad that he has given us this opportunity. Not what he was expecting; he is stunned into silence and quietly leaves our room.

That evening Paunch and Puppydog enter our room. Paunch is carrying the kitchen knife and threatens that he will use it if we are not good. Even so, they seem mystified by the necessity of the manacles. We explain about the interrogation and our journey to Chechnya. They relax and sit on the beds with us as though we are telling them a bedtime story! Before they leave Puppydog unlocks the manacles and takes them away. Phew! We can stretch and turn over and curl up into a foetal ball and sleep.

9–26 October

Most of this period we spend in grey light, with no electricity or running water for ten days. HC has sent us to Coventry, not eating or communicating with us. As he is a late riser we have mornings in the kitchen with GA, but as soon as HC arrives we scurry back into the gloom of our bedroom. The only streaks of daylight come from the edges of the grey blanket covering the window. If the sun is shining we manage to play backgammon with pips and cotton strips on the parquet floor. Sometimes they allow us to leave our door open so we have more light. HC is trying to become more religious. Someone has lent him a tape of a Mullah speaking the Qur'an. Every day he listens, head bent. He has also begun praying five times a day, wearing the most fantastic, glittering, jewelled skullcap. The only contact he has with us is when he beckons Jon to perform the late night massage.

Our food is going downhill, a week of eggs (a constipating experience), followed by a week of vermicelli 'soup' – tiny white stars of pasta boiled in water forming a white cement gruel seasoned either with salt or sugar, the most unappetizing food imaginable.

One day as we are playing backgammon on the floor I find I can't sit comfortably; the lips of my vagina and the area around my clitoris are swelling up. The day before had been another day of violation and I guess my body has had enough.

I . . . am . . . so . . . angry.

I pace around the darkening room calling Paunch all the expletives under the sun until the fury is exhausted and tears bubble up and overflow. I lie down. The glands in my groin have swollen to broad bean size, tight and painful. I don't know what kind of infection it is but I know I'm the only one who can heal it – there are no doctors, no medicines to rely on. So I calm myself, tensing and relaxing my body, starting at the feet and working up to the top of my skull, easing out the stress. Then I hold my hands over my groin and focus the healing energy through them and smile into the pain.

I say nothing but I feel as angry as Camilla about the pain caused by the relentless invasion of her body. I know I could fight Paunch even though I believe he is stronger than me and as time passes my muscles are weakening. If I fought, what would happen? I'd probably be chained up, maybe both of us, and treated like animals. I feel safer staying with the non-violent way we have chosen rather than going down the path of violence into unpredictable waters, especially with these unpredictable men.

The next day Paunch beckons me out of the room, fingering his 'glow in the dark' prayer beads. I have been composing myself for some hours, meditating and asking for help to give me the courage and strength to say 'Niet'. I know that if he tries to violate me in any way I'm in so much pain I would scream and fight like a caged animal, and I don't want this to happen. I stare into his bloodshot eye, looking into his soul with the calm strength of truth and say 'Bolit! (pain)' and I refuse to move from the doorway. He stutters, shifting his gaze away from mine and asks if it's really true. 'Yes,' I say, and feel an amazing powerful energy coursing through me. He looks into my eyes again and starts backing down the hallway. I turn and go back into our room and say a prayer of thanks, thinking how true is the saying 'Every cloud has a silver lining.' My 'cloud', this painful infection, has given me the strength to say 'No'. The following day GA and HC ask me why I had made Paunch so angry – he had complained to them that I had been 'uncooperative'. Again, with quiet strength I say I am ill and they are silent, they believe me. Another miracle.

In the following days Paunch shows his displeasure through little mean acts. At one time there are potatoes but Paunch insists on us eating vermicelli cement instead. The good thing is that he often doesn't stay in the kitchen to watch us eat and if Puppydog is out we secretly boil up some potatoes while the vermicelli is cooking, sprinkle them with salt and silently carry a heaped bowlful to hide under our beds. Then return to the kitchen, eat the cheerless white sludge and wash up. Later we gorge on potatoes in the grey twilight of our room. I'll never forget the taste of those succulent potato skins and salted flesh, totally and utterly scrumptious.

Lack of running water begins to be a real problem in the use of the loo. We can only spare half a bucket a day to flush it and sometimes it gets into the most grotesque state, particularly after being used by Paunch. I think he has problems with his bowels. Puppydog is given the job of cleaning it but he hands the task to Jon and me. Not an easy one when you've only got rags and water and no disinfectant. Jon copes with the stomach-heaving much better than I and becomes chief cleaner.

What's wrong with these people that they can't even look after themselves? In their culture it seems that the women do all the dirty work and here there are no women. So it's down to us, the prisoners, to do the dirty work.

Even Puppydog's more balanced temperament shows signs of stress created by boredom coupled with Paunch's foul temper. On his duty nights he takes to coming into our room and shining a torch into our faces saying 'What is your mission, spies?' 'Who sent you? CIA?' in a 'trying to be gruff' German accent. He has obviously been talking to GA but is not such a good dramatist. He only succeeds in irritating us, like a mosquito buzzing persistently around our bodies looking for a nice suck of blood.

Puppydog and GA take it in turns to stand at the bottom of our beds and do mock interrogations. I think they have seen too many spy movies. They say if I tell them the truth we'll be freed in a few days. I tell them the truth. 'No, no, not that . . . the truth!' they snarl. Maybe I'm a Russian pretending to be an Englishman? Who knows what thoughts go through their minds. Many times I feel like not answering at all but then I think they might resort to using violence rather than psychology. So I quietly respond to their endless questions, playing the game. Maybe it's the way I calmly answer them that makes them think I truly am a spy, a really good one!

One night Puppydog brings in a syringe. This is more scary, they have obviously got the medical contents from our wardrobe. 'Truth, truth, or this!' He gestures with the syringe pointing to our arms. I'm uncertain how much of this is humour. I feel fear grasping me deep inside and I politely gesture 'after you'. His resolve wavers, and he starts telling us how bored he is and eventually leaves us in peace.

HC decides I need to behave like a proper Chechen wife and now whenever we go to the kitchen I have to wear a scarf and sweep and clean the floors the Chechen way with a knee-high reed broom and wet rags. There is a perfectly good tall broom and mop handle leaning against the wall of the kitchen but these are too Russian for their liking. One morning GA asks me to clean all the floors including their bedroom where HC is still sleeping. Before I go in GA says 'Sshhh, Gerner sleep'. He doesn't realize he has told me HC's real name; it sounds German, not Chechen, very strange. The names of the other three we have known for some time – GA is Zabba, Paunch is Isa and PD is Amma – but HC's has been a mystery up to now.

GA provides the only glimmer of light during these dark days of pain, grumbling stomachs, distended bladders and constant stress. He decides to entertain us with tales of 'Silver the bank robber', the main character based on me. He has renamed me Silver after Long John Silver, which he finds very amusing. His flair for drama has us chuckling, even bringing a wry smile to HC's lips. GA is also getting excited about his forthcoming 30th birthday, talking about how his friends will take him into the mountains, screeching round bends in white Ladas and how they will have a feast and he will be toasted in vodka and beer. The day of his birthday dawns and we see GA sitting at the kitchen table with his head bowed in boredom; it was all one huge fantasy and we feel so sad for him.

There are rumours abroad that we are on the move again. HC has perked up; he thinks the move indicates that we will be released soon.

However illogical it seems, our hopes are always raised. There have been more visitors lately; we recognize one gravelly voice, with its tone of authority, the bringer of news from 'above'. So we pack again, the damp pants steaming above the lamp, sheets and all.

9

Bleak House

27 October

In the early hours of the morning we're led blindfold into our new dwelling. The first room smells quite lived-in but the room that is to be our bedroom is damp and chilly. My first view is more brown-painted floorboards, so inspiring. When the blindfolds are off we see, in the half light, pale blue walls, one covered in black mould. The room is large and empty with two big windows and some double doors. HC and GA bring in two iron bedsteads, a chair and a light bulb to put in a ceiling candelabra. Wires poke out of all the sockets, but HC doesn't think there's any danger and climbs up to put it in. Sparks fly, HC screeches as an electric shock shudders through his body and he stumbles off the chair, fortunately not hurt but it means no electric light for us. GA brings two grey blankets, some nails and drawing pins to obscure our view out onto the world and a dented metal bucket for a toilet. It's getting bleaker by the minute. With a mixture of odd words he indicates 'You might think we're bad but if you escape there are far worse groups out there who would snap you up,' and mimes a hole in the ground, chains and no food.

We've brought sheets, quilts and pillows from the pink crystal room. The bases of the beds are made of metal links that have stretched over the years. They sag forming uncomfortable hollows between metal struts looking more like torturers' racks than beds. HC interrupts our bed musing and invites us to the kitchen to eat. There's a frying pan on the table filled with sizzling eggs with four forks hooked over the edge. This is an honour, HC cooking and inviting us to share their meal.

HC leaves the table and we hear the drone of television voices coming from the next room. He tells us to leave the washing up until morning and invites us to watch television. It must be about 3 a.m. by this time and I would dearly love to disappear into our bedroom despite the sagging beds but this is an honour that we cannot decline. It's cold. We huddle on a mattress with our backs against the wall, subjected to some of the worst American movie trash.

Another hostage movie, what fun! This time 'Sadism in the Sewer' would be a good title. The only funny bits are when the Chechen censors attempt to blank out all the kissing, sex and nudity often far too late. Of course all the violence is left in. Finally we are allowed to go to bed as a grey dawn creeps around the edge of the blankets.

We wake a few hours later; the metal struts have dug grooves into our calves and backs. Stretching and twisting our bodies in all directions helps the blood flow to our cramped muscles. I'm still feeling a bit tense after watching those hideous films so decide to do a walking and breathing exercise to help me cope with the day ahead.

Late in the morning there is feverish activity. HC and GA decide to nail up the door between our bedroom and the kitchen. We hear a knock and a woman's voice, low and muffled. There's clanking in the sitting room and we guess she is moving a pile of belongings we had seen the night before. 'Does she knows we're here?' I'm thinking. The front door closes, silence, then we are let out through two rooms to the kitchen. A door leads from the kitchen into a room with a bath along one wall, an old gas boiler and some rickety tables covered in empty storage jars, a bowl full of apples and a jar of beehive cappings soaked in honey. We surreptitiously hide this jar at the back and whenever we get the chance of being alone in the bathroom we dip in our fingers, sucking the honey and chewing the wax, so delicious. Dirty dishwater goes down a drainage hole in the floor, next to some enamel bowls stacked against the wall. The best thing about the bathroom is the window looking out onto a garden. If I stand in the bath I can see an area of clodded earth and wild grasses with a chicken wire fence beyond. When it's sunny I let the warm rays heat my body and bathe my face.

After a bit of fiddling with the boiler there's hot water and someone has left a towel and shampoo. GA nails a piece of cloth over the windowless door to provide some privacy – things are looking up. We are given the task of sweeping and mopping the whole house. The kitchen has a brown cracked linoleum floor, a gas cooker and a small metal sink beside it with a tap but no pipe to take the water away. The plumbing in this house and the hot house defies logic. The table is covered with a plastic flower-patterned cloth fractured by knife wounds. The sitting room has a dresser against one wall and a dressing table in the corner facing the kitchen door with a huge mirror triptych. HC uses this sometimes to keep an eye on us in the kitchen while he watches his favourite sport, boxing. The thin net orange-brown curtains are drawn to shut out the world. HC has rigged up a contraption of rope with a long aluminium curtain rod to keep our doors shut at night. They give us an electric fire and we find a square piece of wood to cover our stylish bent bucket.

End of October, beginning of November

During the next few days there is scant electricity. GA tells us the Russians are demanding money from the Chechen government as all the electricity is provided by a power station in the Stavropol region. A bit rich, I think, as they are the ones who destroyed the infrastructure and have given very little compensation in return.

HC brings his belongings to our house because he has no money to pay the rent for his lodgings. He props a painting of Chechen woods on the dresser in the sitting room with a photo of Shamil Basaev (a Chechen warlord) in front of it. I help him move one iron bedstead from our room to the sitting room and HC makes up a bed with his own quilts and sheets. A large radio is placed near the window with a wire as an antenae squeezed through a crack, so now we have Russo-Euro pop blaring out most days. He has a mirror with a transfer of a Toulouse Lautrec style woman on one side. That night he excitedly brings the mirror into the kitchen where we are all huddling near the gas cooker for warmth and shows us a transfer of a girl dressed in cowboy boots, hat and mini skirt with revealing boobs that he wants to put on the mirror. He picks up a faded red plastic jug from by the door and asks me to hold it.

This is the jug they take to the 'dunny' in the garden and without a thought I commit a terrible crime. After HC has used some water to soak the transfer I place the jug on the table. Now for a few moments no one notices then GA erupts. He swipes the jug off the table and lays into me: 'How can you put the jug of water used for the toilet on the table which we eat off? You have no manners, unhygienic son of satan!!!'

We are banished to our room.

My mind reels. How foolish I was to forget their etiquette and ideas of hygiene! Just a simple mistake of placing a jug on the table has lost us a hundred 'brownie points' in the eyes of our captors just when our relationship was bordering on normal. I feel bad within myself.

The next morning HC, who has been brooding on the crime, calls me out of our room.

I innocently walk out towards the kitchen thinking that last night's events have been forgotten. Not so. HC places his left hand on my shoulder and gives me an almighty punch to my solar plexus. I stagger back a pace, I am totally surprised. 'Understand?' He growls. I hope that has got it off his chest. I am sent back to our room. All privileges removed: no food, light or warmth.

We curl up together on the single iron bed trying to ignore the iron struts digging painfully into our muscles. Early evening they allow me out to do some sweeping and have bread and tea. Left alone in the kitchen for a few minutes I hide some bread in the sarong wound around my head to take back to Jon.

A few days pass and HC and GA forget the water jug incident. HC notices that we have moved our thin quilts to the floor. I explain that the uncomfortable beds are making my leg a lot worse. He brings us a padded quilt mattress, sheets and pillows from his own belongings. Such generosity from HC is quite exceptional. One reason for his good mood is that he seems to have found a penfriend. Every day he spends hours happily writing letters. Puppydog also has the writing bug but it only lasts for one letter that takes him a week to write. HC also gives us a paraffin lamp. We use it sparingly to guide us to the bucket – it's unlikely we will be given any more fuel.

It's cold. Often, as we sit basking in the heat from the two-bar fire, the orange glow fades into darkness – time to hibernate. Curling up together with one quilt beneath, one above, a pair of foetal twins with cold noses. Slowing our blood flow, slowing our minds to quicken the time in darkness.

Soon it becomes obvious the electricity situation is not going to change very quickly and we are all beginning to suffer with colds. Puppydog decides to do something about it. Clanking and hammering come from the bathroom as he wrestles with cutting equipment and gas pipes. He has brought two ancient gas fires, two rubber hoses and a roll of shiny blue plastic tape. We hear someone sawing into the nailed-up door and a rough hole appears through which a snaking black tube slivers. It reminds me of the Beatles film 'Help' when a similar hose was pushed through a hole and red poisonous gas billowed out causing all the guards 'Trooping the Colour' to fall flat on their faces. Luckily it doesn't quite happen like that for us, although it gets close!

Puppydog comes into our room with four bricks and an iron grid with holes in it and I help him connect it to the hose with a bit of slicing and tape binding. The moment of truth, Puppydog rushes off to turn the gas on and I have a match ready to strike. Blast off, we have blue fire with orange tips and warmth. The natural gas hasn't been filtered so our room slowly fills with poisonous carbon monoxide fumes. We wake up with stabbing head-aches in stifling heat because of the lack of ventilation and complain to GA who opens a tiny window, high up, shaking his finger: 'No speaking, no spy-ing.' Then he goes to town, ripping up all Puppydog's bandaged pipes in an attempt to lower the gas pressure. It doesn't work. HC eventually plugs the gas pipe into the cooker so the heat is controlled by a valve. We sit in our room at regulo 1.5, a slow bake.

Oh no, here we go again. Paunch locks me in, keeping Camilla out, I guess he's up to his sordid acts again. I've slipped into a state of resignation, resigned to the fact that I can't take any action, the fear of response too great. My only resource is prayer and hope.

He takes me to the bathroom, moonlight pouring through the win-dow. I tell him I still have the infection, although, in fact, I have man-aged to heal myself. He's too scared to go the whole way, and ejaculates on my thigh. I close my body down, my mind and soul are soaring to the moon away from this sordid scene. He bruises himself badly on the taps, a small retribution.

Jon is still being called out every other night to massage HC's legs. Our relations with HC and GA are good, the water jug incident forgotten. One cold morning GA allows us to watch a cowboy and Indian film with him and is telling us how he feels the Chechens are akin to the North American Indians in the persecution they suffered. Then there is a loud knock on the door. We scurry back to our bedroom and when we are allowed out again the television has disappeared. I felt a bit miffed as it was one of the better films and the television has kept our captors occupied at times when they would have looked to us for their entertainment.

With no television for distraction HC just loves calling me out of our room and playing the torturer while I peel potatoes, asking me over and over again who I work for, what my mission is, what my target is. Over and over I tell him I have no mission, no target. I have come to work with the children, your children, the ones traumatized by the war. 'How dare you impose your Christian ideas on our culture,' he replies.

In many ways it reminds me of the bullying I experienced on the building sites. I was not interested in wolf whistling girls, talking cars and football and going to the pub every night. That was the image of the bricky and I didn't conform so received loads of verbal and physical abuse in the form of swearing, flying half bricks or trowels full of mortar. Sometimes I dreaded going to work but the fear of not having enough food to keep my son fed or a roof over our heads made me continue. The fear was unfounded because I always had a home with my parents if I needed it. How hard we push ourselves, allowing people to trample on us. For me it began at school being an unrecognized dyslexic. So I learnt to persevere with bull-like intensity, part of my Taurean nature. And here I am captive, confined mainly to one room with no access to the outside world, free movement or fresh air. I'm at the call and whim of these few men, themselves tortured by war, passing on their own torture to me, abusing me with their words, their punches, holding me against my will. Perhaps I should thank those brickies for helping me to cope now.

In the evenings HC and GA invite us to the kitchen for long discussions lasting deep into the night, mainly taken up by HC's monologues. He's begun bringing trashy Russian newspapers full of stories of mafia atrocities and photos of dismembered bodies; he uses them as a basis for his theory of the satanic nature of Russian society. His views are fuelled by the Russian propaganda against Chechens that calls them animals, without morals or culture. When conversation turns to religion we have to be more on our guard. 'What are you, Protestant or Catholic?' 'My family is Protestant, Christian,' I reply. Jon is more daring: 'I have no religion, just me and God.' Of course HC can't understand that at all. 'Then you are aetheist,' he replies. Jon denies it but HC uses it as a sneering taunt for the rest of the time we are together.

One night HC has a painful headache and I offer to give him a head massage. I ask all the universal healing powers to flow through my hands and help relieve the tension that has built up from the traumas he has suffered. Energy flows through me and, for the first time, I feel HC relaxing. Afterwards he thanks me and says it was very good, the headache is gone. Then his eyes takes on a sly look. 'Good fingers, feather light touch, must be good at erotic massage!' Of course this becomes a huge joke and they talk about hiring me out as an erotic masseur to make money. I quietly hold my corner repeating again and again, 'Niet, niet.' So my good favour is nearly turned on its head. From that moment Jon and I are asked to give HC and GA head, back and leg massages.

They call us out every other day, one massaging in their bedroom, the other in the sitting room. We used my 'mistake' to give them healing. During the next few weeks they treat us with respect and don't take advantage of us. Sometimes they give us a massage in return. But we know that their minds are still highly unstable; the foundations of their lives have been shattered. All that we can achieve is 'damage limitation' for them and for us.

HC makes derisive comments about me being a woman because I like cooking, especially as it breaks up the hours of monotony. I think he's just provoking a response – he wants to use me to light his volcano of anger. I ignore him, suppressing my irritation. But it is so tiring, especially as I have a heavy cold and a pounding headache.

I'm cutting a loaf of bread, feeling pre-menstrual and irritable; HC is on at Jon again about being a woman and I can see his comments act like a tropical worm under Jon's skin, eating away at his feelings of self-worth. I lose my usual self-control, slamming the bread down on the table. HC punches me in the solar plexus while giving me a lecture on the sacredness of bread. 'You daughter of satan!' I'm banished to our room for the rest of the day and that evening Jon brings me a chunk of bread that he has surreptitiously slipped into his pocket.

Boredom is our greatest enemy, not our own but our captors'. It is now Puppydog's turn to get bored. He has written his letter, given up on his frenzied keep fit regime and fiddled with the handcuffs to distraction and their complete destruction (much to our delight). Perhaps inspired by his own letter writing he decides it's our turn to write a letter to help them get their money and us our freedom. We spend hours around the kitchen table composing a letter to our parents. Puppydog wants us to exaggerate the awfulness of the situation. He doesn't realize the irony, considering how awful the situation actually is! Our problem was to play it down so as not to worry our parents should this letter ever reach them, so I tried to word it as truthfully as possible:

128

Chris,

Please please move quickly and bring the money.

We are kept in a cellar and there is often no heat, light or water and only a little food. Camilla's leg is partially paralysed and she has a glandular infection. Jon's chest is bad. We have no access to medicine or a doctor. Our captors say they will cut off our hands and send them to you if the money doesn't come in a week.

Please, please move fast

We are desperate

Jon and Camilla

November 9th

We didn't think the letter would get anywhere but when we were eventually released discovered it had reached the Foreign Office and our parents.

12 November

HC is in an interrogative mood. Once again, 'Spies, who are you working for? CIA? MOSSAD? Little Star must be a cover.' He is speaking in a bored, slightly sneering tone, not putting a lot of energy into it. Then his face becomes animated, he has an idea and looks at me, 'I'll keep you up all night until you tell me the truth. One hour talking, one hour you give me massage, alternating all night.' My heart sinks; this is going to be a big battle. Have I got the stamina, the energy to hold my own? I don't know.

Jon is sent to bed. GA disappears to his room. No electricity, the one candle is burning low. We sit in the sitting room, side by side on his bed with the dictionary between us, our skin orange in the light of the gas filaments. The usual questions flow followed by my denials, then a period of me massaging his back. My worst hours are around 11 p.m. to 2 a.m. I'm fighting weariness, using all my wits to parry his questions and turn the conversation from spies to Chechen history. Then even HC gets bored and begins to tell me his life history. My stomach, which had been churning, begins to settle down. At one point he goes outside for a pee and comes back holding something delicately in the palm of his hand. It's the first snowflake of winter. I feel honoured. We start having breaks in the kitchen drinking his special Nescafé Gold Blend. The candle has long since died. HC produces light using strips of cotton as wicks sticking out of a saucerful of ghee. Someone has brought a five-litre tin of ghee from the bazaar, a food-aid product from Norway that has found its way onto the black market.

He asks me about my right leg, which is still numb, and offers to give it a massage. I'm dying for a pee and say so, knowing that it would be difficult to control my bladder during a massage and, amazingly, he allows me to go outside into the garden. What pleasure to squat in the fresh crisp air with the snow gently falling. So the tables turn and he gives me an in-depth, very painful muscular massage. At one point I nearly blow it by involuntarily kicking my foot in the air, narrowly missing HC's nose.

I don't know what on earth is going on out there with HC and Camilla. I heard GA going to bed hours ago. I just hope and pray it's not my mind's worst scenario. I do hear voices talking very quietly and in the early hours of the morning I can stay awake no longer, I make my prayers that no harm will come to her as I drift into uncomfortable sleep.

Just before dawn, we abandon the massage and sit in the kitchen. I'm quite alert by now and HC is flagging. He tells me about his teenage years, his prowess at sport, particularly gymnastics, and disco dancing. His meeting on the street with a 36-year-old woman who invited him home and seduced him. Her husband was away in prison. The affair lasted for two years until HC had to join the army. He told me about his time there, mostly about how many women he had managed to seduce (200 or more!). Finally about his wife whom he married when he was 28 and she only 19. He says he will never marry a young woman again because you have to spend so much time training them! But he loved her and misses the conversations he used to have with her. Finally he talks about his three-year-old son who likes drawing, and as the dawn fingers its way into the room he says he'll bring me a photo of his wife and child, then sends me to bed.

I whisper to Jon that I'm OK and dive for the bucket – the release from the intense night has caused my bowels to work overtime. I feel elated, another battle won, and spend hours watching the snowflakes fall outside our little window.

The massage from HC along with some 'pulsing' massage given by Jon helps the muscles and nerves to re-align themselves, so gradually feeling returns to my leg.

For a long time now I have been taunted about my long hair (now in dreadlocks). 'Men don't have long hair. You are not a man.' Until now I have resisted getting it cut, after all it took years to grow, and I didn't want to give in to their teasing. But the lice have multiplied and the word sleep doesn't exist in lice vocabulary. So when GA offers a hair cut I accept, much to his surprise, so much so that he asks me a couple more times to make sure we have understood each other. Off to the kitchen, a towel around my neck. First cropping with scissors and comb, whilst we wait for some hot water. Then out comes the razor, this is the first time I have had my head shaved. What a relief, no more combing, no more labour-intensive hair washing. Much to my captors' surprise I now look like 'Shamil Basaev' with my new baldness and beard. I am still sat in the barber's chair at changing of the guard. Paunch comes in and gives a double take as he's not sure who is sitting there. 'Shamil Basaev copya!' he exclaims.

When GA takes Jon to the kitchen for a shearing I'm not allowed to watch: this is a male domain. In Chechnya all the men in the family cut each other's hair and are very skilled with the 'cut-throat razor'. Jon reappears, bald, only a couple of tiny blood nicks mar his shiny round scalp. It suits him, he has a very neat skull and it emphasizes his large blue eyes. Now one of my favourite occupations is watching his hair grow. Fascinating little whirls of tiny black hairs appear, circling around his double crown.

Puppydog takes advantage of my new 'Chechen look' and late one afternoon, disguised in a black woolly hat and a big overcoat, he instructs me to take the bucket to the dunny. 'Act normal, don't speak to anyone, head down, go to the toilet, empty the bucket and return.' A day or two later I mention this with GA and HC and they are shocked that Puppydog has allowed this to happen. They are afraid I might be seen, an unknown person in a small, tight-knit community, bound even tighter by the terrors of war. Questions would be asked: 'Who is that?' 'What is that person doing in that house?' But it gives them the idea of allowing me to take the bucket out at night. The first trip was a bit of a mess. I have strict instructions to make sure I'm not seen, keep my head down and just do the job. But the feeling of being outside when you've been confined for so long is amazing, the wind on my face, the smells of autumn dancing in my nose, the feeling of space around me. GA escorts me the first 20 yards and stops. Their cultural attitude toward going to the toilet takes priority over their security concerns and

I am left to negotiate the last dark ten feet on my own. I could easily jump the fence. My senses are highly sharpened, listening for any sound. I look up to glance upon the stars – oh the eternal stars, one day I will walk beneath you a free man. In the dark shed I miss the hole – an error that had HC up in arms but thankfully he calmed down without lashing out and made sure I had matches on following trips.

As the power cuts are becoming more frequent and the days shorter I start gathering up all the little bits of wax I can find including the chewed wax from the bee's cappings. With a razor I cut the bottom off an anti-lice shampoo bottle, then twist together several cotton threads unwound from a frayed bedcover to make a wick. I melt the stubs in a jam jar lid on the hot brick which supports the gas fire then pour the molten wax into the upturned bottle. This takes a while as I can only melt a small quantity at a time. It's not very efficient, not very tidy, but when there's a power cut we still have light from my homemade candles. On at least one occasion Puppydog has entered our room during a power cut and been astonished to see we have light and they don't. It's a great distraction, an expression of creativity that whiles away many hours of our empty day. The candlelight is also comforting, helping us relax and feel warm and cosy.

December

The kitchen door bursts open, brilliant sunlight shimmering on the lino. I can see blinding white snow around the silhouette of HC in the doorway. He's beaming, he's holding a litre bottle of milk bought in the bazaar, fresh from the cow. We have a fair inkling of the reason behind his jaunty step: GA had earlier whispered secretively, 'He has a girl-friend.' He doesn't spend many nights with us any more, only appearing in the morning with a voracious appetite, bringing out the tray of eggs he has hidden from Puppydog and Paunch in the dresser, frying a pile of them then flopping onto his bed to sleep the day away. He's even taken to wearing a turquoise tracksuit instead of his customary black jeans and jumper. HC's perky mood makes him generous, allowing us a glass of milk each before gulping the rest. Our diet is very limited. We have a sack of potatoes, a sack of onions and sometimes a few carrots, so the milk just cooled from the cow's udder is supped with reverence.

HC has a great idea. 'Wouldn't it be good if Camilla has a baby! They would definitely send money then.' It's the end of the day and all four are crowded in the kitchen, they laugh and joke about it, little knowing, apart from Paunch, that I could have become pregnant all too easily and Jon would not be the father (he's had the snip). News reaches our parents that I'm pregnant.

In the evenings we help GA learn English. One time he brings a plastic pellet gun and is having fun trying to shoot a tiny tin bell attached to a string from the curtain rail, and a candle flame on the window ledge. When he lets us have a go he's peeved because we're better shots than him! We're given the job of searching on our hands and knees for all the tiny plastic red and green pellets scattered around the floor.

Puppydog and Paunch decide it's time to exert greater authority over us, particularly me because I'm a woman. The slush in the streets means their shoes are often caked in mud and this brings a bit of variety into our daily routine. They tell Jon to sit while I do all the chores and the cooking. This frustrates him a lot, but luckily they lose interest in imposing this rule after a while. No electricity means no running water, but there is a well in the garden. If Puppydog is in a good mood we ask him if we can wash our clothes, which involves him bringing in a couple of buckets of water to heat up (it's no good asking Paunch – he only grumbles and uses it as an excuse to sexually harass me). Washing is one of our greatest joys. We spend time in the bathroom with the chance of being in natural light, pounding our clothes in the steamy heat and making sure we have a hot wash as well. We make full use of the limited time we are given, forming routines – swift body wash, then hair, followed by small items, my one pair of pants and hankies, which we hang on a string line rigged up by Jon while we wash dress, shirt and trousers. Of course we cannot share our washing sessions – far too dangerous, we might leap out of the window together (it has no bars). My washing session always ends with a fingerful of honey cappings, chewed with relish as I wind my sarong around my body and carry the dripping washing back to our room.

The next joy is the drying. Jon has made a couple of cotton-thread washing lines attached to pipes and radiators as near to the gas flames as possible. I arrange my lilac dress, now more grey than lilac, like a sail spreadeagled over the uneven lines: I love gazing at the curves and undulating folds in the material and drawing it in my mind. Then I inspect it, re-arranging it when the parts nearest the flames are dried. Whole afternoons are spent in contemplating our washing.

Puppydog takes pity on us living in darkness and rigs up a light bulb, twisting wires together in a broken socket and winding the flex around a radiator pipe so the bulb can hang at thigh height. 'Health and Safety' would have a field day in our house. As well as live wires sticking out of walls Puppydog has stuck a knife into the electricity meter in the kitchen. One morning it shoots out embedding itself in the floorboards, its jagged tip melted and scorched.

HC has left a newspaper lying around with an article about the death of Princess Diana. I ask Puppydog if I can borrow it and aided by our wonderful new light source, I can read all about the various accusations of who was to blame, the paparazzi, Prince Philip, MI6 or just an inebriated driver. It's good for my Russian but I only manage a few sentences a day, the Russian is so complex and my eyes get so tired.

Our food supply is diminishing rapidly, Puppydog and Paunch have gone foraging in the outhouse. We hear a whoop of joy through our window as they discover a cellar with some jars of pickled vegetables and apples. This certainly adds some spice to our diet. Sometimes Puppydog and Paunch play games like throwing small objects through our window and then rushing into our room accusing us of throwing things out. What fun!

HC starts washing his sheets and clothes and one afternoon he asks me to iron them. He chose the wrong person, for however much I labour I do not reach his high standard of perfection and in the end he shows me how to do it. That evening he decides to mend the frayed collar of his jeans jacket. He asks me if I can sew and I reply 'No'. Fortunately he is in a good mood and doesn't hit me for being a 'good for nothing' woman. The evening turns into the most compatible and relaxed that we ever spend with them. HC sewing his jacket ('As a fighter you have to learn to do these things,' – justifying himself doing a woman's job), Jon mending a pocket of GA's leather jacket, GA making a Chechen medal out of some tin for Jon, me absorbing it all and basking in the gentle energy. The whole scene is worthy of a Vermeer painting.

GA is the only one who appreciates me – I think the others feel their masculine values are challenged by what I do. GA sometimes comes into our room especially to chat to me. Sitting on the edge of the bedstead he regales

Jon and Camilla before travelling to Chechnya, April 1997.

Grozny, May 1997.

Jon and Camilla arriving at their home in Grozny.

Jon and Camilla dancing with children at Little Star.

Camilla, Chris, Adlan and Jon in the Caucasus mountains.

Jon and Camilla after one year in captivity.

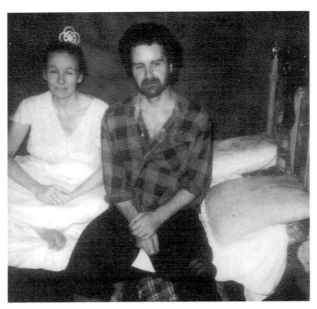

Jon and Camilla after two months in 40 degrees night and day in the 'King's Chamber'.

Arriving back in Britain September 1998.

me with stories. Once he came in wild-eyed and unshaven, in deep distress. He had been driving through a settlement of prefabricated huts, each one the size of a small garage housing a family of up to 12 people. He is appalled at the conditions in which they have to survive. Occasionally he feels like an old buddy to me. When he is occupied in this way there is less chance of him being bored and picking on either of us. It's the same when they have visitors – any distraction for them means more peace for us.

Some card-playing visitors arrive; I can hear the deep tones of Dark Chocolate. Finally Puppydog unties our door and tells us we must walk with our heads lowered so we don't spy on their friends. I go first giving them a wide berth but then find I have to cross the prayer mat. I carefully step over without touching it, however, that's not enough, Paunch has seen me and with the speed of light kicks me hard in the bottom. He shouts at me, probably something about committing a blasphemous act. I shakily continue walking into the kitchen and make some tea. As we go back to our room I can feel Dark Chocolate staring and catch a glimpse of his face out of the corner of my eye. I sense that he pities me. I'm trembling, black ideas gnawing my mind about the type of punishment I will be given if they feel I've seen his face. Nothing happens.

The number of visitors is increasing all the time. We don't see them but hear lengthy discussions in the kitchen. We catch the word 'mediator' many times. GA and HC finally enlighten us. The mediator they had used had demanded thousands of dollars but not done his job so the group decided to choose someone to assassinate him. Apparently Paunch offered (they snigger, miming his bad aim with one eye) and was turned down. The chosen assassin broke into the mediator's house and shot him in his bed. The next mediator had become scared and disappeared so they had lost their line of communication with the British Embassy in Moscow.

This is not good news. With the connection to the Embassy broken and no mediator around to re-establish it we are adrift in a sea of unknowing – knowing that there was a mediator had given us a sense of hope, and now that's gone. Back to prayers.

Our captors are getting tetchy and frustrated. The fact that it is Ramadan doesn't help: they haven't even got eating to distract them during the day. We continue to massage GA and HC. One day when HC is out GA beckons me out of our room, leaving Jon locked in, and asks me to give him a back massage then he says he will give me one in return. I say

I don't need one but he insists. He sits on my thighs and starts to massage my back. The movement gets more vigorous and I can feel him getting sexually aroused. I struggle desperately to get up but I'm pinned down under his weight. He ejaculates on my skirt and immediately gets up, refusing to look me in the face, allowing me to return to our bedroom. I'm angry and tearful. What ignorance causes men to treat women in this way? I really didn't expect it from GA, I thought he had more sense.

I know GA is trying it on with Camilla and I feel frustrated and angry, but I'm unable to take action in any form without reprisals. That same evening after the changeover Camilla, Puppydog and I are sitting in the kitchen drinking tea when Paunch calls Camilla into the sitting room. After a while I become aware that something is going on in the other room. The months of hyper-vigilance have made my hearing very acute. At that moment Camilla returns, we look at each other and sense that something has changed.

When I enter the room Paunch is lying on the bed exposing himself. He gestures for me to come over to him. I refuse and kneel on the floor across the room and begin to cry. This is just too much, it all has to stop. I'm given strength by the fact that Puppydog and Jon are in the kitchen and I'm pretty sure Paunch doesn't want Puppydog to know what he's playing at. Paunch looks startled; perhaps I have finally touched his heart. I dry my tears and go back to the kitchen. If Jon wasn't my partner I think I would lose faith and trust in the male species, or at least their ability to control their hormonal instincts and their understanding of what it is to be a civilized human being.

Later that night and early the next morning while Jon sleeps I pray hard for help. Somehow Paunch has to understand what suffering he is causing. Let a miracle happen. And it does. Paunch calls me out; Puppydog has been sent to the bazaar. He asks me to bring the dictionary. 'What's wrong?' he asks. I fumble through the dictionary. 'No sex. No violence.' I point out the words. His eye opens and it looks like a light has been switched on in his brain. He apologizes, saying that because I'm a 'western woman' he thought I would not mind. Would not mind! What has created this type of thinking? Probably the effect of watching trashy American films and reading Russian pornographic magazines.

Paunch never sexually harasses me again and I forgive him, in his ignorance. At least he has had the courage to apologize but I can never forgive the act of rape. He wants my friendship and still calls me out, but this time to tell me his dreams of owning a market garden and buying a four-wheel drive. He starts appreciating me as a human being rather than a sex object. It doesn't stop me having flickering thoughts of 'What if . . . What if I had confronted him much earlier after the first couple of times? Would he have stopped then? But I know how unstable he was and is. He could have used violence against me or Jon or involved the others. Recently he has seen how the others want our friendship and he doesn't want to be left out. I am lucky it has come to this conclusion now.

GA does have a conscience, although it appears in the ugly form of paranoia and guilt. The next evening he's on duty he bursts into our room accusing us of telling Puppydog and Paunch about our massage sessions. Of course we deny it and are saved from a long interrogation by a doped HC who decides we are telling the truth. HC asks Jon to massage his calves so GA and I are left together. We sit side by side on our 'floor bed' watching the gas flames. GA has calmed down; I am concentrating on filling the room with healing energy. He starts talking about his family and the difficulties they are having with so many mouths to feed. I know he wants me to be his friend and to forgive him but doesn't know how to say it. I forgive him.

They have all taken to preening themselves in front of the mirror, arranging their hair, checking their smiles, squeezing spots and tweaking out nose and eyebrow hairs. Often they congregate in the kitchen at the time of changeover. They squat or stand around the walls like a flock of crows while Jon and I eat our bowls of mashed potato and onion.

The conversation often turns to guns – men's talk – their favourite marque, prices, which bazaar to go to. They give me very detailed descriptions of how to strip them down and maintain them. GA seems to think that I would be good with guns and often jokes about us fighting the Russians in the mountains. I think he wants me to join them in their fight for independence.

15 December, evening

HC enters our room and sits on the edge of the iron bedstead, stiff, straight back, chin jutting out. I think he has some important news to impart. He points at the dictionary and picks out two words – telephone, satellite. One of us will be allowed to ring our family, tell them how badly we are being treated and give them a number of a new mediator who can be contacted to send the money through. Then we will be released. We have mixed feelings, wonderful to have the opportunity to speak to one of the families but not so good to convey threats and worry them. Anyway we have no choice.

The next night we are woken around 2 a.m. Puppydog and Paunch are on duty. Dark Chocolate has brought the telephone; I notice he isn't masked and look to the ground, but he gestures that we can look at him. He is tall, has a long sensitive face with kind brown eyes, only in his early twenties. He's wearing a big overcoat and impressive fur hat. We have decided I will ring Mum as she goes to bed later than Jon's parents and it is already past 11 p.m. in England. Puppydog keeps suggesting things to say like cold, damp, diseases, no food. I'm trembling and Dark Chocolate tells me 'Niet problyemi, niet problyemi'. I dial a number and get a German voice, dial again, Italian this time. Damn it, I've forgotten the code.

Not being able to get through is incredibly frustrating. They assume that we know the international codes. I am stunned by how amateur and badly thought out their preparation for this crucial call is. They haven't told us what they want us to say or not say, how much time we'll have to talk, nothing. Dark Chocolate says he will bring the code tomorrow and we are sent to bed. We don't sleep but discuss what to say, how to reassure our families that we are OK without showing emotion, just getting the information across.

17 December

In the afternoon HC sits me down at a table in the sitting room with a pen and paper to compose my speech for the phone call home; he dictates using the dictionary. I'll only have 40 seconds to deliver it because they fear the signal will be picked up by the Russians. They tell us how Johad Dudaev, their former president, was killed by a missile homed in on his Sat-phone signal. Three hours later, after much translation and negotiation, a script is ready.

HC and GA are very excited, they know we will have to wait until 2 a.m. because of the time difference so to while away the time they put on some loud pop music and invite us to dance. So there we are gyrating under the watchful eyes of Shamil Basaev; every so often HC shows off by dancing on his toes, literally, with the toes bent back. GA does a few high kicks and practises his judo throws on Jon. Jon has a bruising evening. A jar of pickled peppers is opened in honour of the occasion and the revels continue until HC announces 'it's time'.

I dial the number and Mum's weary voice answers, she sounds sad and depressed. 'Mum, this is Camilla.' 'No it can't be, I don't believe you, you're pulling my leg.' This really upsets me, I had begun the conversation in a monotone, unemotional voice because I knew I had to speak as clearly as possible and not be overcome by grief. But at this point I leave the script and say 'It *is* me Mum, it's *me*' and then I tell her she needs a pen and paper. She disappears to get them and I have to mime what she is doing to HC who is peering over my shoulder, timing me. I tell her the number of the mediator in France and that money has to arrive by 28 December or it's Goodbye. I try to make the last bit sound like I'm saying goodbye and it isn't a threat. HC took the phone out of my hand and I could hear Mum's voice fading away 'Goodbye darling, goodbye darling'. Click. She put the phone down and I burst into tears. HC and GA looked very concerned and surprised 'Pachimoo, pachimoo? (Why, why?)' they ask me. 'She didn't believe it was me,' I reply. They have a discussion then say Jon can ring his parents just to make sure the message gets through.

I dial my parents' number and get an answering service so I hang up. 'What's wrong? What's wrong?' they ask. 'Wrong number', I reply, I dial again while GA holds the phone; when the answering service kicks in again GA swears at it telling it to 'Fuck off' a few times and shouts 'Get off the line.' Then I hear 'Hello? Hello?' It's my son Ben. They give me the handset and I say 'Hello Ben, it's your Dad.' He replies in a chirpy voice 'Oh hiya Dad.' He's so stunned he speaks like we've seen each other yesterday. I tell him to listen carefully as I don't have much time. I repeat the message that Camilla has given to her Mum, emphasizing its importance, and tell him to ring her immediately to confirm that the call is real.

I have a clear picture of where Ben is when I make the call and see him sitting, stunned, on a wooden chest next to the phone in the hallway as my parents come out of their bedroom to see who has called. I imagine them putting the kettle on and making a cup of tea. But after seven months in captivity I am too emotionally shut down to feel much about this rare moment of communication with home. Ben sounded clear and strong, I feel that he's doing OK despite the stress and worry, which is a relief.

We go back to our bedroom ruminating about the conversations. A voice is so much more concrete than a thought: at the moment of speaking you're feeling that person through the voice. Lines of worry and weariness were etched into my mother's tone. Having to talk in a monotone, an automated message giver rather than a daughter who wants to scream 'I love you and I'm OK' was excruciating. Breaking away from the script to say '*It's me*' was a split second of freedom. Mum's voice had got stronger and I know she's coping, I just wish I'd had time to say 'I love you.'

Hard to sleep. The conversation had brought those back at home into sharp focus. How's Ashok? Would I have dared asked if I was given the opportunity? Yes, even though it would be hell to know he wasn't OK. But would it be wise? I need to believe that all our loved ones have found the strength to cope, to carry on living with some joy to balance the sadness of our absence. I remember Ashok's words at five and a half after Marcel and I had split up and the decision that he would be brought up by Marcel. 'You are always there, you are like a ghost, I can see the door through you, but you are always there.' I'm hoping that he feels me there now, every new second of now.

Over the next few days the sun shines; I see icicles hanging off the gutter outside our window, sparkling and shedding rainbow drops as they melt. Our captors have become less vigilant. None of them wears a mask any more and they leave the curtains slightly pulled back in the sitting room so they have more light, which means we can see out across a street to some houses on the other side. Occasionally a well-wrapped figure walks past, head bowed against the biting wind. We still have to be careful our surreptitious glances to the windows are not seen by our captors. One morning I pause in my sweeping, stand up to stretch my back and glance at the window. No one is in the sitting room but GA catches my glance in the mirror and wags a finger of disapproval. 'Spion (spy),' he says quietly. I lower my eyes, nothing more is said; I'm lucky.

Saturday 20th we're sitting around the kitchen table. The radio is on, music blaring. Suddenly the news starts and amidst a stream of incomprehensible Russian we hear our names and then 'Scotland Yard'. HC lets out a whoop of joy. I feel a wave of relief and tears well up. Thankfully they are as excited as we are and don't give me any grief for my tears. HC explains, with the help of the dictionary, that two officers from Scotland Yard are in the neighbouring state of Ingushetia, negotiating our release. Our hopes rise. Could we be free soon?

No more is heard during the next few days. I am more concerned about my menstruation as I have nearly run out of tampons. I have been asking for new supplies but they refuse to buy any themselves and refuse to ask a mother or sister as it would give away the secret of our existence. They don't trust women to keep secrets, they explain, GA miming a gaggle of gossiping women. I have run out of pads so I use the hankies instead and this leads to another gruelling episode.

One evening I ask GA if I can have a wash. I have hidden the hankies up my sleeve. By the light of a paraffin lamp I fill a small enamel bowl with soapy water and soak them while I strip-wash. I get dressed and am just finishing rinsing the hankies when GA pokes his head through the curtain. 'What are you doing?' he asks. His mouth is distorted in a dangerous pout. 'Washing some hankies,' I reply, miming blowing my nose. 'You are using the bowl used to wash the dishes you unhygienic daughter of Satan.' He continues to berate me, brandishing a sharp kitchen knife in my face. The subject of the water jug comes up and HC, who has just appeared from smoking a joint in the sitting room, decides it's time to teach us a lesson. He punches Jon in the chest and puts his thumb over my Adam's apple, pressing until he thinks I can't stand the pain any more. Neither of us makes a sound; we steel ourselves to the pain. The next day Jon is allowed out to eat and sweep while I stay in our room; actually I'm happy not to be in their company.

For sometime now Camilla and I have followed an early morning ritual. We never know what any day is going to bring; our fab four are becoming more unstable in themselves, so we have to try extra hard to keep stable ourselves. This is only possible if we let go of the events of each day by taking deep breaths, breathing in new, revitalizing energy and breathing out the taunts, the mental or physical battering from the day before. We project harmony into the day to come and into our captors using the intention of our thought. It stops us from holding on to bitterness and falling into despair. A letting go and forgiving of each day and a drawing in of strength.

Christmas Eve. HC is morose, he has a large herpes sore on his upper lip and I think his affair has ended. He is becoming increasingly paranoid about being seen rolling a joint. However much we look the other way we are assaulted by a flow of bitter sentences, liberally sprinkled with the word 'Spion'. That evening he's perked up; apparently we have got to make another phone call tonight. He sends Jon to bed saying that I can make the call then he sets up the backgammon board. After many games I wish the phone would arrive so I can go to bed. I'm feeling weary, my energy reserves at a low ebb after months living on adrenalin in a constant state of alertness. HC decides I have to give him a massage then he says it's my turn. I refuse, but he insists. He tells me to take off my dress so he can give me a more thorough massage. 'You can trust me,' he says, after looking up the word 'trust' in the dictionary. I turn away, take off my dress (better than a thump, I'm thinking), and lie down on my stomach. There comes a point when I feel his touch change and become feather light. I leap off the bed and put my dress on. 'What's the matter?' he asks. I answer him honestly, saying 'I've had trouble in the past with men trying to sexually harass me, that's why I am nervous.' 'Our group would never do anything like that, we are *chisty*, honourable!' I smile wryly to myself. If only he knew! Perhaps it's better he doesn't. We retreat to the kitchen and drink coffee. I ask to go to bed, conversation is flagging but he insists I stay until first light. I don't think he can face his dreams.

Christmas Day

I am exhausted and chill inside. Jon curls around me, warming me. My head's full of mucous and my nose begins to flow. What a wonderful Christmas Day! In between sleeping and dabbing my flowing nose we talk about our families, wondering what kind of Christmas they are having and hoping they are having some fun despite our absence.

Christmas is of no concern to our kidnappers, who are still observing Ramadan, but we decide to have a celebration of our own. Camilla finds a walnut in her bag left over from the 'hot house'. I manage to break it open and we each eat one half with as much Christmas cheer as we can manage. Afterwards Camilla teaches me how to waltz and we hug by the light of our gas fire. Happy Christmas!

There's a flurry of activity the following day. Our guard is increased: three people on duty now instead of two. We meet (but are not exactly introduced to) 'Young Soldier' who always wears combat uniform and a mask, and 'Tall Soldier', also in uniform but no mask. He looks very un-Chechen with light brown hair and blue eyes. They spend most days cleaning and oiling their guns while listening to Chechen music rather than the Russian pop that HC likes so much. That night we notice a third masked figure sitting playing cards. As soon as he speaks I recognize him as 'The news bringer, gravelly voice'. GA tells us this man is a brilliant soldier who moves so swiftly and silently at night they call him 'Batman'. Batman beckons us over after we have eaten to join them in a game of cards. This is our first encounter with the Russian card game 'Torak (Fool)'. We are assigned partners and away we go getting totally lost in what appears to be quite a complex game. They find our antics very amusing but Batman sticks up for us, and tries to teach us the rules. He looks rather like a bat with his small beady brown eyes and half mask. I notice his square determined chin with its layer of stubble and his neat mouth. He has an expensive-looking watch on his wrist with a satin blue face, catching the light from the lamp.

The increase in security suggests that we could be moving or leaving which makes me feel optimistic – any movement, even if not to freedom, is a change and would be welcome. With three guards we also feel more secure as we are never left alone with just one which prevents them from getting up to their individual games.

D-Day. There are rumours that someone is flying to Kabardino Balkaria then driving to Chechnya bringing our ransom money. Early evening HC comes to our room to explain tonight's procedure. 'You come to eat then go back in your room, pack bags, wait to be fetched. Then freedom!' A feast meets our eyes – a pile of syrupy wheat sticks and small cakes with hard white icing. Everyone, apart from Batman, is here tonight, all dressed in combat uniform. There's a knock at the door and a flurry of activity, masks being donned, guns cocked and us being ushered back to our room. We hear low voices, swiftly pack our bag, sit on the floor and wait ... and wait ... and wait ...

I eventually give up on waiting and decide that if we are going to move they will have to wake me up anyway so I go to sleep.

I cannot sleep, I sit, I lie, I listen and listen then watch the sky lighten through our little window, my eyes full of tears. It's a beautiful dawn, the reflected light from the sun bright orange on the tree bark against a pale blue sky. A condemning dawn, condemning us to more days of captivity. The window of opportunity didn't open.

I stand up and watch the tree, telling it to take my loving thoughts back to our families, from tree to tree, through roots, earth and sea. I think of one particular horse-chestnut tree that my mother often stops to admire near her home. Let it give her the message that we're OK. I hear when we get out that she used to send us prayers through that same tree.

I awake and, surprise, surprise, we're still here. Nothing is said until we ask GA and he tells us there is a delay. HC just forgot to come back and inform us of the new arrangements. I promise myself not to believe anything until it actually happens but it is a hard promise to keep. That night HC tells us, once more, we may be freed in a few hours. I manage to shut down my listening ear and sleep.

The fractious tension of the last few days takes its toll on my health. I now have diarrhoea and decide not to eat for a couple of days. It's almost a sin in Chechen culture not to eat if there is food so our captors are very concerned and keep knocking on the door to entice me out. But I'm adamant and don't leave my bed. By the second day my stomach is feeling more stable and I cannot refuse to drink some of the fresh milk Batman has brought especially for my health. I think they're concerned about our thin bodies and lacklustre faces so a sackful of large tins of Austrian beef is dumped on the floor of the bathroom – to me a sign we will not be leaving soon.

This is a great change in our diet, Austrian beef and onions for the next month! Our captors jokingly tell us that we can't leave Chechnya until we've eaten all the beef. I work hard at eating my way to freedom. Paunch comes in regularly at night and pinches me around my ribs making snide remarks about fattening me up to make shashlik (barbecued meat). We are the thinnest we have been, all the stress eating up our fat reserves.

Although I have been vegetarian for ten years I start eating this beef; my body is crying out for nourishment. When Batman's on duty he brings food cooked by his wife and he always gives us a share of it. When he arrives he peels off two cheese or sweet pumpkin pancakes from a buttery pile. Because it is still Ramadan they eat about five in the morning and we get what's left over the next day, usually some rice and meat balls or bits of fried chicken. Deluxe food!

New Year's Eve

We're invited out about an hour before midnight. GA and Batman have prepared a little celebration (HC nowhere to be seen). On the table there is half a chocolate swiss roll, two satsumas, one banana and a bottle of 'Mona

Lisa' white wine. Seeing this food on the table is bizarre and the alcohol a complete shock as they're all Muslim and don't drink it (not in front of each other anyway). Neither Camilla nor I are big drinkers but we have to finish the bottle. It's a special present and they stand over us smiling as we drink the sickly sweet wine. Over the next couple of hours we get vaguely drunk; I have to drink most of it because Camilla can't stomach it. On the stroke of midnight we all toast to 'Cveboda! Freedom!' for us and for the Chechen people. They open the front door and tell us to listen. We hear a muffled bang and a wizz. GA tried to set off a firework rocket but it fell over and shot dismally along the ground. A traditional but surreal New Year!

January 1998

No more long evening discussions with GA and HC, no more daytime tête-à-têtes with Paunch, no more washing shoes, no more sweeping. Our time is more regimented: one hour in the kitchen in the morning for breakfast and the occasional wash, and one hour in the early evening for supper. We play a lot of backgammon and do some exercises although we don't have much physical energy. We spend hours sitting, meditating and praying for a swift release. Every morning I wake early, Jon still sleeping as he's on the alert every night. I contemplate the square of window, our living painting, watching the framed trunk and branches changing colour – orange to grey to greeny brown to dark silhouette. Occasionally a crow enters the painting, its black cawing weight swaying a branch or two before it flaps off into the blank, unseen, unpainted canvas beyond the window frame. This is the time I commune with members of my family, telling them how much I love them, willing them to have the strength to cope. I cannot see or hear them but I feel waves of loving energy pouring through and around me like a huge comforting blanket. Often I cry, silently; this is the time I can release my pent up grief without distressing Jon or causing a reaction of guilt-ridden paranoia from our captors, resulting in mental torture and thumps. I ask harmonious energies from all the spheres and dimensions of existence to help us survive this day.

Dark Chocolate has become another of our watchmen. He has a quiet gentle energy, not as unbalanced as the original four. He brings books to read or plays cards with the others. As time goes on he becomes more tense and jumpy with dark rings under his eyes. One day he has a massive headache and asks me to give him a head massage. I stand behind him as he sits on a chair in the kitchen, placing my hands gently on his head calling healing energies to flow through me and take away the pain replacing it with peace of mind. I know this is one thing he has very little of. He thanks me, saying the pain has dissolved.

He seems to be the 'gofer' of the group and is the one to bring a faxed sheet of proof-of-life questions, questions such as 'What's the name of Jon's son?' and 'Where does Ashok's father come from?' It is addressed to 'Dear Zakir' and signed 'kind regards Vincent'. We spend a morning composing our answers and looking up the Russian equivalent so they know what we are writing. HC tries to interfere: 'What does Zakir mean?' We tell him it's a name. 'I don't believe you, tell the truth, the truth or . . .' He grinds one white knuckled fist on top of another, our nerves are frayed and I start shaking. The others admonish him in Chechen and he disappears into the kitchen to smoke a cigarette in sulky silence. The next day Dark Chocolate brings a video camera. Puppydog and Tall Soldier are on duty and they have fun dressing me up in Dark Chocolate's winter coat and scarf and Jon in a blanket. They stand us in front of the mildewed wall in our bedroom telling us to shiver and shake as though it's minus 5 degrees celsius instead of plus 25 degrees celsius. They want us to say how cold and hungry we are, and plead for the money to be sent for our freedom. I'm told to hold the sheet of proof-of-life questions. I look into the camera and say, 'Please send the money soon. It's really cold here and we've had enough.' Jon continues, 'We want to go home.' We hate this deception but hope our parents (if they ever manage to see the video) take some comfort in seeing us alive.

HC is losing it. For the past month he has been getting me to do his washing, making remarks like 'You come to Chechnya to work so I give you work.' Usually he's grateful but one day he's ironing some black trousers that I'd washed the night before and finds a white mark. It's only dried soapsuds and I offer to wash them again but he grabs me by the arm and leads me to the kitchen area where he delivers an almighty blow to my lower chest – 'Huuhh.' In total shock, the air knocked out of my lungs, I stagger back a few paces. The sound has alerted Tall Soldier who comes into the kitchen holding his gun to find out what's going on. HC tells him why he has punched me and Tall Soldier appears baffled by his actions. I am dismissed back to our room and leave them talking. I'm glad Tall Soldier has witnessed this instability and hope he will tell his superiors.

The death throes of HC's scorpion tail happen a few days later. He is still desperately trying to find ways of maintaining his authority over us. Perhaps, subconsciously, he feels it is his only reason for existing. He arrives early for his stint of duty and sends the other two away. He calls me out and demands a back massage which I give him, although I can sense by his restlessness this is not the main reason for calling me. He gets up and says, 'Now, it's your turn.' I reply, 'I don't need one – my leg is better now, thank you.' He stands in front of me, defiance and challenge in his eyes. 'If you don't allow me to massage you, you will have to sleep with all three soldiers on duty tonight.' He pulls out a packet containing three condoms. 'Just the right amount, now you have to say yes,' he says, placing one foot over mine and pressing down on it, harder and harder. I have reached the point when I don't care how much pain he inflicts, I'm not going to let him take advantage of me. Internally I speak to the honourable part of HC, almost smothered by his distorted, trauma-born sense of reality. I look him directly in the eyes, into his soul and say 'Niet'. He looks away and releases the pressure on my foot. 'Chai?' I ask lightly and start lighting the gas before he can reply. There's a knock at the door and I go back to our room as the rest of the night watch come in.

> Chris
> Please, please move quickly and bring the money
> We are kept in a cellar and there is often no heat, light or water, and only a little food. Camilla's leg is partially paralysed and she has a glandula infection. Jon's chest is bad. We have no access to medicine or a doctor
> Our captors say they will cut off our hands and send them to you if the money doesn't come in a week.
> Please, please move fast, we are desperate
> Jon + Camilla
> November 9th

A letter we were forced to write, sent via a mediator to Britain November 1997

10

The Ice Palace

On 17 January we're on the move again; a jelly wobble of fear runs
through my innards. I have got used to this house and our routines.
We pack our things and are guided out to a waiting car. HC arrives just
before we leave, in a red-eyed stupor. He wants to come with us but Batman tells him to stay, the conversation is in Chechen but the meaning is
very clear. No Jeep this time and we slide and slither all over the bumpy
icy roads. When we arrive we are guided over a snowy bank before coming to the door of our new home. After being led through a couple of
rooms they take off our masks. We are in a small bedroom, the single
sofa bed has been made up with a sheet, feather duvet and two pillows.
There's a wardrobe in front of a boarded-up window. By the bed is a
table covered by a plastic cloth, grimy with dust and ancient grease. We
fit a dented metal bucket next to the wardrobe and cover it with a plastic
bag. The worst thing is the lack of space – there is only a narrow piece of
free floor in which to move. I'm feeling depressed with no fresh air, no
natural light and no space to exercise, only the freshly-washed bed linen
makes it bearable.

The house must have been occupied by a Russian family as there is
a small Russian icon above our bed. Slotted in the frame is a scroll of
religious scriptures hand-written in tiny Cyrillic letters. Above the table
there is a print of a seascape at Dubrovnik. Legs of a plastic doll splay out
from the top of the wardrobe. Under the bed we find a kettle: inside is
a reel of yellow cotton, a needle, a pair of scissors, some safety pins and
a box of matches. Useful stuff. Behind the kettle is a large net sack full
of walnuts. On the table is a wonderfully kitsch candle in the form of a
Father Christmas. We light it and it bubbles and squeaks before splutter-
ing out – the paraffin wax is full of water.

The room next to ours has a bed, above which are shelves full of knickknacks dominated by a large 1950s radio. The walls are covered with family photographs: stilted, unsmiling, moustachioed husband and bunned wife rigidly standing side by side. To the right as I look out from our room there are double doors leading to a sitting room. Here we have breakfast on a shiny cherrywood table. There is a large dresser with glass doors, the shelves twinkling with cut glass bowls and sherry glasses and a piano sits in the corner covered in dust-sheets. The windows have inner shutters that are closed – no peeping out. The most intriguing room is the kitchen that only has a small gas cooker with no gas pipe. Where did they cook and prepare the food?

The cooker is ingrained with dirt and looks like it has been sitting in a garage for years. Batman and GA ask us to clean it on our first day; at least it relieves the boredom. I open the oven door and find it full of small glass jars of dried up paint. Batman gives us some rags and a packet of soda 'grit' and we set to work. It's hard. The ancient grime doesn't want to let go and the soda is scratchy and gets under our nails. GA takes over from Camilla – she hasn't got enough elbow grease. It's a pleasant chore. I scrub and I scrub with the soda crystals, slowly getting down to the enamel beneath. My main aim this day is to make this cooker shiny, as shiny as the day it was bought. All we need now is some gas to fuel it.

They have got a treat in store for us. 'When you have finished you can have a wash,' GA laughs in a conspiratorial way (we know there isn't a bathroom in the house). Batman goes out, coming back 20 minutes later, saying 'It's ready. There's a bath-house in the garden. I will take you there, one at a time, no masks but keep your eyes on your feet.' I am given the first turn. On the way I glimpse rows of coats on pegs, porkpie hats on the shelf above, and four walking sticks in a rack. Maybe the elderly couple had been driven out as spies, their child flown the nest years before, leaving her '60s toys stuffed on top of the wardrobe. Out of the door into daylight. It's snowing! Even in these straitened circumstances I feel the excitement of a small child experiencing snow for the first time. All around is silence except for the hiss of the snow crystals falling through the air. I follow Batman's footsteps imprinted in the snow, seeing white-laden pine branches out of the corner of my eye and feeling as if I'm in the middle of a Grimms' fairytale.

The bath-house is a square brick building. An ante-room leads to a room which contains a huge boiler and bath with a rose shower head high on the wall. The boiler is humming away, the room is warm and cosy, green and blue tiles decorate the walls and luckily there's a tablet of old cracked soap. Dust and sooty smuts cover all the surfaces, but it doesn't take long to shower the dust and spiders out of the bath. I'm nervous about undressing in front of Batman, however he has anticipated my dilemma and withdraws to the ante-room with a book. I stay under the shower for a long time, cleansing every pore of my body, warming my muscles and bones, washing the horror and tension of the past few months down the drain so I have enough strength to face whatever we have to face.

It's my turn. I'm led out of the house and along the snow covered path to the bath-house. Batman sits down on the chair with his book and points me to the bathroom. I don't need any persuading, I turn on the shower and relish the sensation of hot water flowing over my tired body. As I scrub myself clean I am shocked again at how many layers of dead skin come off, but it feels like I'm shedding more than just dead skin cells as I wash several months of imprisonment away. I scrub and scrub but after a while I become concerned about how long I've been in there – previous bathtimes have always had a time limit and I am concerned about them giving me a hard time. I finish swiftly, dress and wait to be escorted back to the house.

My menstruation comes with a vengeance. We have spent most of the previous day cutting up strips of the bottom sheet to fold into sanitary pads. Jon hems the cut sheet with yellow cotton. That night my body is wracked with pain and I toss and turn, weaving in and out of nightmare escape dreams. The heating is on and there's a burning hot pipe next to my head. I feel as though I can't breathe; darkness and pain envelop me. Dawn arrives, a shaft of grey light creeping through a crack at the top of the boarded up window. I sit up, careful not to wake Jon, wretched tears streaming, my mind screaming 'How much longer? How much longer?' There is no answer.

The pain recedes and our life takes on a semblance of its former routine. We live on a diet of pasta, bread and tea. Someone brings a pot of 'Rama' margarine to enliven the pasta. GA has fixed a gas pipe to the enamel cooker so we can heat up our food. They allow us to cook. There is only a thin white sheet covering the window so after hours in our dimly lit room we bask in the natural light. The day after our shower the electricity is cut off, no more running water, no more warm showers and we have to rely on them to give us a candle to light our room. We take some hot water back to our room after washing up to soak and wash my sanitary towels in the old kettle and wind them over the hot pipe to dry. When the Rama margarine has been devoured I use the pot to soak them. We use the remaining water to splash-wash ourselves over the toilet bucket – we have no other choice.

We have been discussing who we should tell about the walnuts. It has to be someone who won't immediately take off in a tirade of 'Spion' accusations. Our choice falls on Dark Chocolate. Fortunately he's on his own the next morning and is delighted with our discovery. We take the sack into the kitchen and use the walnuts to supplement our diet, although they are rather old, many a shrivelled nut turning to dust.

I have been telling GA how much I love playing the piano. I nearly come to grief over this. He invites me to play, Young Soldier removes the dustsheet and I sit in front of the keys. Now I stopped learning the piano when I was 14 and am not very good at improvising, especially with an audience. So I fumble around and they burst out laughing. 'You lied, you cannot play.' Young Soldier takes my place and plays a jaunty little tune. I am led back to our room. The piano becomes a source of amusement and they all have a little tinkle. Someone discovers some music but no one reads it. I summon up my courage and say 'Please let me try, I read music.' They allow me to have a go and luckily there are some simple tunes that I can pick up. What a joy, it certainly helps to take my mind off our desolate circumstances and gives a boost to my sanity.

We don't see much of HC at the piano house, he drifts in and out, looking dishevelled and lost. Late one evening he opens our door and peers in; we are already in bed. I think he meant to ask Jon out to massage his legs but he says nothing and closes the door again. The next day he asks me to give him a head massage; his hair is greasy and unkempt, very unusual for dapper HC. I overcome my disgust at touching it and massage his scalp and forehead feeling enormous compassion and sadness. He thanks me quietly.

25 January

Electric light, yes! We ask GA if we can have another trip to the bath-house. 'After us, if you are good,' he says with his gappy grin. We wait patiently, playing backgammon on the bed. Our turn comes, what joy! Batman sends me back to the house by myself to get Jon. He knows I'm not going to fly away and it feels good to be trusted. I can't stop myself looking up (without moving my head) and see a wrought iron gate, other houses across the street with snow laden trees, the icy road in between. It looks like a pretty neighbourhood with houses built for those with professional jobs. GA asks me to teach him how to play the piano. I have been practising a piece called 'The Carnival' and so I sit next to him teaching him the first few phrases. He thumps the keys, sweating in his concentration.

Without any request from us and in an amazing act of kindness Batman tunes the radio to the BBC World Service. There is a commentator describing a first division football match. I am not the least bit interested in football but hearing an English voice describing such an English event suddenly makes me acutely aware of where home is and how far away from it we are. I bring my awareness back to the room, to the surreal situation that we are in – me listening to an English football match and Camilla playing the piano, both of us under armed guard. Our reverie is interrupted by a knock at the door and we are sent to our room. There is much talk and scraping of chairs then Tall Soldier calls us out. He mimes an aeroplane taking off and we turn to gather our things. 'Niet, niet,' he says, shaking his head, so we go out leaving all our precious possessions. The sitting room is crowded: Puppydog, Paunch, Young Soldier, Tall Soldier, Batman and GA.

GA beckons me to come into the adjoining bedroom, where there's a big wardrobe full of a woman's clothes. He tells me to take off my clothes, he can see I am distressed about this and he turns his back on me saying 'Go, go. I won't look.' He rustles through the clothes in the wardrobe and pulls out a knitted blue dress. He turns around and sees I haven't taken off my pants and says 'Off, everything.' I protest, saying 'Menstruatie,' but he insists. 'The ignorant bastard!' I'm thinking. He pulls out a pair of khaki nylon bloomers, thankfully with a cotton gusset sewn in by hand. I put them on and feel like a 1930s footballer; they sag and flap around my thighs, having been made for a larger frame. Then I put on the blue dress, which itches dreadfully. I am sent out to show the others and luckily Batman comes to my aid: he says something about it not suiting me and takes me back to the wardrobe allowing me to look with him. I find a simple, white cotton shirt and he brings out a pink skirt and jacket.

Apart from being a little big it's quite comfortable. GA tells me to take off my sandals and hands me a pair of low-heeled dark blue pointed shoes and thick woollen socks. The shoes don't fit over my feet and socks. GA looks as if he's going to blow a fuse so I take the socks off, stuff them in my pocket, and squeeze my feet into the shoes. I go out and do a twirl with a wry smile. Tall Soldier asks where my scarf is – 'Platok?' I gesture back to the wardrobe room and he allows me to get it and wear it. I am forever grateful to him, for that 'scarf' (my sarong) is one of my most precious and useful possessions.

Whilst Camilla is being dressed they size me up and tell me to take off my black trousers. I start to do so but as soon as they realize I have no underwear I'm quickly told to put them back on again. There is a short discussion after which they hand me a pair of green camouflage combat trousers that I have to put on over my black ones. I also get a purple and black checked cotton shirt, green combat jacket and some trainers. Their eye is good and everything fits fine. Once we have our new gear on they start getting excited, flapping their arms pretending to fly. Part of me is hopeful, but we've been here before. Batman looks at his watch and says, 'Time.' They hand us black balaclavas, with no holes, which we put on. Taking us by the arm they guide us out of the building – the compacted snow makes the ground uneven and I find it difficult to move at the speed they want me to. There is a sense of urgency but they are not too rough. We are put in the back of a car and told to keep our heads down.

Young Soldier guides me out, and because I am slipping and sliding so much in my new shoes he picks me up under his arm and carries me to the car. Just as we reach it he skids and we both end up in a tangled heap. I'm not hurt and find it rather amusing – it must be the bubble of excitement that I am trying to contain. We drive steadily for about ten minutes, then the car stops and we are led out, our hands guided to hold onto a wire fence. All kinds of thoughts fly through my head, 'Will the next vehicle take us to the airport or is this the end of the road? Perhaps there's a firing squad behind us?' Someone lights a cigarette, then we hear another engine approaching and we are pushed into another car. New voices. Have we seen the last of our 'friends'?

11

The Base

25 January – 1 February

The second car races towards our next destination, whatever that might be. Eventually we stop and hear a squeaky gate being opened. The car rolls slowly forward and then comes to a halt. They help us out. There is a slight echo and I guess that we are in a courtyard of some kind.

Many of the richer Chechen households are constructed with buildings on three sides, the fourth side being a high wall with large metal gates in the middle; I imagine we are within one of these compounds. We're guided gently over tarmac covered in uneven ice, difficult to negotiate in slippy shoes and mask, but they don't get frustrated with my hesitancy. Then through a doorway, down some concrete steps into a room. I feel heat and see flickers of flames through my mask. We're taken through to another room and gently pushed down to sit on a bed with a whispered 'Sediti (sit)'. I reach out to find Jon and someone puts my hand on his arm, 'OK?' Jon whispers. 'Yeah,' I whisper back. He's sitting on a bed at right angles to me. Above our heads is a continual drone of men chanting and stamping feet. With that and the flickering flames and heat I feel we have entered Dante's Inferno.

I am wondering when we are going to be getting on the plane that they have been talking about. There are a few moments of silence, then a voice speaks in halting English.

'Where do you come from?' ' What music do you like?' I listen to the voice and sense this person is genuinely interested, not about to interrogate us. Someone else is fiddling with a gun in the background but that doesn't feel threatening either. I answer 'We come from England, and I like many different types of music.'

'Do you like Queen?'

'Yes,' I reply.

'*Freddie Mercury was a brilliant singer,*' he says. '*Do you like sport, foot-ball?*' he continues.

'*I used to run a lot and play squash, but I am not very interested in football.*'

'*What is squash?*' he asks.

'*You have a racket like tennis but it is played indoors, no net and very fast.*'

'*Ah, I understand,*' is the reply. Then more silence, but this opportunity to communicate is a rare relief.

Someone comes in and whispers urgently in Chechen. They start fidgeting and I sense an air of tense anticipation. Footsteps descend and a loud voice barks some orders. Our masks are immediately removed. In front of us is a man, fairly broad and stocky, standing very erect, military style. He's wearing a grey uniform and an enormous grey-wool Cauca-sian hat. He has blue eyes, a broad face with slightly pink chubby cheeks, and a full-lipped mouth surrounded by a greying clipped beard and moustache. His face gives the impression he's only in his mid thirties, just prematurely grey. Perhaps he's the 'Boss' GA used to tell us about in those early days in the Kiva. He told us the 'Boss' was only 32 and had a young son brought up by his mother because his wife had left him for an-other man. I remember thinking how unusual that must be in Chechen society. GA used to go around to shave the little boy's head to keep the lice away.

He smiles at us and talks in Russian assuming we can understand which, with the help of his hand gestures, we do. 'Look, no mask, you can trust me, I mean you no harm. You will be here for a short time be-fore you are released. Chai? (tea?) Couchette? (food?)' 'Da, pajalsta (yes, please),' we reply. He barks an order to one of his entourage that have descended with him then wishes us 'Spakone Noche (good night)' and turns on his heel leaving an awed, stunned silence.

Now I see we're not in a dungeon, but a room half below ground level with peeling wallpaper and lino floor, lit by a single light bulb. Beside the beds there is a low table. A tall, well-built man is sitting next to Jon, dressed in black. He has a wide forehead, light brown hair and eyes and a mouth of perfectly straight white teeth (very rare in Chechnya). He introduces himself as 'Genghis Khan'. His black, pointed ankle boots are highly polished. Leaning against the wall is a boy of about 16 with short black wavy hair playing with his gun; he's dressed in combat uniform with heavy army boots. Through the doorway (there is no door) a gas pipe is balanced on a large dumb-bell, threaded through the handle. A flame shoots out of its nozzle, source of the heat and very sooty fumes. On the wall behind the flame I can just make out an enormous photographic poster, nearly the size of the wall, with a forest of autumnal trees surrounding a dark, rippling lake. During the days to come, in the many hours of sitting on my bed I take myself for a walk in this forest imagining the red, yellow and orange leaves above my head dancing in the wind and dip my hand into the cool refreshing waters of the lake.

Another young fighter, looking about 18, carries in a tray with a kettle, small teapot, some cups, a bowl of sugar, a bowl of cherry-plums in syrup and some teaspoons. He says something in Chechen to Genghis who translates for us. 'Sorry, no food is left, you will have to wait.' 'Niet problyemi,' we reply. The tea is wonderful, the cherry-plum syrup sweet and delicious. They put the syrup in their tea but Jon and I prefer to eat the plums out of a spoon, savouring the taste.

I can feel blood seeping through the bloomers on to my skirt. Genghis seems friendly enough so I summon my courage and say, 'Adeen problyemi, mye menstruatie is y hotch material (one problem, I have my menstruation and I need material).' His eyebrows rise up but he gives an order to the 18-year-old. After a few minutes he comes back with a very small piece of clean white cotton cloth. I smile inside – they really have no idea. 'Thank you, but it will not be enough.' Jon mimes cutting up lots of material. Genghis shakes his head. 'There is no more.' Jon pulls out the edge of the sheet on my bed, miming cutting a strip, 'OK?' he asks, and Genghis nods. 'We need scissors,' I say, and Genghis gives another order. The 16-year-old goes out and comes back with a small pair of scissors. They will do and Jon cuts a strip from the edge of the sheet; at least it doesn't look too dirty, although not pristine. My legs are tightly crossed and I'm wondering how to attach the material to the inside of my bloomers. I'm still smarting at GA for putting me into this awkward position. I feel inside my pockets – only my socks. I open up the jacket, and miraculously there is one small safety pin attached to the lining.

Once more into the bloody breach improvization.

The next question is, 'Where's the toilet?' Genghis stands up and beckons me, 'One at a time.' I have to put my mask over my eyes but not over my whole face which means I can see my feet, a great advantage. He leads me to a small brick building on the other side of the courtyard. A porcelain latrine rather than a hole dug straight into the earth. There's ice inside on the tiled floor, but the jug has just been filled. Afterwards he asks if I want to wash my hands, 'Da, pajalsta.' I am led to another room that contains, to my amazement, a large empty plunge pool and a sauna. There's a metal bucket of warm water on a table and a saucepan. The whole room is tiled and near the wall surrounding the plunge pool there is a large drain in the floor. Genghis gives me a cake of soap and I wash my hands over the drain. 'Later you can both have a proper wash,' he says.

Genghis is more communicative and open, more confident and less paranoid than the previous Fab Four and has a smattering of English.

Eventually he takes his leave with a 'spakone noche' and the two young fighters are left to look after us. We moved to our new location early in the evening, which was unusual. Previously moves have happened in the middle of the night and I wonder if we'll be moving again to another location or to the promised plane before dawn – these thoughts make it difficult to sleep. Time passes, the fighters bring in a carpet and roll it out in front of the opposite wall. They lean their backs against the wall, sitting on the ground, watching us. 'spit? (sleep?)' they ask, more as a question than an order. So we decide to lie down, since they obviously think there's time to sleep.

Morning and no freedom. I am feeling depressed, especially as the middle finger on my left hand is infected. It started after we were given the task of cleaning the cooker in the piano house. Some dirt must have got lodged under the side of my nail and now the whole top of my finger is swollen, red and throbbing. I send healing into it through my other hand and pray it doesn't spread. Genghis creates a welcome diversion from my sombre musings by bringing breakfast. Bread, biscuits, tea and he sends the 16-year-old running off to get some butter. I'm a real 'butterite' so this is a great treat. 'Later there will be some soup,' he tells us; 'it's not ready yet.' The conversation turns to music and cars then, quite unexpectedly, to dentistry. 'How much does it cost to have a filling done?' Jon plucks a figure out of his mind to keep Genghis happy. 'It is very expensive to go to the dentist in Chechnya, and now impossible because much of the equipment was bombed or stolen by the Russians,' he informs us.

Our conversation is interrupted by the sound of many feet approaching. The 'Boss' or 'Commander' as they call him enters noisily, followed by two hardened looking fighters. 'Kak di la? (How are you?)' 'Harasho (good),' we reply. He plumps out his chest with an air of importance. 'Soon you will be free, it is being arranged. What do you need? What can we get you to make you feel more comfortable?' I think he means it! We explain in halting Russian and mime that all our possessions were taken from us, even our clothes, so we need toothbrushes and paste, soap, brush and comb, shaving equipment, clothes that fit us and shoes for me. He barks an order and one of the men goes off to find a paper and pen. He flings Jon's jacket and trousers behind him into the other room; one of the young fighters picks them up and takes them out 'at the double'. (Jon had taken them off because they were tight and uncomfortable in the heat.) The man with the paper returns and writes down an order. The Commander storms out after signing it. A bit of a play act, I think. Not real anger, he's just trying to impress us. It looks as if they have a credit system working in the bazaar. I quickly mention sanitary towels and underwear to Genghis and he tells the man with the order, who blushes and replies in Chechen. We do not understand the words but the meaning is clear, this request will be difficult to fulfil. No Chechen man would dream of asking for sanitary towels or female underwear in the bazaar.

A couple of hours later Genghis returns and I ask if I can have my clothes back, they weren't that bad! But it's too late – they have already been incinerated. One of the fighters, whom we nickname Round Boy due to his shape and round cheerful face, appears with our 'order'. He takes great pleasure in being the bringer of gifts and presents us with a brand new toothbrush each, two tubes of 'Blend-a-Med' toothpaste, a brush with a mirror on the back, two combs, a razor with two packets of blades, two plastic bottles of shampoo, one with green liquid, one pink, a carton of three blue and white marbled cakes of soap, powerfully scented, and matching 'his & hers' towels, one blue and one lilac, with a satin heart sewn in a corner of each.

Round Boy likes his 'Father Christmas' role and has put a lot of thought into these purchases; my heart warms to him. However, no new clothes or shoes or sanitary towels, this is our lot. But what a 'lot' it is, more precious than any Christmas gift. Genghis chats to us while we finger our new possessions. The two young fighters come in and start 'rough housing' like puppies on the carpet. I smile at them, I'm glad they're having fun. The 18-year-old says something to Genghis who tells me they don't like me smiling at them. I look down at the floor and shut off my smile. Oh God, can I never show any feelings without them being misinterpreted through a paranoic haze of insecurity.

We are given thick vegetable soup with bits of mutton floating around in it, and more bread and tea. Afterwards I ask to go to the toilet and they say 'wait a moment'. There are people moving about in the yard and they don't want me seen or me to see whatever or whoever. Over the next two hours I repeat the request several times and each time the reply is the same. I am desperate. Finally one of the guards takes pity and to my great relief finds me a plastic bottle.

In this place there seems to be much more wealth. It's a base of some sort with many men moving around all the time. I've no idea what they're doing but it seems to be a kind of coordination centre. All the men we've met so far appear more balanced than most of our previous captors. None of them go out of their way to engage with us but if they have to do so it's in a friendly, non-threatening manner. No 'spion' accusations, room to breathe.

Late evening. 'You want a wash, yes?' Genghis asks us. 'Yes, please,' we reply. Genghis gives the 18-year-old some instructions and he disappears for half an hour. On his reappearance we gather our plastic bags of goodies, don our masks and follow Genghis to the sauna room. There are two steaming buckets on the table. Genghis leaves us, saying he will wait in the other room. Leaving our clothes on a bench by the table, we sluice the water over each other. The intimacy of washing together, helping each other with shampooing and showering without the fear of GA or HC accusing us of some other crime, is invigorating. An inch of freedom.

Two days pass, no release. My nerves are taut, my finger throbbing. The fighters play backgammon with Jon, but I am excluded because I am a woman. I have to move, so I put on my socks and begin to dance. Stretching my arms to the ceiling, spinning and whirling. They look on with incredulity. 'She's dancing!' I hear one whisper in Russian. They don't stop me. I feel so much better.

I admire her courage just to take the opportunity to use the space to dance. I wish I had the courage to do the same. But my joy in dancing has been dented by the forced dancing we were made to do with GA and HC. Dancing to crap music, against my will, against the desire of my whole being. In

earlier years I had been known as 'the dancer'. Now the only reason to leap
puppet-like to their strings is so as not to incur their wrath.

The young ones are beginning to get very bored having to be with us all
day and night, so they vary the watch. Sometimes Genghis takes over in
the day bringing along a friend whom we call 'The Sensitive One'. At first
I wasn't so sure; he's thin, dark and silent, and spends a long time taking
an automatic machine gun and tripod apart and cleaning it. I watch his
deft hands with their amazing flexible thumbs, so lithe and strong. But
then he begins to talk. With a mixture of Russian and English he asks us
why we came, what were our jobs in England, what was England like to
live in. He is under the impression that everybody is rich there, so we tell
him about the homeless on the streets. There are some very rich people
but the wealth is not evenly spread. We talk about life in general and our
own journeys within its flow. It is such a relief to talk with someone who
is genuinely interested in us and our life without having some ulterior
motive. We ask him about his life. He was in his last year of school when
the Russians started bombing in 1994; he had wanted to go to university
and study English but didn't have a chance. His family live in Grozny
– he has 7 brothers and sisters and 60 cousins. When he and his elder
brothers began fighting in the war their family moved to a cousin's house
in a village as the food in Grozny was running out. It wasn't much better
but they survived. We ask him what all his brothers and sisters do now.
'Work in the Bazaars, work on farms in the country and I do this,' he
replies, with a sweep of his arm indicating the gun, us and the building.
I'm dying to ask him what 'this' is but I don't think he will elaborate and
we could be accused of spying again.

He brings us a radio and tunes it to a Grozny channel. It plays a lot of
English pop music from the sixties, seventies and eighties, much of which
we really like – Peter Gabriel, Roxy Music, the Beatles, David Bowie. Much
better than the Russo-Euro pop we were subjected to in the 'Bleak house'.
Music played a major part in my teens. In our isolation we discover how im-
portant information is to our minds, hungry for stimulation. In our modern
world we are subjected to information overload with adverts thrust upon us
through commercal TV and radio, but music . . . gentle, lyrical, classical or
swift electric rock, music is food for my ears.

We have another guard for the night watch. He must be really fearful, he has a mask: his body is shrouded in garlands of ammunition and

he clutches a Kalashnikov. He does not threaten us with it, just salutes us with 'Dobri Oodra (Good morning)', and slumps down against the wall with a lot of clanking. His trust in us grows and on his second visit he leaves his garlands and mask behind. He has such a soft young face with an aquiline nose and downy black beard just sprouting. His head, which is shaved, is adorned with a white skull cap. He plays backgammon with Jon and starts talking about the war. His father was killed so his family went to the mountains. As the eldest he was now responsible for the whole family and foraged in the woods for edible nuts and berries to feed them all. For a couple of nights we have him on night duty. Our guards have been given a scanning radio so now one of them sits with it in the next room. The second night we have 'Garland Man' on duty, on his own; someone tries to call him on the radio but there he lies, gently snoozing while we are totally awake. Jon goes over and nudges him into consciousness but before he gets to the phone one of the young soldiers comes bounding in to see why there's no response. Garland Man gets a good scolding and is not trusted with night duty again.

The radio becomes a useful plaything and time waster. They record little rhymes and ditties and play them back amidst hoots of laughter. In this way we learn the names of some of them, Isa the young 16-year-old, Osman, the 18-year-old, and another called Ali Khan, a lanky 20-year-old with white spotty socks. Also they can tune in to other people's conversations and interject. One woman was having a conversation with a man about apples and young Isa entered their conversation making absurd comments. We don't understand all the words but the meaning is clear, especially the increasingly irate tone of the woman who finally slams down the phone. They all fall about in hysterics.

Early one morning Osman accompanies us to the loo – this time no masks. We pass a large black BMW with dark tinted windows and no number plates with its nose tucked into a portico which, strangely, has some pale green garlands of grapes painted as a border pattern near the top of the cream plaster walls and a couple of trompe-l'oeil fluted columns. The plaster is cracking and the paint faded like a forgotten Italian fresco; it seems totally out of place here.

Osman has started talking to me about his past (they mostly direct their conversation towards me because Camilla is not their kinswoman or their wife). He tells me that during the last war, when he was 15, he was captured

by the Russians and imprisoned in Kabardino Balkaria in a small concrete
cell containing two wooden benches and ten men and boys, ranging in age
from 10 to 70. The elders slept on the benches in rotation while the rest slept
on the floor. There was a tiny window above eye level and a hole in the floor
for a toilet. He was there for three months and fed only on stale bread and
water. He also told me that many women were captured and sometimes held
in the same cells as the men which was shameful for both. We had passed
this prison on our way back from Moscow a couple of days before we were
kidnapped; it's strange that now we are meeting one of its former inmates.
Now he lives in a shell-damaged block of flats with a broken lift. He asks if I
have any idea of how to mend it. I have to say that I don't.

We get a new guard. He is short and stocky with shoulder-length black
hair and a beard. He grunts and snuffles like a bull and is full of nervous
energy. He sits on my bed; his gilet is bulging with ammunition that must
weigh at least a couple of kilos. When he's not talking he's tapping out a
rhythm with his fingers on whatever surface he can find, or drumming with
his foot on the lino. After an hour or so it becomes deeply irritating.

I notice that our new guard periodically holds his right side and is in
some pain so I summon up courage and say 'Bollit? (pain?)'. He explains
that his kidneys are not functioning well after spending too much time
outside fighting in the cold winter of 1994–95. He relaxes for a while,
then starts pacing around the room like a caged animal; fortunately
Genghis comes to relieve him and take over the night watch. He brings
with him an old cinema chair with a flip-up seat, its brown velvet covering faded and worn. I wonder from whence it came and how many
hundreds of people had sat on it watching all those flickering films, a
whole spectrum of emotions running through their minds. He sits on
the old seat, stretching out his legs, looking tired. 'We lost three men in
an exercise last night,' he tells us but doesn't elaborate on what kind of
'exercise' it was.

My birthday is approaching. We mention it to Genghis and he asks
if we want any vodka. No thanks! The day arrives, 31 January 1998, my
40th birthday. They leave us on our own for stretches of time; we've been
here a week and they trust us not to flee. What a relief to be on our own!
We can do some tai chi and yoga and play backgammon together. Most
days we spend time sitting crosslegged on our beds in deep contemplation and prayer, which they find extraordinary. It is the end of Ramadan

and some of the guards have gone home to their families to celebrate. Young Isa returns and presents me with an orange for my birthday – he remembered! I feel honoured. The colour alone is enough to inspire and uplift my spirits; it seems to radiate energy, fed with sunlight and rain water. We watch it glowing on the table before beginning to peel it slowly, ceremonially. I smell the oily juices of the peel on my fingers. The orange aroma gets stronger and stronger, I peel the white pith away from the flesh of the fruit, and reveal its round segmented form. I offer some to our captors but they decline, so I split it, half for Jon, half for myself. Biting into the juicy flesh, savouring every euphoric moment. Then I carefully store the peel in the pocket of my pink jacket. What a birthday present.

1 February. Oh no! They tell us we are going to move again tonight, just a move, not freedom. I feel the fear pit in my stomach growing. We have a special meal, a bowl of sweet rice mixed with raisins and bits of dried fruit followed by a plate of biscuits, a treat to mark the end of Ramadan. Neither of us has much appetite, the impending move lying heavy in our bellies – a new place, new guards to adjust to.

Late in the evening Genghis comes in with Round Boy and another man with a huge scar running from his left eye back to the top of his ear. They are dressed in black, carrying guns, very relaxed and chirpy. Genghis looks at his watch: time to go. On the road again, off to a new holding place. After a few miles Genghis removes my mask and gestures that I remove Camilla's. They don't care what we see. Maybe they understand us better than our previous guards, understand why we are here and are just doing what they feel they have to do, duty bound to look after us. The Jeep smells new and expensive. There's a clock in the ceiling for the passengers, and air conditioning. It's 3.15 a.m. I get mesmerized by all the fluorescent green dials on the dashboard, which are like Christmas lights to my information-starved eyes. Round Boy is driving and operates the music, making jokes we don't understand and we bounce along to loud Russian rock. There's another man crouched behind us in the luggage compartment chewing gum. It seems like being on some kind of festive nocturnal outing. The night is frosty and the dirt road sparkles. We pass a mud-splattered white van with no back lights weaving across the road and a number of ancient Ladas going about their nefarious business.

The Jeep dips downward beneath a wide bridge; this is the underpass where Hippolada had become 'Lada Brilliant' having managed to float through a flood, the engine still revving. So we know we are heading west towards Ingushetia and away from Grozny. As we reach the outskirts Genghis tells us to put the masks back on. We remain on the main road for some time and then turn off left into the hills. After a short time we arrive at another secret destination. The Jeep rolls quietly through a village – I can see the flicker of streetlights through my mask – and we brake. Silence. One of them gets out to see if the coast is clear. When they are satisfied they guide us out and through two doors, our shoes creaking on the powdery snow.

Jon's wall decoration

12

The Sauna

We are standing in a room with an empty concrete plunge pool, a wide wooden bench and an empty metal water tank. There is a large drain in the concrete floor covered by a wooden slatted pallet. They point to a door next to the tank and we enter the sauna. It has two wooden levels, the top one the width of a single bed and the lower one half the size with the earth floor below. A stove fed from outside has four bricks taken out at intervals to let heat into the room. Round Boy comes in to inspect and immediately sets off to find a piece of wood to cover a small window. They don't seem to worry about the sound of hammering waking the neighbourhood. As he hammers, he gestures to the stove and says, 'You will have a warm night.' But they don't light it and we are cold. We are given a red quilt just big enough to have under and over us, our combined body heat keeping us warm, except for toes and noses. We have the old problem: where is the lavatory? We are getting wiser and ask before they lock us in. They obviously haven't thought about it, and have a discussion with the answer being we can use the drain and they will bring a bucket and a plastic bag. The bucket and plastic bag don't last a day. They don't know where to dispose the bag without arousing suspicion and decide they will have to take us out in the middle of the night to relieve ourselves. The one with the scar lies down on the bench next door; we hear him sneezing and coughing during the night. An old woman wakes us up shouting 'Isa, Isa' in a cracked ancient voice and she knocks on the outer door. Our guard grumbles and stomps out. We guess it's his grandmother calling him and we are guests of his family. After that we nickname him 'Young Farmer'. He reminds me of an old farming friend with his weathered cheeks, blue eyes and thick corn-coloured hair, not very Chechen in appearance but extremely Chechen in nature and culture.

Young Farmer re-appears and unties our door, rolling away a tree stump that they use to wedge our door shut, and indicates that we can use the drain. He disappears into the ante-room that later on we discover is a washroom with lots of enamel bowls and home for a brand new shiny red generator. We return to our new bedroom and sit on the top ledge surveying the surroundings and listening to the sounds outside. We hear cows mooing in a nearby shed, someone hammering and sawing, a woman shouting instructions, and an elderly male voice answering. Our stomachs are beginning to rumble. Are we going to be fed today? Footsteps, a clink of china and doors squeaking – sounds promising. Genghis pokes his head around the door. 'Dobri oodra, kak di la? (Good morning, how are you?)' 'Harasho (Good),' we reply. He wedges the door open and presents us with a tray laden with a vast array of culinary delights. Our eyes are on stalks, jaws hanging in amazement, it looks too good to eat. There's a plate of fried potatoes surrounded by pieces of mutton on the bone, two half-moon pieces of homemade sourdough bread, a lump of butter on a saucer, two cut glass pedestal bowls, one containing a handful of sweets and the other, crystallized pieces of plum in syrup. It's the latter that really makes me gawp. This was a Christmas delicacy when I was a child and during one of our storytelling times I had given Jon a detailed description of the Christmas feast my grandmother would prepare for all the family, including the joy of eating crystallized fruit. This is a lovely late birthday present!

We're left alone, listening to children playing, occasionally peeking at the outside world through small holes in the boards covering the window. We can move them a little which gives us a bit more light but it's too risky to pull them far enough to increase our view. There is a light bulb in a glass shade and because of the generator we are only ever in darkness for a short time when there are power cuts. More food! This time it's macaroni in milk. Daylight is fading and the temperature is dropping in our new home. We mention to Genghis that we are getting cold again. He goes out of the building and we hear the 'thud, thud' of wood being loaded into the stove, then the roar of flames as the fire takes hold and quite quickly our room gets warmer . . . and warmer . . . and warmer . . . From one extreme to the other!

Camilla has retreated to the floor, crouching by the door in an attempt to get some cool air to breathe, and I lie down on the lower shelf. Oh no!

Someone is still loading wood so I grab all the bits of material I can find, including our brand new towels, and stuff the holes, but this only slows down the increase in temperature. We hear someone coming back into the outer room so we knock on the door. Genghis comes in, realizes what the problem is and lets us go into the outer room which is comparatively cool and we jokingly ask him if he was trying to roast us alive. He laughs, saying 'No, no, it was a mistake.'

Even the plunge pool chamber is now getting hot. I don't believe it, more wood is being shovelled in! Someone is trying to open the outer door that they have locked from the inside. We hear a young woman's voice calling. Our captors don't respond. Perhaps this is a communal sauna used by different families from the same clan and only a few know about us. Later Genghis tells us that not even the woman who cooks our food knows who she is cooking for. Genghis and another man, possibly the one sitting behind us in the Jeep, are sitting on the bench and Jon and I are on two mini wooden stools near our door. But we migrate nearer the plunge pool, as far away as we can from the source of heat. We are all dripping and sitting in wilting heaps. Thank goodness it's cold outside and draughts are sucked under the doors keeping our feet and ankles cool and preventing our blood from boiling. The silent fighter gets up and ambles out; he's had enough, his shaved head glistens, rivulets of sweat running through his thick black eyebrows. It can't help that he's still in combat gear. We later hear him being called 'Idris', so 'Ginger Beer' becomes his nickname. He's the silent one, barely exchanging a word with us. His dark blue eyes are quite piercing and show no feeling. I sense that he could probably pull a trigger without a thought, bypassing all his emotions in the cause of duty, the perfect soldier.

Eventually the heat begins to subside and Genghis asks us to go back into the sauna. We protest that it is still far too hot for the door to be left shut, and he grudgingly leaves it open a few inches. The heat only becomes tolerable as dawn approaches and the turkeys start gobble-gossiping in their high trilly voices just the other side of the walls. I love these turkeys – it's such a pleasure having them as our early morning wake-up call. It helps me feel part of the farmyard, expanding my consciousness beyond the wooden walls of our prison.

This morning there is rice pudding, tea and biscuits for breakfast. When we ask, they also bring a bottle of ice-cold spring water, just the tonic for our dehydrated aching heads. The change in the quality and quantity of our food, although welcome, is challenging my digestive system and by mid afternoon I am in extreme pain so I ask if I can go to the loo and am met with amazement and a definite 'Niet!' Later as the hours roll by, I ask again. 'Not possible.' I am now bent over double with the pain of holding, my body temperature's going up and down like a yo-yo. Finally the guards notice my extreme distress, Idris goes out to see if the coast is clear, it's just getting dark and they swiftly organize a military-style manoeuvre to the dunny by the cowshed. On my way there I manage to get a fairly good view of our compound – the sauna building is attached to the house and next to several outbuildings, including the cowshed. After the months of closed air in closed environments the whiff of cow shit is a pleasurable experience.

We are to have a visit from the commander. Our captors are as excited as we are, all of us hoping for news about our release. The tread of many heavy boots approach and our door is opened, the commander stooping a little to peer in at us. 'Kak di la?' 'Harasho,' we reply.

'Couchette ochi harasho, spaseba (the food is especially good, thank you).'

'I have a satellite phone and I will be calling London at midnight, to-night. Very soon you will be free.' He smiles at us benignly. Perhaps that's why they have brought us out of Grozny nearer the border to Ingushetia. The fluttering wings of freedom beat softly in our hearts – he is the com-mander, so this must be the truth.

Later that night we are led outside, one at a time. No masks but heads lowered carrying a plastic bottle of water. We turn right out of the sauna building to wait silently in the shadows while Genghis checks that no one is around. The snow has melted but the air is freezing and there are icy patches on the path. I glance up and see a half moon above an open field with a large building in the distance. To the left is the cowshed and beyond a high wall bordering the property with a metal gate above which I can see an orange street-light. We are told to go around the side of the building past the scorched brick opening of the sauna oven to a space just in front of a wire fence where we can squat. As I walk out of his sight I glance up again and see fields beyond the wire sloping downwards and a series of smaller rounded hills rising up. In between their sloping sides, in the distance, car headlights are moving along a straight road. Could this be the road to Sernovodsk and the Ingush border? I like to think so.

I take long gasps of breath; the air is chill and vibrant, nourishing my being with its vitality. Just a few precious moments and then it's time to go back into the still, musty air of the sauna.

Red letter day! It comes in the form of an excited 'Ginger Beer' bursting into our reverie, and making an announcement, roughly translated as 'I have seen your parents with a big birthday cake for you' – he points at me – 'and many people singing, and your sister, very beautiful, very beautiful, blond with blue eyes, asking Russia to help in your release. It was on the news.' A flurry of emotions run through my body: joy, grief, resignation. Joy at hearing about our families, sadness at our separation and resignation as my sister's words don't bode well for a quick release. I ask if he saw any children but he doesn't remember. He turns to Genghis and talks in Chechen; Genghis tells us they are going to try and bring the television so we can see the next news broadcast. And sure enough they bring in a mini television and set it up in the sauna. We watch the nine o'clock news avidly. As each item finishes we listen intently for the content of the next one, our hopes beginning to fade. The powers that be have decided it is not important enough to show again. I imagine the scene, a huge cake with many candles surrounded by our beloved families singing 'Happy Birthday'. I send love and gratitude to them from my heart, love to give them strength to cope and to know that we are still on this planet and surviving well and thanks for all the efforts they are making to help our release come swiftly. I think of Ashok and the tears trickle silently out of my eyes.

Wow, our folks are working really hard to get our situation publicized. It's even made Russian TV. It's good to know they are alive. I feel a twinge of emotion but I've been suppressing the sadness for so long now, numbing myself in order to survive without going mad, that I cannot respond with any great joy, or with any feeling at all. I am running on automatic pilot. They don't take the television away but move it into the plunge-pool room, balancing it on the tree stump, using a piece of wire as an antenna to improve the quality of the picture. This provides entertainment for us and them – a good thing, as they are getting bored.

The first programme we watch together, sitting rather stiffly side by side on the bench, is an old black-and-white 1950s Russian film. Although we understand very little of the language it is a fascinating film to watch. There are scenes of the vast wheat-growing steppes and cameos

169

of life in an agricultural collective. It has a surrealist touch to the ending with a large combine harvester driven by a farmer, his girlfriend by his side, headscarved and dark-lipped, towing a trailer with an old woman dressed in black bouncing up and down singing to herself. The machine stops and they get out to look at a screen set up in the field playing back the last scene of them on the combine harvester.

We haven't seen Young Farmer since our arrival and Genghis tells us that he has flu, most likely helped by that freezing night he spent in the plunge-pool room. To avoid that happening again they have found a massive suede coat lined with thick grey wool from a long-haired sheep or goat; they lie on it or pull it round themselves. I imagine the coat being used by a shepherd for warmth during the cold nights high on the hills, surrounded by his flock. Ginger Beer takes many breaks for trips to the bazaar to buy Marlboro cigarettes. Even though he's not captive he feels like he is. After a week he disappears and we don't see him again. Only Genghis wants to be our friend and stays to chat, asking about our life and gradually revealing more of his own. He was studying dentistry before the war. Now we know why he was interested in the price of a filling! He also did a lot of sport, particularly football and weight training; he still looks very fit. He is sad and angry that he cannot follow his ambition and sees no other route except to fight for liberty. He has a girlfriend in Grozny whom he saw for the first time on a bus and wanted to say something to her but was too shy – she was another student at his college. Then a year later he met her again ('fate' he says) and they plan to marry. He shows us a gold chain and a cotton friendship bracelet that she has given him. Now she looks after her parents, having given up her ambition to be a dentist's receptionist, and he thinks she'll make a good wife. He definitely doesn't want a career woman.

Genghis is the only one who directs his converstion to both of us; all the others speak only to me. He asks us to describe who we were with before: 'were you beaten?' Camilla decides to trust him and starts telling Genghis how we were treated by the fab four. I'm not sure if it is wise.

I tell him about the interrogations and how we were kept but not about the rape. 'Please don't tell anyone; they said if we speak we will be shot.' It felt wonderful to speak to someone about those hideous seven months, to let it all gush out. He replied 'I didn't take you, I wasn't part of that group and I don't think it is really a good thing but I am part of this big group and now we have to look after you, the commander thinks it is dirty money.'

Genghis starts to make the plunge-pool room more comfortable. There's a large window at one end covered with a piece of wood, which he removes and replaces with newspaper. The wood is used for the base of a bed covered by a thin mattress, some quilts and a pillow from the house. He presents us with a new pack of cards and teaches us how to play the game 'Fool'. He is patient, not getting angry when we are slow to pick up the rules. It's a good game because there is always the element of chance as well as strategy. This new diversion is very welcome in a week that has been long and thick with expectation. In the sauna there is no room to exercise, except a few stretches on our bed. We use a Sufi breathing practice to clear our minds, meditate and pray for help and guidance. Often we feel waves of love and know we are not forgotten or alone, although sometimes despair descends like a Dartmoor mist, especially when I discover I have a lump the size of a large marble under my right armpit. My immediate thought is cancer in my lymph glands and I think about my father, who died from a malignant melanoma. The infection in my left middle finger is nearly healed but the lump could be related. I lie back in the sauna staring up at the ceiling, tears trickling out of the sides of my eyes. Will I never see my family again, or is it my fate to die here? I take some deep breaths to calm myself and focus on my armpit, breathing in golden healing light. Jon comforts me but I know it is my battle to fight. We tell Genghis about the lump and let him feel it, hoping it might quicken our release.

Towards the end of the first week, when our captors disappear to eat they allow us the run of the sauna and plunge-pool room. I manage to do some tai chi on the wooden pallets. My pointed, dark blue, fake leather shoes wobble in the gaps between the slats. Better barefoot, but the air is icy at ankle level. It feels so good to move. We peep through the cracks in the door and see the washbowls and generator. Sometimes they leave the outer door open and we catch glimpses of a small plump woman with a bowed back, wrapped up in woollen jumpers over a long dress with winter boots and a headscarf tied tightly around her wizened face. Perhaps this is our wonderful cook? Quite often an elderly man passes, small and bent with a pickled walnut face, carrying wood or a bowl of meat scraps that he leaves in the washroom for the cat. When it is sunny we gaze out, drawing the reflected light off the snow into our eyes, an unusual form of sunbathing. We hear the old woman calling the man in a sharp, commanding voice, 'Vitri, Vitri!'

Our days of being boiled are not over. We ask for heat when we become numb with cold and the fire stoker gets to work. Unfortunately he doesn't know when to stop. We're just warming up nicely when another load of wood goes on. Genghis then leaps outside to take off a log or two before they get too hot to handle. We hear him calling Vitri and talking softly to him. So he's our stokerman. The word must have got around that the sauna is out of bounds because we don't have any more visitors calling at the door.

Sitting in the sauna one day I remember the orange peel in my pocket. Tearing the peel into spirals, we pierce holes in the skin with the safety pin and tie them with cotton onto ragged lumpy cement in between the bricks on the chimney. Little twirling mobiles, fun to watch, although they get very brown and brittle in the heat.

Normally they go out every morning so we can have a quick splash in cold water and use the drain. After a few days we ask if we can have a full body wash and shampoo our hair and they bring a vast enamel bowl full of hot water. We have great fun soaping up and showering each other. The sensation of feeling well scrubbed invigorates us out of our captive stupor. How wonderful it is to feel volumes of water flowing over my body, washing away not only the grime but emotions as well. What a magical element water is – so healing, so earthing, clearing the mind, washing away stress.

We usually have two meals a day. One is a bowl of 'kasha' (semolina) with a dob of butter in the middle or rice pudding or macaroni in milk. The other is a large meal with meat (chicken, steak or mutton) or fish along with rice, potatoes or pasta twirls. Occasionally we have little apples that have been stored from the autumn. One morning we are presented with a slice of vegetable cake. This is gourmet food; I cannot believe my eyes, perhaps it is someone's birthday. The cake is made up of layers of grated carrot, beetroot, cabbage and flaked egg mixed with mayonnaise. I've never eaten anything like it before. Sometimes we have a Russian national dish of boiled pastry parcels (they look like ravioli) with white salty cheese inside or mashed potato steeped in butter and garlic. Once there was a big plate with leaf-shaped dumplings and slices of kidney arranged around a small bowl in the middle containing garlic butter. We have a different meal every day for ten consecutive days without repetition, an enormous change from our diet of the last seven months. We eat in solemn, sacred silence focusing on each nourishing mouthful. There is a full-length mirror in the plunge-pool room and we notice our scrawny forms filling out. The down side is constipation and training our bowels to work at 3 a.m. One night Genghis is in a particularly good mood and takes me around the side of the cattle shed and allows me to look up and gaze at the Great Bear, Orion's Belt, the Pleiaides, the vivid glowing moon. I store this sparkling picture of the heavens to give me solace in days to come.

Our nightime toilet visits don't work for me. My body won't readjust to this imposed timetable and I become constipated, which is uncomfortable and frustrating, but the nightly dose of fresh air and views of the stars and moon are very welcome. After some time our guards don't wake us any more, we have to wake them. One of us has to stay awake until it's time and we massage our bellies to activate our digestive systems. Then we are led out by a grumpy Genghis or Ginger Beer through a gate into a field with a large house at the other end. On these nightly visits we trudge gladly through deep white snow, enjoying the space. Sometimes I make a snowball and take it back with me into the sauna; it makes a good ice pack for my hot head. I get a lot of headaches here, a toxic build up from the lack of movement and the constipation.

Our gourmet cook is having trouble with her new microwave. Genghis seems to think that I'm 'Mr Fix-It' after I'd helped him wire up the antenna for the TV. He brings me the owner's manual to see if I have any good ideas. I make a few suggestions but he says they have tried them already, I say that they had better take it back from where they bought it. He tells me that isn't possible because it came from Moscow.

Genghis has unwittingly provided us with new spy holes by taking the wooden board away and covering the large window in the plunge-pool room with newspaper. It has tiny drawing-pin holes and when you put your eye up close a whole vista of the outside world appears before you. There is the wooden gate that we go through on our nightly sojourns, a small red-brick hut to the right, next to the wire fence, a pile of roof tiles leaning against its walls and the snowy field beyond. In the distance is the enormous red-brick house, the porticos and garages alongside it still half built. In front are an open-backed lorry and a couple of cars. The snow falls heavily in the second week and as soon as Genghis goes out to eat I dash to the window to watch the snowflakes dancing their way to earth. We take turns to feast our eyes and lose ourselves in the beauty of the dance.

In the third week the snow begins to melt and they let some cattle roam in the field. They are scrawny beasts, their red-brown skin stretched over their withered hocks. Sometimes we are fêted by human figures entering our moving painting. One bright sunny day an old woman walks into the field followed by two small children, two wrapped bundles skipping and jumping along the well-trodden path leading to the mansion. An old man wearing his tall grey-wool Chechen hat comes out of the large house to greet them. Occasionally we hear their high shrill voices through the plunge-pool wall.

Genghis comes in one day and tells us that he is going back to Grozny for a couple of days – 'I need a change of clothes and to see my family and girl-friend.' He asks me to trim his hair. I agree and offer to do his beard as well but he prefers to do that himself. He talks about his acne'd back and asks for advice, saying that before the war he had no problem and how during the war he had little or no food and much stress and now skin problems. I suggest he keeps off the fried food and eats fresh fruit and vegetables as much as possible. He considers these options. In another unexpected act of friendship he brings a tape and disc player with some CDs by Queen. Listening to the music is a welcome distraction and colours our environment. We have music, we have cards and we are no longer locked in the sauna room except at night, unless it is too hot.

The rousing strains of Bohemian Rhapsody *are interrupted by Round Boy, who has come to look after us while Genghis is away. He spends most of the first day resting on the bed. 'Night exercises,' he says, as an explanation for his weariness. He is a large chappie and seems to fill the room with his boyish energy. Soon he becomes restless and leaves us alone. We hear gunshots nearby. In the time I have been in Chechnya I've learnt to recognize the sound of different sized weapons and this one sounds quite hefty. We hear the angry shouts of a woman and the mooing of the cows – I guess she's telling him off for scaring the animals. He comes back in and shows us a tin mug with two holes in one side and one in the other. With a big smile he says 'Not bad at 50 yards, three bullets, two holes into one.' Then he naively hands me the pistol he was using – it's a Smith & Wesson 45. I've never handled a gun before and am surprised by its weight. I hand it back to Round*

Boy and he puts it back in his holster. He's glad when Genghis gets back and quickly dismisses himself from this boring job. Genghis becomes so relaxed he leaves the ammunition for his automatic rifle under his bedclothes when he goes out to eat. Of course I am curious about the suspicious-looking lump and have a look.

The Winter Olympics have started in Japan. The opening ceremony brings tears to my eyes with the thousand-voice choir singing around the globe connected by satellite. All those bobble-hatted faces with pink cheeks and angelic O-shaped mouths. Genghis is bored by the skiing and ice skating but allows us to watch when he is not around. We manage to see many ice hockey matches, something I have never really watched before but I'm feeling nostalgic as my father used to play for the Royal Air Force. The Dutch are coming out top in the speed ice skating and as my son is half Dutch it provides another link home. It's not really a very interesting sport to watch; I get mesmerized by the shape of their thighs, ballooning out with massive muscle power resembling frogs' legs with skates on.

17 February

Ashok's birthday. He is 12 years old. We light an imaginary candle for him and sing Happy Birthday softly. I make up a prayer wheel in my mind, drawn in beautiful, gold calligraphic lettering, and send it to him on the ether. My beautiful son. I think of him with enormous love and great sadness.

Young Farmer comes in to talk to Genghis. You can feel the air of intimacy between them, close comrades. Genghis turns to us and says, 'You are moving tonight, it's too dangerous here, too many spies.' Again that cavernous feeling in the belly. Once more journeying into the unknown.

13

One-Night Stand

No Jeep this time but a humble Lada, masked heads on knees. Genghis makes us a gift of the playing cards. After ten minutes or so on the bumpy lane we reach the highway and turn right. I get a sinking feeling: maybe we are going back to Grozny. After about an hour we change to another car. 'Johnny, Johnny, how are you?' delivered in a sinister tone. I recognize that voice. I sink lower, it's GA. Another voice says something in Chechen – it's Batman. Then silence. Eventually the car stops and we are helped up some steps into a building.

Someone taps heavily on my shoe and I crouch down thinking there is a trapdoor to go through. 'Niet, niet, tufli (No, no, shoes).' The voice of Paunch. Someone starts taking my shoe off a bit roughly so I complete the task quickly. We are led down a passage and into a room. Masks off, the room is empty apart from one mattress with a pillow and blanket and a bag of plaster in one corner. The floorboards are rough, warped and bare, rotting into holes and powdered with plaster. A large window is covered with thick opaque plastic. There is no door, just a moth-eaten velveteen coverlet nailed up in the doorway.

GA and Puppydog come into the room with us. Oh shit – I didn't think I was going to see these guys again. Is this a step backwards? 'Kak di la?' enquires GA. Thankfully he has given up his Jack Nicholson impersonation and this is said with sincerity.

We tell them about the sauna and the wonderful food. 'Sanitori!' GA laughs. There are many sanatoriums in the Caucasus where the Russians spend a few days rebuilding their health and having a holiday. They usually have doctor who suggests various therapies such as body massage, hydro massage and herbal teas. Sometimes, as in Sernovodsk, they use local hot sulphur springs. Puppydog and GA seem genuinely pleased to see us, grinning away at our stories of life in the sauna, the heat, tele-vision, music and my birthday party. I was worried that they might have heard about me blabbing to Genghis about our earlier time with them but I can tell they know nothing of our sauna 'friends'. Time for sleep. I ask for a bucket and Puppydog brings a faded red plastic one with a white lid, looking very like the one we used in the Kiva, and a plastic jug of water and soap. What relief – at least now we can relieve ourselves with-out having to train our bowels to work at a set time. The blanket is not smelly and the pillow has a clean white pillowcase. I'm buoying myself up, looking for the positives.

Morning comes and we wake at dawn hearing the Muslim call to prayer and cocks crowing, light diffusing through the plastic. I look around and find it hard not to cry; my view is coloured by my hor-mones doing their premenstrual thing! All night there was coughing and sneezing coming from the other side of the curtain. I can see a blue rheumy eye studying us through a hole in the curtain and Paunch pokes his head around the side. He is unshaven and deep black rings surround his eyes. He looks very rough and his paunch has shrunk. 'Chai?' he asks in a gruff voice. 'Da, pajalsta,' we reply. Eventually he returns with a plastic bottle full of hot sweet tea and two chipped mugs. The plastic is beginning to contort with the heat so we pour it out as hastily as pos-sible. This is the last we see of Paunch. Maybe apart from feeling ill, he also feels some guilt and shame. When he gives us the tea he avoids our eyes. I send love through the curtain, I feel compassion for him and also a touch of 'just deserts'.

The day drags on. We play a few games of cards but I cannot concen-trate, for my heart is full of grief. I lie on the mattress gazing into space, aware that the lump under my armpit is still there even though its size has diminished. I try to pour healing into it but haven't got the energy, just tears and more tears. Jon comforts me but cannot quell the grey despair that engulfs my being. Our room gets lighter, the sun is shining out there with the bird song and there is the occasional screech of a bus braking for the potholes. Out of the depths comes a shining angel in the form of Puppydog bearing gifts: hot boiled eggs wrapped in newspaper, a pile of 'Chechen doughnuts', a twist of salt and a small bowl of sugar, followed by more tea and a smile.

There have been many times in these places of isolation when I have started sliding down the slippery slope of depression and Camilla says, 'Are you OK? Is it OK for me to talk?' And I brush my depression to one side to hear Camilla's. In talking Camilla through her dark places I assist myself on a journey through my own, coming to understand that my thoughts and emotions exist in a quiet ocean, a quiet space of calm, of no thought. I quell the storms; I do not wish to be too happy, I do not wish to be too sad. I enter the place of mediocrity, the middle way, boring. Surviving in a monotone land.

The daylight begins to fade and Puppydog brings a candle stuck in a bottle. GA arrives and they both come in and play 'Fool' with us. They are mightily impressed by our newly acquired skill in playing the game. 'Good teacher,' we say. 'What was his name' Puppydog asks and we tell them 'Genghis Khan' – even though we know his true name was Ruslan, we don't want to be accused of being 'spies' again. GA informs us, with some mime, that HC started losing his mind and had to go and see a psychiatrist. This is no surprise; I feel compassion for him and the difficult road he has chosen in life, and hope he finds a way to release his traumas and find some solace.

There's knocking at the door and they quietly go out. We hear a conversation in whispered Chechen and the front door closing. GA and Puppydog reappear to inform us that we are leaving tonight; maybe freedom, maybe not, they don't know. Puppydog goes out and brings back a broom. 'Sweep yourselves out, it's good luck.' We tell him there's a similar superstition in England and he smiles.

I try not to hope too much that this journey will lead to freedom – too many times the word 'freedom' has been preceded by disappointment, and I do not want to sink into despair so I try letting go of any expectations and stay in a state of acceptance whilst still praying for release.

We say our goodbyes, hands are shaken and I give them both a Chechen side-on hug that they find amusing. I hope it really is goodbye this time. Masks on and heads down, we are driven out of Grozny in the back of yet another Lada. Out on a straight highway, half an hour later we pull over and wait. Another car purrs to a halt and we are transferred across. New unknown voices in a car with dying shock absorbers.

There is a man sitting next to me who keeps pressing my neck down. Feeling sick I ease my mask up so I can breathe and begin chanting a healing mantra in my mind to calm myself: 'Ra, Ma, Da, Sa, Sa, Se, So,

Hung' (roughly translated as 'May the divine powers of the sun, moon, earth and stars heal me and keep me safe and in trust and in remembrance of who I am').

14

The Farm

We turn off the highway to the right this time and skid through potholes and over icy lumps of compacted snow, eventually coming to a stop. Out we get and I have one man on each side guiding me through a muddy snow-slush field urgently whispering 'Boostra, Boostra! (Quick, quick)!' But my shoes keep sticking in the mud until one is left behind. ' Stuck!' I tell them, trying desperately to point down at my feet and finally they realize the problem and pick the shoe out of the mud and hoist me under my armpits for the last few feet until we reach a building. It has a wooden floor and a slight echo so I imagine a high roof. Quite a big room to cross, then we are pulled to an abrupt halt. Someone presses gently on my shoulders; this time the message is to squat and he takes my hand to feel a metal rim that I have to climb over still in a squat. Are we going underground again, I wonder with trepidation. No, my guide follows me and pulls me upright and Jon follows. Masks off and we have the first glimpse of our new home.

The man standing next to us is smaller than Jon, wearing a full mask with beady brown eyes shining out of two holes. He gestures around the room pointing out a proper lavatory hole with brick steps to place our feet. This is just opposite the 'Alice in Wonderland' door we have crept through. The door has been cut out of an aluminium corrugated roofing sheet which is now a wall separating us from the rest of the room. The other walls are made of mud, straw and manure. The width of the building is barely four metres and the distance between the metal wall and the back wall, two metres. There is a large single iron bedstead made up with sheets, pillows and a duvet, with two small towels draped over the end. By the loo is a plastic tub of soap and a jug full of water. Opposite the bed is a small white wooden table, a child-size plywood chair, a gas tripod (looking rather homemade with its knobbly welded joints), a galvanized bucket and a kettle. On the table are plates, cups and cutlery, a small bowl of salt, a bowl of sugar, a packet of tea and a box of matches. Underneath the table are two marbled-blue plastic buckets full of water that match our soap from The Base and a washing up bowl. This man has thought of everything and my heart warms to him.

'Ruskie?' he asks. 'Niet, Angliski' we answer. 'Couchette?' he asks. 'Niet Spaseba,' we reply. Then he explains slowly in Russian that we will be given food for the next day every midnight and goes off to collect some. He returns with a large casserole dish of thin vegetable soup with meat balls floating in it and two rounds of home-made soda bread and, most delicious of all, a litre tin mug of fresh cow's milk. I am looking forward to the morning and a nice steaming hot cup of milky tea. We have one light bulb above the bed and, after 'Farmer' has gone with a friendly 'Spakone Noche' Jon climbs on the bed with a towel and unscrews the bulb. We curl under the covers and roll together in a big dip in the middle. Oh no, not one of those back-breaking beds again!

Woken by joyous birdsong, we have natural light seeping over the top of the metal wall. Jon puts the kettle on to boil and I await the delight of a nice hot cup of tea! But first I have a mouthful of milk, sweet and creamy. We survey our new home. Locked in, without guards, we can talk in normal voices for the first time in eight months.

A tractor is going about its noisy business outside, so there's no chance of us being overheard. There are a few screw holes in the metal wall that we can see through. We are in a large farm shed with a wooden floor. The room is empty except for a camp bed with a sheepskin covering that 'Farmer' slept on last night, and a pile of yellowing pumpkins in a corner. There are three windows. Through the nearest one we can see an area of muddy ground and a concrete building with a metal roof; through the next, part of a tree and some sky. The angle is too great to be able to see out of the third, only reflected light on the back wall. Perhaps we should call this our holiday home! We can wash, eat and go to the loo whenever we like; sing, dance and meditate to our hearts' content.

But I still have thoughts of escape. Mentally I scale the metal wall thinking 'Could Camilla climb this?' I could squeeze over, but the drop is long and there would be no return. Then what? The building is locked but maybe I could climb through a window. I look up at our ceiling. There is a thin layer of adobe, then a space before a metal roof. We can see daylight shining through holes in the adobe but where is the light coming from? It could be seeping in through tiny cracks nowhere near big enough for us to crawl through. But what's beyond? How visible would I be? They have a dog or two who might bark before we manage to give them some meat scraps and there might be a wall or high fence to climb over before we could leave the farm compound. We hear speeding traffic in the near distance so we know there is a major road nearby which would be a big advantage if we could reach it and hitch a lift. We hope that it's the main road west of Grozny heading in the direction of Sernovodsk but this is all conjecture.

Washing is one of our favourite daily rituals, boiling water in the galvan-ized bucket and scrubbing our clothes and ourselves with our blue-marbled, highly scented soap. We have to wash our clothes three days in a row before the water stays milky rather than turning dark grey. I make a washing line by tying together Camilla's sanitary strips of sheet and hanging them from nails in the wall near the gas tripod. We can only dry one bit of clothing at a time. Camilla takes charge of turning the clothes over like meat on a spit till every part is dry. The floor is pretty grubby and I decide it needs a good scrub, especially if I am going to be walking on it barefoot. On his next mid-night visit I ask Farmer for some rags and a dustpan and brush, miming my intention to clean the floor. He goes away and returns with them immedi-ately. I get stuck in right away and manage to complete three quarters of it before I run out of steam. Camilla completes the job. It is so satisfying to see the clean pale beige boards emerging from beneath the grime.

When Farmer pokes his head through our door he seems rather sur-prised and pleased by our efforts. I decide it is safe to ask another favour: 'menstruatie material and material for making underpants pajalsta' – the last request done with mime as I don't know the words. We have heard his wife in the background helping him carry food and water so I know she knows we exist and there is a greater chance he will let her provide me with my needs. The next night I am presented with a large sheet of new white muslin cloth, two large pieces of stretchy cotton material, a reel of yellow cotton thread with a needle, a pair of scissors and two safety pins. I am beaming!

I lay out the material on the bed and have a discussion with Jon about how to design the pants. Sewing is not my métier and Jon is quite a dab hand at designing and sewing so he gives me some good tips. I use thin sheet strips to make ties on each side so they can be tightened or loosened as required. The finished product wouldn't win a design competition, but they are the best pair of pants I've ever had. If my mother could see me now she would be grinning from ear to ear. My period arrives and I put my new 'hostage designer' pants to the test. Perfect.

25 February

My son Ben's 18th birthday. I was hoping to be out by this time to celebrate it with him. I feel emotion stirring deep inside. How much I love him, how much I miss his company! All the adventures we have been on, camping in Wales and on the wild and wet isles of Scotland, canoeing down the river Wye.

I remember the extraordinary meeting between Ben and his Mum after 13 years of being apart. I was not feeling too good after going through a relationship breakdown and felt it would be a good idea for Ben to have contact with his Mum and have her support as well. I discovered that Debbie and Chris, her husband, had moved from Norfolk to Cheltenham so Ben and Debbie started exchanging letters. In the spring of 1995 Ben's drama club won a competition and performed at the Everyman Theatre in Cheltenham. Ben had the lead role in The Dark Tower. *I thought this would be a good opportunity for them to meet, so there we were, face to face; the atmosphere was truly magic. We all felt we were old friends coming together again after travelling our different ways through time and space. I certainly felt there was a massive healing process going on, lots of joy and not too much grieving. He will now be in his final year at college doing his 'A's, and I won't be there. I am saddened, I hope my captivity hasn't clouded his world too much. All we can do is send our love and hope he manages to enjoy himself despite our absence. We light an imaginary candle and sing Happy Birthday to him.*

We have taken to sleeping top to tail, which is slightly more comfortable than side by side. We contemplate sleeping on the floor but there isn't enough space. Camilla's right leg is beginning to go numb again. I ask Farmer for some board to put under the mattress. After a complex and extensive mime in which I describe my intention, Farmer disappears and returns with five long planks and three short ones. He must know the measurements of the bed because they fit exactly. I lay the timber on top of the metal frame and then with tremendous trust he hands me the hammer, handle first, and a

fistful of nails. I ask if it's OK for me to make some noise and he gestures
that it's no problem. So, at about 1 a.m., I'm hammering nails to secure the
wood together. This simple physical act gives me great joy. In a few minutes
the job's done and we have a new bed base. Voilà!

I don't think Farmer's wife takes such joy in cooking as the woman in
the sauna and also the ingredients are of a lower quality, which probably
means they are not such a wealthy family. Her soda bread is very salty. I
make it more palatable by slicing it in two and covering the insides with
a layer of Rama margarine and sugar and steaming them in an empty
Rama carton floating in boiling water – my version of 'Shrewsbury butter buns'. Nearly every day we are given meat, either lumps of mutton on
the bone in soup or gristly rissoles, 'grissoles' we call them. Farmer brings
us a plastic bag full of eggs for us to cook ourselves. What a luxury to
have a soft-boiled egg. He also presents us with a packet of 'mechanically
separated' chicken sausages made in Canada. I think this was meant as a
treat. The idea that anyone would think of creating such 'food' makes us
laugh and feel sad at the same time. We only try them once: apart from
the whole idea being quite horrendous, a few bites give you indigestion
for the whole day. Another treat is 'cardboard cake'. It appears in the
form of a swiss roll with an unidentifiable white cream and flavoured
jam in the middle and a shelf life of about five years! The best bit is the
colourful wrapping paper that we use for a wall decoration.

This is the season of 'honk'. It grows wild in the woods; the stalks are
boiled and served with butter. It has a strong garlicky flavour and the
Chechens consider it a very healing food, a good blood cleanser, energy
giver and aphrodisiac. Our energy levels certainly zoom up, nerves tingling, eyes bright and clear. At the beginning of our stay we are given a
welcoming present of a handful of toffees. Black and white cows knee
deep in green grass roam across their wrappers. We smooth out the
paper and hang them with cotton on rough lumps in the adobe wall.
I compose a 'Rap' song all about trying to hang a picture on a crooked
wall. Jon hangs an empty Rama carton on a nail to hold our combs, cards
and sewing kit. Empty Rama cartons have a thousand uses.

I usually wake up before Jon and hear the morning call to prayer while
bathing my face in the steam of a hot cup of tea. Slowing down my breath
and calming my mind I think of my family at home, strengthening the
bond of love between us all, and ask guidance for the day from the purest,

most loving energy in the universe. As a child I couldn't feel much love in Christian dogma and especially all the talk of 'sin'. Singing hymns was the best part for me, in particular the ones that lifted my spirit. As I grow older I see the same teachings in all the religions I come across, only they are dressed in different clothes; some of them I wear more comfortably than others. 'The beauty of the universe is in the diversity of its creation and the wisdom in the knowledge of the underlying unity.'

I muse on all the teachings I have had and how they help me accept where I am now, in captivity in a small country wracked by conflict, caught in the 'maya' of existence. Whatever happens, whatever pain and degradation we experience, nothing can affect my eternal self, the god within. Of course it is easier to think on these things when you are not subject to mental or physical torture or the draining expectancy of horrors to come. Then you bear it and do what physical and mental exercises you can to maintain your sanity and release the daily trauma. Now my mind can relax a bit and contemplate.

No guards hovering behind the door, on our own. No one overseeing us or asking questions, the emptiness of the days giving us space to move around at will in our tiny world. The pressure off, I feel I can start to unwind and begin to heal from these past months. The softness of the adobe walls and wooden floor make this a gentler environment. Once the farmer and his tractor start ploughing we are able to talk without fear of being heard. It sounds strange to hear my own voice at its normal volume again. It is all crackly and I quickly get a sore throat, I guess through lack of use. Over the next few days my voice becomes clearer and stronger. I make sounds like a didgeridoo – deep earth tones; exploring these strange sounds gives me a sense of pure delight and I feel myself enter into a different state. I have a vision of an Aboriginal man in a desert landscape. He is standing on one leg supporting himself with a spear and I am filled with a feeling of friendship. I get a sense that I know him from somewhere, that he is a great friend, that we had made a pact to help each other and that we would use a didgeridoo to signal our need. It is as if through my vocal explorations I have unknowingly made a call for help. I need do no more.

We begin our programme of healing, gaining much more ground than the 'damage limitation' that we had achieved in the past few months. After my 'communion', while Jon is having his cup of tea I go through an exercise routine stretching all the parts of my body, then some yoga or tai chi. While Jon does his exercises I peer through the screw holes in the metal sheet watching an old black dog sunning himself or a woman putting up some washing – dresses, trousers and colourful, woollen tights flapping in the wind – or a boy and a girl chasing each other then sitting on the doorstep by the dog, stroking him. Watching these little cameos reminds me of the time we met a family high in the Chechen mountains during a weekend break from Little Star.

We had set off from Grozny on a hot, overcast morning in late May. As the mountains approached, the roads became a gravel mud track with big shell holes. We passed through a village that was completely destroyed by the Russians – just a few ruined walls remained, with all the telegraph wires adrift in the wind, hanging from drunken posts. So bleak, and such a contrast to the deciduous wooded slopes with their leafy green branches redolent of new life. Further on we came across a rusting wreck of a Russian tank lying at an angle of 45 degrees, its back end wedged on a scree slope leading down into a steep ravine; Jon clambered over it dangerously. This tank was part of a Russian column completely destroyed by the Chechens. None of the Chechens were allowed to live here between 1944 and 1957 after Stalin exiled the whole population to Kazakhstan. Brezhnev allowed them to return in 1957 but by this time many Ossetians had taken over their homes, and the Chechens were still denied access to the mountainous region until the early 1990s.

We arrived at the home of Said Hussain who moved here from Sernovodsk in 1991. His home was built into the side of a slope. It had a roof of corrugated asbestos with large stones placed all over it to weigh it down. Said gave us a tour of their land and ruined family tower, built over a thousand years ago. There was much talk of the war. The Russians sent bombers up the valley dropping shallow and deep vacuum bombs. Said's wife was out in the fields with her eldest daughter in the summer of 1995 when a bombing raid came up the valley; they had no shelter, and she was killed by flying shrapnel and her six-year-old daughter wounded. The little girl still suffered from nightmares and other psychological problems and Said wanted to send her to Little Star. We bought a lamb, which was killed and cooked for our supper, although I declined, and planned a walk for tomorrow.

We began our walk clambering over a stream and through some trees on a gentle path to an alpine meadow with flowers, butterflies, horseflies and a wonderful view. What a relief to walk, after days in our 'open prison' in Grozny! Chris chose a route straight up at an angle of 75 degrees. Earth, scree and trees. Most of the time you could scramble from tree to tree, but there was one point where I froze, for I had to let go of the tree I was holding and the next one was about three metres away with a very steep drop of scree and crumbling earth in between. Jon coaxed me and in the end I looked down at all the ants walking without fear and decided to behave like them. I did it – yippee! We climbed like this for 900 metres. When we reached the high, grassy top there were cheers while we looked up at the snowy peaks still far above us and then lay down watching the clouds and eagles.

Farmer steps into my thoughts with a hammer and nails covering the cameo windows with material. Can he hear me think? Twice he brings his wife and daughter in to collect some pumpkins. Through a screw hole Jon catches a glimpse of them taking furtive glances in our direction; they walk like mice and talk in reverent whispers as though they are in a church. His wife looks drawn and haggard, a lot older than she probably is. When they have gone I sing one of my 'heart' songs, improvised and spontaneous, singing my deep grief, my love, my joy. Tears flow, calmness descends and my inner peace is strengthened.

We start holding our prayer circles again. We wait until we hear the tractor outside then Jon stands up, arms raised in salutation, hailing and calling in the healing energies from all directions. Then we sit opposite each other on the bed and visualize who wants to join our circle. It seems to be getting larger and larger: we see all the children from Little Star and others we know in England doing drawings and paintings for us (this actually happened). As usual we put our captors and their families in the middle of our circle and shower them with love.

The smell of our food has attracted some little furry friends, 'Long Nose' and 'White Paw'. There's a small hole in the adobe, three quarters of the way up the wall, through which White Paw makes his entrance. Long Nose comes up through a broken floorboard. Their noses twitch and sniff, searching for breadcrumbs. When they notice each other they get a little angry and chase each other around the room. This is our live entertainment, a bit of mouse soap opera. Sometimes they make a truce and decide to ignore each other, nibbling in separate corners. We put crumbs down for them on a Rama carton lid. But Long Nose gets a little too adventurous and starts climbing on to the table so Jon puts a stop to that by rubbing scented soap on the legs – not very tasty, we think, and Long Nose agrees!

Our sleep is broken by the crashes and bangs of rowdy rat parties in the other part of the room – I didn't realize they were such noisy beasts. Only once did one come to visit us. It poked its head, followed by an enormous furry body, up through a broken floorboard near our door. I stared it in the eye and said 'Go!' with such vehemence that it turned tail and never reappeared. Mice I can cope with, but rats . . .

Farmer was the only one of our captors who had the patience to teach us the name of some objects in Chechen. 'Hee' for water, 'bepka' bread, 'ash' apple. Sometimes we talk of the situation in Chechnya; he tells us there is still so much suffering. We ask him what he thinks about Maskhadov, the Chechen president, and he says Maskhadov is doing the best he can and is a good man. This is a very different view from all our other captors who said he was too weak. On 19 March Farmer comes in earlier than usual and tells us we will be leaving tonight. 'Freedom?' I ask hopefully. He lowers his eyes. 'Ya niesnayo (I don't know).' We gather our things, feeling sad that we are leaving this healing place, and steel ourselves for another blindfold journey.

15

The Carpet Room

We hear the sound of a tractor engine and some grumbles from the driver. 'What's a tractor doing out in the middle of the night?' I'm thinking; it must be blocking the lane. Then our engine stalls. What now? Two men get out and fiddle in the engine and talk to the tractor driver. The driver engages the starter motor and after a few tries the engine splutters into action. The tractor moves out of our way and we are off again. We halt, the engine dies and we are guided into a building. Masks off and we are in a small room with two beds in it. Before they leave us Camilla asks for a bucket and a masked man brings a small red one with a white lid and a plastic bottle of water. There is a curtain covering the doorway which leads to an ante-room and we hear them locking us in. The first thing we do is quietly push the beds together so there is more floor space, then look around. The end wall has a spray of red plastic roses. A longer wall behind the beds is mostly covered by a large patterned carpet. Opposite is a blank white wall, one third of it covered by a shiny metal sheet, the back of a fireplace. The floor is the usual matt brown but the ceiling makes up for what the floor lacks: it is white, speckled with tiny blue spots that look as if they have been spray-painted. Camilla comments that it looks like an Impressionist's view of a dreamy summer sky.

We lie on the beds. Thankfully the mattresses are on wooden bases and are fairly comfortable and we have control of the light, the switch being by the doorway. I use my pink jacket as a pillow and Jon uses the purple/black check shirt Paunch dropped through the trapdoor all those months ago in the Kiva. There are two thin covers which we pull over ourselves. In the early hours of the morning it gets very chilly so we curl up together on one bed.

We wake to the chirpy sounds of a small child who is just learning to talk. The smell of fried eggs reaches us and the sound of sizzling oil in a pan. A man and a woman talk in low voices. We hear the door being unlocked and a masked man pulls back the curtain and presents us with a stool, then a plate of fried eggs, two forks, some slices of bread and two bowls of tea; sugar, salt and freshly churned butter follow. 'Barkal (thank you)' we say in Chechen and are greeted with silence. He looks suspiciously at the beds and asks us in Russian why we have moved them. We reply, with a bit of arm swinging mime, 'For the space,' and he accepts our explanation.

Well, we are being fed, that's a good sign. We listen to the sounds of washing up and the child playing with some kind of toy car making the engine noises 'Brmmmm, Brmmm'. This brings tears to my eyes – his (I'm making a presumption here) gentle innocence, memories of two-year-old Ashok. I don't really know why I cry but I feel my heart opening and relaxing as the tears flow. The noises cease except for distant hammering.

We feel adventurous and poke our heads through the side of the curtain. There are two small windows facing us, covered in clear plastic. To our left is a table with a lacy cloth and an electric sewing machine on the top. I want to look further and Jon warns me to be careful. On my right is a large wardrobe; I can see a black mask hanging off the top. Opposite, near the door, is a shoe rack. I look at the shoes with fascination. A pair of tiny red high heels for a woman with fairy-size feet and three pairs of lace-ups, toddler size. Under the window is a large sack of sugar. Through the plastic I can make out a large white sheet blowing in the wind on a washing line and the smudges of red-brick buildings a few yards away. I dare not look further and retreat into our room.

At least we have access to some daylight. Not for long – the next day we learn the reason for the hammering. The man and friends have been constructing a door to fit the doorway to our room. They spend a large part of the day measuring and fitting a doorframe to which the hinges and door can be attached. I am getting panicky and tearful, the electricity is off and soon we will be in darkness again with no ventilation. Jon tries to comfort me in my despair. I do some deep breathing and Jon points out when the men have gone that the doorway is crooked and there will always be gaps for air to penetrate through. When our meal of thin vegetable soup with mutton arrives we ask the man for a candle so we can see the food we are eating. He brings back a two-inch white stub, enough light to eat our meals by for the next few days, though not enough for playing cards or anything else.

We start creating a daily routine, exercising in turn before breakfast. Camilla has just enough room to do this comfortably, although I'm a bit cramped. I'm right, natural light does creep in through the cracks around the door frame, and I manage to hook the curtain over its rail to gain maximum benefit from the light available. While we're digesting our breakfast we massage each other's feet and relate vivid memories from our past in soft whispers, then begin planning our future wedding.

I always said that if I ever got married it would be in the little village church of Litton, in Somerset, where my grandfather had been vicar. But it wouldn't be big enough for our friends so there would be wedding part two in Devon, a camping party with a ceilidh band playing live music. We get totally absorbed in the detail, even down to what kind of sandwiches we would make. It's a good way to use time, a positive focus.

When we've exhausted all our ideas we do a 'smile' meditation which involves smiling into all parts of the body; we feel sure this keeps us healthy. If the electricity is on we play multitudinous games of 'Fool'; sometimes the monotony is broken by a lunchtime treat of homemade doughnuts and a bowl of blackberry jam.

The woman prepares the food and brings it into the ante-room on a tray, placing it on the table next to the sewing machine. We know this because we catch glimpses of her through the cracks between the wall and the doorframe, though she moves almost without sound in her slippers. Wearing long dresses and a headscarf, she is small and pretty and looks very young. Sometimes she comes to collect sugar or wash the floor on her knees, with a cloth. It's so nice for me to feel the presence of a woman in this all male environment we have been living in for the last ten months; I feel an affinity with her even though we are on opposite sides of a locked door and have grown up in such different cultures. Her husband comes in a few minutes after she has left the food, dons his mask, untying the door to hand the food to us and take the bucket away if necessary.

The afternoon pans out, we listen to the sounds outside – clucks of chickens, a cock crowing, two people greeting each other in the distance; and then the sounds within the house – the baby having a wash in the kitchen and being taught the Chechen for various objects. The mother tuning to Russian pop on the radio to accompany her as she does the housework when her husband is out and the toddler asleep. Sometimes she sings along with the music in a clear high voice. She'll never know what pleasure she gives us. One time her husband came in when the radio was blasting out and he turned it to a channel of traditional Chechen music, shouting at her with angry sharp words. As the afternoon light fades we do some qigong; then supper arrives, usually in the form of a soup or pasta with grissoles and hot tea. He also brings us ice-cold water from a spring. Before we sleep we sit on the edge of the bed and do a healing sound meditation, which helps us to shed the worries of the day and sleep deeply.

How strange to be part of a household yet totally invisible. Quite often we hear the voice of a more elderly woman visiting after breakfast – maybe the young woman's mother. After these visits we are given some fresh milk, perhaps from the family cow, and sometimes a dish of salty white cheese that we soak and drain in cold water three or four times before eating. One morning a whole group of women call by for tea and a chat. I love their lively gossip, sprinkled with laughter, and smile along with them, even though I don't understand a word. That evening the masked man brings a friend and they both enter our room. The other man looks a little fierce. 'Kak di la?' he asks in a gruff voice. 'Harasho,' we reply. 'Problyemi?' he continues, and I'm not sure whether he means have we got problems or are we creating any as he gestures for us to get off the bed and stand against the wall. My heart beats faster. He moves the beds, looking underneath them, then looks behind the carpet, pulling it away from the wall. I think they suspect that we have escape plans and have been burrowing through the wall! Satisfied that we are not going to disappear, they leave us in peace.

After a few days we ask if we can have a hot wash. Up to now we have been using a Rama carton filled with water to have a 'light' wash squatting over the bucket. Our thigh muscles are getting very strong but it is tiring and somewhat inelegant!

Our masked man brings a large metal bowl with hot water, a plastic one for us to stand up in, a large green slab of washing soap, a jam jar to shower ourselves with and two well worn towels. We also ask for a cloth so we can wipe the floor afterwards. I rig up a line made of the sheet strips from the Base and hang it in front of the metal wall. As the weather is cold they light the fire most days and our room gets toasty hot though fortunately not reaching sauna temperatures. We wash ourselves and our clothes as best we can with the limited amount of water. I poke holes in an empty Rama carton to make an improvised showerhead that helps us not waste so much water when we help each other rinse off the soap.

I feel the waistband of Jon's black trousers just before he washes them and discover there are still three bits of paper rolled up so tightly that they somehow have survived a few previous washes with the pencil writing still legible, part of my diary in the Pink Crystal Room. It is strange to read my words written at a time when we thought release might not be far away. I decide to stuff them down the skirting board, for the danger of keeping them is still great. In years to come perhaps that little boy will discover them and wonder how these scraps of English sentences came to be in his home.

Later we ask for a dustpan and brush. We have become very aware of the organic nature of our bodies through the amount of skin and hair we shed in our confined little room with so little ventilation. When I have my period I ask for hot water every night and it is brought without a grumble. I know they are doing the best they can to keep us comfortable in our prison, probably hoping for a slice of the ransom money when we are released, and at this moment we are luckier than many other hostages.

The minutes lengthen to hours and the hours into days and it's hard not to let the mind weave its dance in downward spirals through grey-pitted potholes of despairing thought. 'Ashok will have a beard by the time we get out,' I tearfully whisper to Jon. 'Of course not,' he replies calmly. Thank God there are two of us. When one is swooping downward the other is often striding calmly across the hilltops of positive thought and can reach down to haul the other into the light. On one of my 'swooping low' days we are given rice pudding. Now rice pudding has been one of my favourites since early childhood. We are handed two bowls and I study them both carefully. I am feeling tetchy and grumpy, and I am sure Jon's bowl has got more rice pudding in it than mine. I tell him and he immediately swaps them around saying 'Have it.' I look at the bowls again; there is no difference and I am ashamed of myself. I begin to cry and the tears gush down my face. What if I was in a pit with many people and only scraps were thrown down to us? Would I fight for every mouthful or have the courage to starve with dignity? There is no answer. I just pray to be given the strength and wisdom to rise above the basic survival instincts of fight or flight, and follow Jon's example of being more selfless.

Jon finds it hard to cry. I feel the tension growing in his chest around his heart. His movements and voice become more staccato and blunt.

We've been in the carpet room three weeks already and the captors of this place visit us rarely, only to empty our bucket and deliver our food. There's no human contact as such. We've tried on several occasions to engage in casual conversation but the captor at this place chooses not to enmesh himself. I know we're not being harassed physically or mentally but I find this total non-communication a bit like a non-responsive robot. I guess I could understand it if he was a robot, not another human being. I find it quite bizarre and it riles me to the core. Why do they treat us like animals, fed, watered and mucked out but with no communication at all? We're like the goose being fattened up for Christmas – keep the bird happy, keep the bird happy. Well I guess they're thinking one day we'll be worth millions of dollars. Or do they fear us or feel ashamed and too guilty to engage with us as humans? So we are kept alive on this basic level but this lack of communication hits deep into my being so I break down and cry out 'Why do they treat us like animals? Why can't they even just say "Hello" or give us a weather report? Anything just to let me know that I am human. What about going on hunger strike? At least they might engage more and we will be doing something.'

I know Jon wants to do something concrete to give us some sense of control over our destiny but I think it would be a big risk. I reply: 'They might get angry. Look at their history: they have had to go hungry many times and food is considered sacred. I don't think it would achieve much, and I think it's really important to keep healthy. I don't want to come out looking half starved and mentally deranged. Think what our families would feel.'

One night the family have the television on with the volume high and I feel it's safe with this background noise to start to express some of the pent-up energies, the angers I have in myself. So I start swearing, cursing at GA, HC, Puppydog and Paunch, calling them all the names under the sun. I feel some of this venom, this anger in me, is released with all this ranting and raving. Then I manage to cry, squeeze a few tears out. The emotion expressed, I feel happier, a little lighter. Ready to continue into the days ahead, the unknown.

I sit with Jon as we mentally put ourselves in a protective energy dome so that our captors do not physically or psychically pick up on our distress. Our experience in the past with 'the fab four' was that because of their own trauma they were very quick to pick up on our moods or thoughts of escape or me peeping around blankets covering windows. Once again I call on universal powers of healing.

During the many vacant hours between meals we also help each other work through old traumas that we have suffered in relationships in the years before we met. Jon performs a wonderful piece of courtroom drama to help me sort out some confusion, anger, guilt and grief. Strutting around like a cock judge with his chest thrust forward and his elbows flapping to the walls, he passes judgement on the accusations of both sides and has me in stitches. All the tension melts away and my heart feels free to love some more. Sometimes we forget the value of humour.

I strut around like a cock or a character from Pink Floyd's, 'The Wall' and work through with Camilla all that nonsense we've had from past relationships and people we've met. I hack away making fun of all the words – the shoulds, the oughts, the better thans. Then there's the 'wordy turds' and 'sitting ducks'. We clear away accusations and judgements in our pasts, laugh at all the silly situations, laughing at ourselves. It feels good, something we've been lacking for a long time. We've been sitting in this frightened, guarded space and now the tension melts away. My throat feels sore with all this high whisper ranting. At one point our guard must have heard me because I hear him coming to investigate so I stop and sit in silence and he is standing in silence on the other side of the door and we are listening to each other's silence – crazy! When he is satisfied there is nothing untoward going on in our space he returns to his TV programme, closing the door, and we conclude our court room drama.

We get another visit from our favourite food delivery man and his gruff friend and they bring with them a Polaroid camera. Blessings on the invention of Polaroid! I'm handed a brown knitted skullcap that I'm directed to wear upon my head, which I do quite happily. So we sit on the bed, side by side with the spray of plastic flowers on the wall as background decoration. Click. Another proof-of-life photo to send back to England. They return the following night saying the cap was not visible in the photograph. This time they give me a green velvet cap, I hold up my hand and they place the cap over the top of my fingers. Much later we hear that when my parents saw this photograph they thought my fingers or my hand had been chopped off as we had said this might happen in our letter back in November 1997. Happy with the second attempt, our gruff friend gives us a Snickers chocolate bar and says 'Cveboda scora (freedom soon)'. Our reward for being good little kids!

We feel the tension in the house mounting. The little boy has a cold that makes him fretful. His parents have started arguing. In the first couple of weeks they would talk harmoniously and giggle together and play with their son, rolling marbles around the floor (or that's what it sounded like). Now the stress of secretly keeping us is taking its toll. At night we often hear the sound of many men gathered in the sitting room playing cards. I think his wife goes out when they are there, as we never hear her voice – or maybe she stays with the child in the bedroom. During the day we hear her sewing on the machine, having taken it from the ante-room to the sitting room. We are wondering if she is sewing clothes to make some money. Soon we learn it is not for that reason at all. Masked Man brings our supper and tells us we are to leave that night. I ask him what the date is. He looks at his watch. 'The 25th April,' he answers, in Russian. Five weeks we have been here; I thought it was four. This is the first time I have started losing track of days and dates; the monotony has taken its toll. We gather our belongings into a plastic bag and wait. Masked Man and Gruff Man come in. 'Cveboda (freedom)?' we enquire. They lower their eyes to the ground. 'Ya niesniyo (I don't know),' Gruff replies. Their eyes say it all. They hand us two rather amazing masks. These are what his wife has been frantically sewing in the last days. The material is patterned, shiny and made with synthetic gold thread, sewn in the form of two large square tea cosies but without holes for the handle and the spout. Gold masks, well, well, well. They look rather divine but I am already thinking about how I am going to breathe. I feel the material and realize she has sewn one side double thickness so I make sure the single layer covers my face, giving me more chance to take in air. I can see light through the mask but no objects.

The boss of our kidnappers keeps the chain of communication from one place to another very thin; it seems the information about where we are going is only known to a very few. It certainly looks as though

Masked Man and his friends have no idea. We could be going to our freedom, our death, or another holding place.

Heads on knees and another lumpy bumpy ride through the lanes. 'Ra, Ma, Da, Sa, Sa, Se, So, Hung,' I chant in my mind. I have managed to peel the lower half of the mask up so my nose is clear to breathe. We reach a main road, turn right for a short way, stop and pick up another man who gives instructions to the driver, then a few miles further on turn left off the highway and drive the last ten minutes through some hilly lanes to our destination.

Jon's birthday card May 9th 1998

16

The King's Chamber

They guide us into a building and I am told to sit down with my legs dangling into a hole. A hand comes up from the hole and guides my feet until I'm standing on a chair, then helps me down into an underground passage. I take a few steps, am guided onto another chair and up through another hole. Then I am allowed to take off my golden mask. I find myself looking through some horizontal bars into a small windowless grey concrete room; to my right is an open metal door. My helper, dressed in black including his face, leaves me while he goes back down to help Jon. There are two iron bedsteads, one along the back, another smaller one on the side of the door and a small camping table against the other wall. Two stained wilting mattresses adorn the beds with one grubby blanket and one manky pillow. Jon appears through the hole and is followed by a sprightly elderly man – a small elfin figure with a white skullcap over silver hair, white long sleeved shirt, long johns and slippered feet. He has sparkling brown eyes and a huge grin. 'Haroshi miassa (good place),' he says, which makes me giggle a bit inside because I was thinking just the opposite. 'Ruskie?' he asks. 'Niet, Angliski,' we reply. 'What are your names?' 'Jon and Camilla,' Jon replies as the elderly man's question is directed at him. 'Toiliette?' Jon enquires. 'Aah, Da, Da,' he replies, disappearing back down the manhole. A few minutes later he reappears, sweating heavily, carrying a 50-litre milk churn. Our new silver loo. 'Spakone noche.' He padlocks the door, climbs down the hole and pulls down the manhole cover after him. We put both mattresses on to one bed and curl up under the blanket. Fortunately our minds are so weary we spend little time dwelling on our grim surroundings.

Here's home! A concrete bunker measuring about two and a half metres by three, with no windows and barely two metres from floor to ceiling. It's hard to tell if we are above ground, below it, or somewhere in between. The configuration of the access to this room conjures up pictures in my mind of being incarcerated within an Egyptian pyramid. The inner sanctum can only be reached by crawling through small tunnels. As the elderly man retreats down the entrance hole I count the doors that he closes behind him. First the clunk and scrape of the drain cover then the thud of a door in the tunnel followed by a distant clang of the trap door at the other end of the tunnel being replaced and finally the ker-thunk of a heavy outer door being shut and the sound of a key turning in the lock. I name our new home 'The King's Chamber' and I suggest to Camilla we are now in the heart of an etheric pyramid of light.

In the early hours of the next morning my stomach churns and my mind performs its relocation ritual. In my semi-conscious state images flash before me. I hear men shouting, a lorry starting up, cars revving. Are we in another base? Then a flock of sheep seem to be walking above us. A dog barks and a woman calls – thank God there are women here too. I open my eyes to grey concrete and feel a fissure of despair opening up in my heart. I climb carefully over Jon's sleeping body and, using water we have brought from the carpet room, wash myself as best I can. I know it would be crazy to let panic engulf me and tell myself I have the power to control my emotions and change my outlook. I stand in the centre of the room allowing my body to relax, letting all the tension drain down through my feet into the earth. I visualize myself connecting to the centre of the earth via a gold and silver thread which flows up through my body, out of the top of my head, up through our universe and all other dimensions to the source of creation, the pure point of creative potential. I smile deliberately into my body and into my mind. On opening my eyes I know that the only way to stay sane is to remember the essence of love in all things. I touch the grey walls and thank them for being; the rusty metal bars, the floor and the ceiling and thank the little white spiders who were weaving their silken threads in darkness, but are now bedazzled by the single 150-watt bulb. I feel calm and relaxed and think of Jon's words last night. Yes, another home.

I wake up and start exploring the room to see what gifts it can give us. Under one of the mattresses I find some newspaper, two folded sheets out of a magazine with prints of Russian paintings, a tiny white candle stub and two books, one without a cover. High up on the wall above our bed are fifteen scratches. A previous occupant marking out time? Fifteen days or fifteen months? Who knows. The date on the newspaper is August 1996, just before the end of the conflict, so it seems likely that the occupant was a Russian soldier. So we know this is a purpose-built prison, offering no easy escape.

Jon does some exercise while I look at the books. Books! I can't believe it – it's the first time I've held a book for nearly a year. One is a schoolbook with short stories and illustrations; in the middle are some paintings. I look at these for a long time and join Pushkin in his musings, sitting on a rock gazing across the Caucasian peaks that glow purple and pink in the sunset. Smile at the beaming Kazak schoolgirl, a satchel on her back, the hot sunlit plains sweeping behind her. Look across a glittering blue sea with an old sailor and a small boy. Watch the hunter with his black dog, gun slung over his back striding up a field against a backdrop of trees, ablaze with the oranges and yellows of autumn. Feel the spray blowing off the waves of the Black Sea on a sombre squally day. Sense some of the excitement and fervour of young 1917 revolutionaries as they march under their red banner, drums banging and trumpets blowing. And the pride of the young man receiving a medal in a clearing of a silver birch wood, ankle-deep in snow. The other book is of Russian poetry and I wish I had the language to read it.

The tears are coming. Will we ever see the sky again? Or breathe fresh air smelling of the scent of flowers or summer rain? Jon comes over to comfort me. Even knowing I am premenstrual which makes it easier for the greyness to influence my mood, I still cannot staunch my tears. Maybe they can help release the fears of the night move and the fact that we still haven't had any food. As I think this we hear a door being unlocked. The drain cover rises and a black masked face pops up like a mole appearing from its burrow. 'Kaka di la?' he asks. 'Harasho,' we reply as I discreetly wipe away my tears. He goes back underground and a tray appears. Scrumptious gifts from the earth. This mole must have a very hard-working wife or mother. He unpadlocks the door and hands us the tray then disappears momentarily. Up he pops again with a whole array of things to make our life more comfortable. One of my bleakest moments has been transformed; they are not going to let us waste away, forgotten in our concrete underworld. I feel blessed.

The tray is followed by an enormous box of Turkish biscuits with a seaside resort pictured on the cover. Then a large yellow plastic bag with sheets, a blanket, two pillowcases, two towels, two flannels and an extra pillow stuffed on top. A red quilt follows, then a red washing bowl, a cake of soap, a jug (blue marbled plastic yet again) and a bucket of water. 'Blessings on the Turkish plastics industry,' says Jon. Finally a large flask of hot water and a pot of strong tea. The contents of the tray are another marvel: two smoked mackerel in their beautiful gleaming skins, boiled potatoes, grated carrot salad, two elegant bone china cups, a bowl of sugar, a jam-jar of salt, and, wait for it, a jar of fresh cream and a tin of Nescafé. I treat myself to coffee and cream with a sprinkling of sugar, savouring every sip – such a luxury. We shower the food and the person who prepared it with thanks before tucking in.

Being able to make the bed with laundered sheets, crisply ironed and smelling of fresh air, is another luxury. I manage to find some nails in the wall to hang a washing line for our towels and flannels. I look at the plastic bag; it is bright yellow with 'HOLIDAY' written in black and a logo underneath representing the world. 'This'll brighten up our grey wall,' I think, and hang it from the light-bulb fitting. It's brilliant, reflecting yellow light into our grey room and reminding us that every day is a 'holy-day' as well as a 'hostage holiday' if we choose to see our present life in that way. It makes us chuckle, which is always healing. Thinking of our new home as a sacred place, 'the King's Chamber', helps us to accept it with love and not despair.

There is a pipe opening in one corner of the ceiling that I think is meant to be a ventilation hole but we can feel no air flow. Fortunately there is another round hole above the churn, stuffed with a bit of wood. I peer into it and see a glimmer of light and smell fresh air. There is also a drain in the floor between the two beds and through this we hear noises from the outside. Cows mooing, chickens clucking, birds chirping and the low growl of the tractor. As the day crawls towards evening we realize that we need to keep moving to keep warm. When Mole pops up with the evening meal the elder of the household follows and asks if there is anything more we would like. 'More clothes please, it's cold,' we reply, and accompany this with a shivering mime. Elder looks surprised. 'Cold, more clothes? Soon it will get very hot.' 'And two chairs please.' The table is quite low, sitting on the bed leaning over it is not very comfortable and the rough concrete floor is not at all enticing. He says something to Mole who disappears and comes back with a long grey-blue knitted cardigan, a mock-velvet dark blue dressing gown with flowers embroidered on the lapels for Camilla, a padded red and black check shirt for me and two home-made three legged stools. Perfect. That night we snuggle down between our clean sheets, heads resting on pillows with clean covers.

The next day I wake up and hear children's voices through the drain. It sounds as if they are playing tag, running around the building. I catch glimpses of their shadows as they pass by the hole in the wall above the churn. There must be a gate somewhere close as there are lots of squeaks and clangings as they chase one another through it. They are joined by a much younger child, maybe just a toddler, who can't keep up and ends up screaming either in frustration or because he/she has tripped over. The angry voice of a woman booms up through the drain chiding the older children in Chechen for not keeping an eye on their younger brother or sister. I love these audio clips of life beyond our grey walls; my imagination stretches through them creating a film of what might be happening. Mole brings us breakfast of thick vegetable soup with mutton, a huge round of warm soda bread, another jar of cream (I'll be a little plumpette when we leave here!) and takes the teapot and flask for refilling. He is still very much on his guard, cracking knuckles and flexing muscles in a fairly threatening way while waiting for an unseen person to fill the flask. To avoid him feeling any need to show off his fighting skills and use Jon as a punch bag, we've decided that I will collect the food from him. I also wear my scarf on my head in the traditional Chechen manner as a sign of deference and to keep warm. Later that day the light bulb starts to flicker and go dim. The thought of being in complete darkness for any length of time is scary – to my mind, it's a good way of creating insanity. I watch it avidly. Jon's listening and hears the sound of a welding torch, so that is the reason for the failing power – what a relief! We spend a lot of the day doing exercises. When the building appears to be empty and there's lots of noise outside I sing quietly. Jon's voice is too deep and resonant, it's unsafe for him to sing.

As Camilla sings I reflect on our time in captivity: almost a year now. A year living in a pressure cooker of tension fired by adrenalin. At least they are not psychologically or physically abusing us here and our survival needs are being met. I look into my mental toolbox and take out a metaphorical practice taught to me by a friend as we worked in his garden. He would tell me to weed the paths and imagine them as paths of communication, by removing the weeds I was also clearing the pathways of communication in myself. As I turned the soil, pulling out grasses and thistles, he told me to notice how some came out easily and some required a lot of pulling and digging and imagine them representing unhealthy thoughts and ideas embedded in my mind. Now I look for the weeds in my psyche that have grown during captivity; there's definity a few ugly ones. Anger at not being able to protect Camilla from the rape, lack of self worth (all those months with the fab four grinding me down). The roots are deep.

Later that afternoon, hearing someone coming, we sit down demurely on the stools and wait to see who arrives. A white skullcap and silver hair appear through the manhole: it is the elder. He sits himself down on the other side of the bars and lights a cigarette, no long johns this time just baggy blue working trousers, check shirt and the obligatory slippers. 'Why did you come to Chechnya?' he asks. We explain that we came to help the children by setting up a centre where they could overcome the traumas they had suffered during the 1994–96 war. He smiles and says 'Idiots!' There is no reply to that one! We know it was worth it, seeing those young eyes, pained and dull, lighting up with laughter and joy. We have no regrets and smile at him, saying nothing. He disappears back down the hole.

He must have spoken to Mole telling him we are not dangerous because now Mole has a face. Brown eyes, brown hair, with a pattern of adolescent scars on his skin. We guess he is in his early twenties. He seems more relaxed as he hands me a casserole dish of rice and chicken wings, and there is not so much knuckle cracking. As we bed down we reflect on the nature of our new carers. The head of the household seems a well-balanced man, his unmasked face shows he has no fear of us and his manner reveals no trauma. Judging from his age he would have started his life in Kazakhstan and would have known a fair bit of suffering and hunger. Obviously he managed to keep his animals and the farm running during the recent conflict and thereby a way of earning his living. It must give him a focus in these unstable times and keep him sane. His son is a bit more jumpy and unsure of himself; maybe he spent two years fighting and experienced, for the first time, the atrocities of war. There is a silent woman behind the scenes but we know nothing of her.

Mole brings us more presents from the deep: a small digital watch, a calendar pad, a pair of scissors for cutting our nails, a small mirror and a long white candle with matches in case there's a power cut.

I artistically fold and cut some of the newspaper into snowflake patterns

203

and stick them to the wall with melted candle wax. Learning how to fold the paper several times and make just one or two cuts to form intricate shapes gives me satisfaction and serves to alleviate my boredom. A fascinating pastime for someone who has no TV, no radio, no reading matter and no window to look out of. The snowflakes are followed by trees and flowers and a moon cut out of the foil inside the Nescafé tin. Camilla joins in by smoothing out gold paper sweet wrappers that she has saved from our time in the sauna and cuts out a sun to go above the paper trees. I even manage to create a symbol of unity with five intersecting circles. These decorations break up the monotony of the bare, rough concrete walls. We are creating our own world within a world.

I study the calendar pad; it has a recipe or poem or piece of practical advice to accompany each day. We have no dictionary now, but I try to work out the meaning of the words. Today it's a recipe of little boiled pastry envelopes stuffed with meat, potato, or cheese and soaked in melted butter and garlic. Yum! Jon has asked for some black cotton and a needle so he can darn his black trousers which are becoming so thin and worn holes are appearing. When the cotton arrives Jon has a brilliant idea of making a picture rail by attaching a length of it to the iron bars. He makes little metal hooks out of the remaining tin foil in the coffee tin, sticks them through the top of the magazine pictures and hangs them over the cotton line. Wow, our very own picture gallery.

There are four paintings, two on each sheet. The first one shows a father and son reaping a field of corn; they wear clothes of the Russian peasants in the early part of the century, cream smocks and baggy trousers. The boy has pink cheeks and bright blue eyes while the father's face is drawn and haggard after years of hard labour, the muscles in his arms taut and sinuous like the branches of an old gnarled tree, his massive hands clutching the scythe. The wind bends the high corn in swathes of dappled yellow ochres and the sky has a purplish/grey tinge to it signalling an impending storm. On the other side is a dream landscape of sloping hilly fields demarcated from each other by their strong colours; a woman walks in the foreground in a long dress, with a vacant expression on her face. Although the colours are bright there is no feeling of sunlight, in fact it has a sombre, rather sinister feel to it. We rarely show this side in our picture gallery. I have a favourite out of the other two as well, a mill scene. There is a millpond in the foreground with water lilies and a few reeds, surrounded by willow trees and part of a wooden building with the waterwheel in the background. This painting has a deep, calm feel to it. The other side shows a red-brick factory building amongst some fir trees painted in flat tonal colours, it has a strange, empty feeling like the dream landscape.

The next day, after a delicious soup of pieces of fish cooked with vegetables, milk and peppercorns, I cut out the paintings from the school book. I don't use metal hooks for these, just fold the top border over and hang them on the line. Now we have a choice of paintings to contemplate. I start practising some tai chi walking, very very slow with great awareness in every movement. There are six small paces between our bed and the bars. I focus on one painting, walk towards it and enter into the scene losing sense of myself as a separate being, then back away watching it recede until I become the room with the painting as just a small part. This exercise in 'headlessness' is extremely calming for the mind and excellent for working the leg muscles. I lose all sense of time.

It's the fifth day in our new home. I hear women talking and laughing in the outer room leading to our chamber and sounds of metal bowls clanging and water sloshing; it must be wash day. Later we see the ankles of a woman in the underground passage as she passes our breakfast to Mole to hand to us. 'Please thank your mother for the wonderful food,' Jon says to Mole and there are giggles from the underground tunnel and a high woman's voice answers, 'Niet Mama, Siestra.' 'My mother is dead,' Mole adds. This is the first time a woman has spoken to us for ten months and it feels wonderful.

Hearing her voice makes me realize how much I miss being with women, a feminine softness that has not been present in the last ten months of my life. Ten months surrounded by traumatized Chechen males trying hard not to look weak: 'Chechen men don't cry.' Of course there is the same male attitude in our society; the balance of male and female attributes in both males and females is not widely understood. Jon finds it hard to show emotion, probably from early conditioning, but he does allow his softer side to come out which, I believe, helps keep him sane.

Later that day we hear a car arrive and male voices echo up the drain. There are noises outside the hole above the churn and we realize it's being cemented up. Help, what's happening? The natural light, the fresh air are being cemented out of our existence. The elder comes to visit us and rants and raves, arms flying around. 'KGB coming, very important man, Russian Kommandant.' He's very excited and starts examining the padlock on the door and the hole that he has cemented from the outside. Eventually we understand we are to have a companion. Our spirits drop. We have just settled into our new home and have been building up a good relationship with our captors; now, all is to change.

1 May: Valentin's arrival

The elder appears up the manhole with full welding kit, mask, gloves and a torch. The identity of the light-dimmer, the welderman, is discovered and his nickname is born. He cuts a hole in the metal frame of the door and fixes another padlock. It's a long process and the dust is incredible, it fills the whole room. We sit mute, Camilla with a scarf over her mouth and nose, me with a flannel. It's quite an ordeal with so little ventilation and after he has finished we ask him to leave the drain cover open. He sends Mole in with a large air blower (like an overgrown hair dryer) and he trains it up the hole in the corner of the ceiling but it doesn't seem to help the air flow; the metal dust hangs thick, suspended on the still air. Eventually it settles and we wipe the rusty grime from the table and stools and shake it off the beds. Mole appears again with another mattress and some more bedding for our expected guest. The mattress is quite new, red with white stripes; it's too big for the smaller bed so we swap it with the healthier of our two, which fits the other bed, and spread out the sheet and the quilted cover and plump up the new pillow in readiness for our guest.

Supper arrives and no sign of our visitor. We play a game of 'Fool', savouring the last hours of being alone together and having the space to ourselves. As we're thinking about climbing into bed we hear what sounds like a Jeep arrive. Sitting side by side on the stools, leaning our backs against our bed, we face the manhole and wait. There are lots of whisperings, scrapings and shuffling and finally the drain cover grates open and a chair is placed underneath it. A masked man, dressed all in black, guides another masked man to the chair and he sits down breathing heavily. When his breath is calmer he is helped to stand on the chair and to climb up through the manhole, then through the door and is guided to sit on the bed. He is wearing a baggy army camouflage suit and a pair of worn-out black slip-on shoes; they're too small and his heels squash the leather down at the back. The man that has helped him in is more thickset than Mole, his body tense, set for action and his eyes stony brown. He looks around the room to satisfy himself that we have no means of escape then retreats back down the hole after double padlocking the door.

So here we are, the three of us. The man takes off his mask and leans forward resting his elbows on his knees. Then he looks at us and holds out his hand, we shake hands and introduce ourselves. 'Strasvoitye, I'm Valentin,' he says. His body is carrying a little more weight than his frame needs and he's only a bit taller than Jon which is lucky as the ceiling is barely four centimetres higher. His blond hair is shaved high above his ears and longer on top; it looks quite military. He has vivid light blue eyes. There's a small cut and a bruised swelling above his left eye, but otherwise he is unharmed. 'Are you a soldier?' we ask. ' No, I work for Yeltsin, special police,' he replies. We wonder if he means bodyguard or KGB. He looks too old to be a bodyguard (he must be in his forties or early fifties, although his hair hasn't got a speck of grey). He is not keen to enlighten us further about his job and he speaks very fast in Russian so it is hard for us to understand. We offer him food and drink but he declines. It is late so we retire to bed, having pointed out the churn to him. I wake up in the night and see him curled up, facing the wall, calling for someone in his sleep. His whole body shaking, probably more with shock than with cold. I hold my hand out, palm facing him, sending some healing.

The honeymoon week

In the morning we ask for a curtain to give us some privacy when we use the churn. A masked Mole brings us a white sheet and a piece of wood that I manage to wedge between the bars and the hole above the churn. We all feel much happier. At the same time as bringing breakfast and water Mole looks across at our table and gestures for us to return the scissors and digital clock but allows us to keep the calendar and small mirror. We give Valentin a toothbrush and a comb. There is hardly any noise from outside our walls, no washerwomen, they have been directed elsewhere, no children playing, even the dogs have stopped barking. It seems that everyone has been told to keep quiet because of the new important visitor.

Valentin looks exhausted, with big dark rings under his eyes. He lies on his back with his feet sticking through the bars at the end of the child-size bed. I decide to do some tai chi, drawing in universal love and healing energy through the flowing movements and mentally sending the healing to Valentin. It doesn't matter to me what his job is; what I see is a human being in distress and he is very much sharing our world, one of us. His face and body begin to relax, the muscles losing their tautness. I do not (cannot) explain to him what I am doing but without prompting he says he feels better and he enjoys watching the movement. By the afternoon the initial torpid trauma has lifted and he is pacing back and forth in the constricted space, perhaps turning over the events of his capture in his mind. The energy of anger and outrage radiates into the room. The manhole cover grates open and Mole appears with our evening meal. Valentin engages him in conversation. We sit quietly getting more and more anxious as Valentin shows his irritation and says something rude about 'Ichikeria', the name the Chechens choose for an independent Chechnya. Mole errupts with an angry torrent of words and swiftly disappears banging down the hatch. We are furious: Valentin has threatened all our lives with his behaviour. Mole and his family are our umbilical cord to survival; they could withdraw food and water and leave us to starve or come and beat us up and chain us. We have learnt to control our emotions, always finding a neutral stance the most beneficial. We control them now and say nothing to Valentin; the damage is done.

A night on the alert, waiting for reprisals. I have a knot of pain in the centre of my forehead. I do not want to see or know what will happen in the morning and the tension of anticipation is enormous. Luckily this family is much more in balance than our 'fab four' and breakfast arrives as usual, delivered by a mute and angry Mole with the help of Welderman, equally mute and angry and now wearing a mask, but they throw no punches. I ask what the time is and Welderman waves his arm in a dismissive gesture, saying nothing.

Valentin seems to have calmed down after venting his spleen and we have a merry meal together of smoked mackerel. I am beginning to relax, sensing that this is not a man who will abuse me as a woman, in thoughts or actions. He talks to me as a fellow human being regardless of my sex. He teaches us how to gut the mackerel using one of Jon's razor blades. For us it is gourmet food but Valentin has been brought up on fish caught in the White Sea and he is a little dismissive and doesn't eat a morsel. I think it is also because of the shock; we had no appetite the day after we were kidnapped. We ask him about his home. 'I come from Arkhangelsk (Archangel),' and he draws a finger map of Russia on the grey concrete wall and points out Archangel on the edge of the White Sea, in the far north. 'Luche? (better?)' I ask, pointing to the cut and bruise above his left eye. 'It's nothing,' he replies and mimes how he defended himself when gunmen surrounded him as he bought some things from a roadside bazaar. They took him to a forest and stripped him of his clothes, giving him the army camouflage in exchange and some food to eat, then told him they were going to ask for two million dollars. After nightfall, they brought him to join us.

We ask for any recent news and he tells us about the death of Linda McCartney. We are quite shocked, having felt a link with the McCartneys when we saw the photo of them in Moscow. It also reminds us that we have had no news of our own families, that one of them may have died or had an illness or accident and we would not know it. He asks about the yellow plastic bag hanging below the light and we explain that it says 'holiday' and is also our internal sun. This makes him laugh. Ah, good, humour is raising its healing head. That night I have a vivid dream where Linda McCartney is laughing happily and telling me all about a beautiful white horse she is stroking. The strange thing is I had no idea that she even liked horses until after our release.

Valentin is lying on his back one day, stripped to his waist and I can see his sun tan line so I point at the light bulb, saying 'The sun's hot today; ten minutes then you'd better turn over.' Valentin gets the message and his stomach heaves with laughter. There's a square piece of grubby white cotton material hanging over the top bar, our dishcloth, I go over to it and turn an invisible knob. 'Televisie,' I whisper. 'It's a Western.' I start describing the film with plenty of mime and Valentin and Camilla join in, inventing different programmes as I change channels. For these few precious minutes our bellyaching laughter lifts us out of our grim thoughts.

A couple of days after Valentin's outburst he asks for new clothes to replace the army suit. Welderman grumbles a bit but returns with a pair of dark blue tracksuit bottoms and a black and white horizontally striped nylon pullover. He also brings a chessboard. Valentin teaches us how to play. At first he is quite patient but fairly soon his mood turns to frustration as his play is of a high standard and we are novices. Twice I manage to beat him and he's not a very gracious loser! After a few days he refuses to play with us and so for the next few weeks we end up playing between ourselves, about six games a day, sitting cross legged on our bed with the board balanced on a pillow between us. A nice change from cards and backgammon.

Valentin has been watching us practising tai chi and qigong with great interest and asks us to teach him. I think he realizes how much it helps us survive healthily. We teach him all the exercises and a simplified version of the smile meditation. 'I'm a quick learner aren't I?' he says, and he is, he has natural talent. He also practises skiing exercises to increase his fitness and has started eating less; soon the extra body fat disappears and he looks years younger. He tells us he has a problem with his heart, a heart murmur, and from time to time he asks for pills that they bring. But I think he's a bit suspicious of taking them and, in our increasingly humid atmosphere, they disintegrate into white mush that he discreetly chucks into the churn. Eating with Valentin is another eye-opener. We hadn't realized how much we were warping time to help the days pass more quickly by slowing down all our movements, including eating. Valentin gobbles and slurps his soup before we have swallowed one mouthful. We come to a happy mean with us speeding up and Valentin slowing down.

The calendar proves to be a good source of entertainment; every afternoon I read some of its poems and Valentin attempts to explain the meaning, with some gesticulating. There is a poem about gathering mushrooms in damp woods and one about the first cuckoo call of spring as the buds and leaves unfurl their trembling, delicate forms, pale green and sticky. I love the images they conjure up: wet bark and moss, bird song, trees shivering in a breeze dislodging a shower of rain drops. The grey walls around me disappear and I'm standing amidst tall tree trunks in the dappled light of a forest or in a field of hay with my head raised to the yellow sun warming my skin.

Some more readable material comes our way when Valentin asks for loo paper. None of your triple velvet, double layered soft pristine white rolls but damaged library books. Valentin picks up the first one looking aghast. 'This is classical Russian literature!' he gasps and Welderman makes a dry comment on how all the libraries have been destroyed by Russian bombs damaging millions of books. The book contains Russian myths and legends; of course Jon and I cannot read it but we enjoy looking at the illustrations. Jon's birthday is coming up and I decide to choose the most appropriate illustration I can find as a birthday card. There is one dreamscape of an eagle soaring over the tops of tall square family towers, the ruins of which are commonly found in the mountains of Chechnya and Ingushetia. A man stands on the back of the eagle with a mane of white hair, holding a spear, and beside him is a horned bull with a full moon above. Jon was born in the sign of Taurus and the eagle has always been an important symbol for him, so I think he'll like it. I don't have anything to write with but I do have black thread and a needle, so every day when Jon is having his siesta I add to a sewn message: 'Jon Happy Birthday Love Camilla'. I sew a border around the picture. This is a labour of love – I am not a seamstress and it's pretty tricky sewing backstitch letters through paper without drawing them first or tearing the fragile paper. However, it gives me loads of pleasure.

It's time for a hot body wash and I devise a way of organizing the room by draping the sheet across a cotton line and moving the furniture so we can all have privacy during our ablutions. The following hot-wash day Valentin decides the room rearranging is too much of a palava and says he will lie on his bed facing the wall while we wash. We get into a routine of asking for hot water every five days. It arrives with supper, so the chunks of chicken steam on the rice while I help Valentin with a shampoo and rinse. Camilla sits on a stool facing the wall, combing her hair. Our room becomes a steam bath with condensation running down the walls.

As the weather grows hotter outside and the atmosphere within more humid we ask them to bring cold water. At first Welderman cannot understand it. 'There is plenty of hot water, why do you want cold?' We point at the glistening walls and the dark tide of dampness threatening to cover the floor. Before the heat there was rain and the cement of our two outside walls sucked in the wetness until they took on a darker hue with a film of white spotted mildew forming vistas of snow-covered mountains on the uneven surface. Valentin begins to cough, his bed is lower than ours and the mattress is touching the damp wall and becoming saturated. He decides to move his bed across the room to the dry inside wall, so Jon helps him swap around the bed and the table and stools. Valentin asks Welderman if his mattress can be taken outside to dry and has the brilliant idea of asking if our clothes can be washed and dried also as there is no way we can dry them in these climatic conditions. Owing to our previous experience we never even considered this as a possibility. His wish is granted.

My heart's beating, it's the middle of the night and I can hear a distant door opening and some whispers, then a 'thump' as someone jumps down into the underground passage. I hastily wind my sarong around my head and pull on the pink skirt, tucking in the white shirt. Jon grabs the checkered shirt from the bedpost. The manhole cover slides back and up climb Mole and Welderman, Mole carrying a video camera. Welderman tells Valentin to turn to the wall. No script is given to us but we are still wary about what to say and how our words will be used.

Jon begins to speak: *'I'm Jon James and as you can see I'm still alive. Still wanting to come home . . . please soon.'*

'I'm Camilla Carr and yes, I hope to be free very soon.'

'Please send us a newspaper or book. We have nothing to read or any pictures to look at.'

'Ten months now,' I whisper.

'And please make this the last video we have to do.'

'And we love you all very much, think of you all everyday.'

''Scuse us, we've just woken from our night's sleep.'

Afterwards, I feel quite upset, thinking of all the other things I'd like to have said. I realize my responses are still conditioned by our time with the fab four, and I'm still expecting retaliation for speaking freely.

The shit hits the fan

It's the end of our honeymoon with Valentin. I knew it would be coming: he has been far too jocular, putting on a 'good front', secretly (I suspect) expecting a miraculous release after a few days, just as we had. Now I think he is beginning to see it could be months or years before freedom comes and realizes he could be spending all that time cooped up with a couple of English people of whose language and culture he only has a smattering of comprehension. He gets more and more grumpy and derisive of our ways. 'How come you have so much to talk about?' he asks curtly. We say that for many months we didn't have much chance to talk at all and that it helps us to heal, but it's too difficult to explain all that we suffered and I don't think he really wants to know. It is obvious to us that Valentin must have had a job involving telling other people what to do as he tries ordering us around but we won't play; as far as we're concerned we are all equals in our concrete box.

'You're 40 years old with responsibilities and children. How could you come to Chechnya and work for so little?' he asks accusingly. 'That kind of thing is for young people not people of your age.' We understand that we have different beliefs and value systems, neither of them being more correct or better than the other, just different, so we are not drawn into an argument. But when he starts being critical of Jon my sense of justice is ignited. It begins with the chess games: 'Plocha Domit (bad thinking),' the usual muttering from Valentin, even when Jon beats him. Then it becomes more frequent, and considering Jon has taken on all the gruesome cleaning jobs, such as cleaning out our washing bowl and the outside of the churn when it reappears after being emptied, I am not impressed. One day I blow a fuse. 'Tye plocha domit (you bad thinking),' I whisper angrily to Valentin, and point out all the things Jon does to make our lives more comfortable. He listens and there are no more 'plocha domits'. However, there is one time when Valentin grumbles at Jon that I find very understandable. Jon decides to do a yoga sequence in the space between Valentin's bed and the table, not once but five times. When he's in 'the dog' position with his bottom raised to the ceiling, it's barely 30 cm from Valentin's head! The combination of our airless room and the sweat of his body creates none too sweet an aroma. Straight to the washbowl and soap for you m'boy!

Jon's birthday is drawing near and we tell Mole, who asks Jon if he would like anything special. 'Juice please,' answers Jon, and I add (with the help of some mime), 'Flowers would be nice to brighten up the room.' The 9th of May arrives, no juice, no flowers, only my card. However a couple of days later some cool apple juice pops up from Mole's tunnel.

Valentin is sinking into a depression. He has decided to cut off from us and pretends we don't exist – not even a 'good morning' comes out of his mouth. He has stopped doing the qigong and other exercises, is eating little and spends most of the time on his bed, curled up, facing the wall. I watch him holding up a shaky hand, looking intently at the lines on his palms as though trying to read his fate. We feel great empathy for him and try to break through the wall of silence, knowing how hard it is and how alone he must feel, but he chooses not to communicate. He stays in this inert state for some days. Then something compels him to pick up the Russian poetry book. He walks up and down the six paces reading some of Pushkin's poems out loud in a low melodious voice. At first his voice cracks out of lack of use. Perhaps the fear of forgetting how to speak gives him the energy to rise out of his torpid state. I feel an expansive feeling in my heart hearing him reading the poetry so beautifully and knowing that he has the willpower to survive. Gradually he reintegrates himself into our world.

Jon and Valentin spend a lot of time being awake at night and so after breakfast they usually sleep, which gives me space to do some movement and also to sit at the table, pour myself a cup of coffee laced with sugar and topped with fresh cream, and disappear in my mind to a café in Bath, chatting to my mother over a cappuccino. On Wednesday mornings I join her meditation group, feeling myself there, sitting in the circle, joining in the shared silence. I greatly value this time to myself. In such a confined space when we are all awake one can almost hear what the others are thinking, not necessarily the words but the energy and intention behind them. It can be a busy and exhausting environment with nobody moving at all. One day Valentin is lying on his bed and I can feel heavy black thoughts circling around his head. I don't want to feel them; it makes me irritated. Minutes later he talks to Jon about some ideas he has had of how to overcome Mole when he brings a meal; they are very violent. Although I understand his frustration and desire for freedom, violence only breeds more violence and logically there is very little chance of us escaping even if we manage to get past Mole. Jon talks him out of using any action. I want to cleanse the room of these thoughts; I am scared our captors will sense the energy and become paranoid and retaliate.

When Jon and Valentin wake they take turns to do some exercise. Skiing exercises for Valentin, pumping his arms and bouncing on his heels. Some kundalini yoga for Jon. The 'squatting frogs' look far too strenuous to me. Valentin has been asking for some books; he explains to Mole that it is harder for him because, unlike us, he has no one to talk to. Perhaps in retaliation for Valentin's outburst of disrespect for Chechens, Welderman demonstrates a wicked sense of humour by delivering two books. One is about the '94–96 Chechen war, written by a Russian journalist who is critical of the way the Russians handled it. The other is a Muslim

Encyclopaedia. Jon and I are very amused and wonder what Valentin will make of them. He flicks through the book on Chechnya and barely touches the encyclopaedia. A few days later he passes them back to Mole and asks for some different ones. An odd assortment is sent through the bars. When Valentin reads, Jon and I play our marathon chess games on the bed; when he's dozing we sneak a look at them, the more illustrations the more interesting for us. One book that doesn't interest Valentin in the least is all about farming. There are intricate diagrams of how to build the most efficient slurry drainage channels under cowsheds – not a topic we've had any interest in before, but now it keeps us amused for hours. Another rather ancient and mildewed hardback turns out to have been published in 1921. I open it and see a drawing of a large country house set in a beautiful garden with an enormous cedar tree. Somehow it looks familiar, very English, so I turn back to the cover and decipher the title, letter by letter, 'William Morris'.

While Camilla's studying the William Morris illustrations I look at the painting of Pushkin, sitting on a rock gazing across the mountainous landscape. I'm so glad we had the opportunity to take a couple of outings into the mountains and experience the beauty of the Caucasus for ourselves. Memories of a gentle summer breeze blowing through our hair, across our skin. On our second outing we were with the three Norwegian mine clearance experts. As we reached the foothills Camilla and I asked Adlan to stop and we rushed off into the bushes to have a pee, followed by angry shouts from the Norwegians – they knew there could be live mines lurking in the undergrowth. How naïve we were! Later, climbing the slopes, Gaier, who had been in the Norwegian military, pointed out a small bomb embedded in the hillside, he told us to walk away, slowly, as it could still be live. The fuse generator is as simple as one in a cigarette lighter – one heavy footfall could trigger it.

Further up the steep slope, Camilla left far behind sniffing the alpine flowers, we met some locals who were grazing sheep and horses on the high summer pasture. They sent down a horse taxi to pick up Camilla and invited us for tea in their little stone house tucked into the side of the mountain. We gazed out at the snow-covered peaks. What a view!

Not much of a view now in our small concrete box. The days are beginning to blur in the endless routine of chess and card games, yoga, meditation, conversation and silence.

Into the heat

I become acutely aware of ourselves as living, porous organisms made up of about 80% water. The outside heat is penetrating the concrete walls and our bodies are responding by sweating, causing condensation, more steamy heat and more sweating. It gives me the illusion that most of the air is being replaced by water, making it hard to breathe. We know we can't survive in these conditions without a fan so Jon mimes to Mole that we need the wind up fan that he had brought in when our room was full of welding dust on the day of Valentin's arrival. The next day a pristine white electric fan appears. They take the cable down through the man-hole to reach the main electric current. It has three different settings and a small light on the stand under the fan. This we find extremely useful as we can leave it on at night, our 'moon', and it provides enough light to guide us to the churn instead of holding on with aching bladders until breakfast when Valentin screws the 150 watt light bulb back in.

My knitted cardigan and dressing gown are lying redundant over the bedstead; they are beginning to smell mouldy so I hand them back through the bars. I watch sadly as dark, damp patches spread out from the walls over the floor; each day the island of dry cement is smaller. The floor is now too damp for me to exercise in my socks so I take my shoes from under the bed. A sheen of mildew decorates the plastic. Jon's train-ers are growing a rare pale green forest around rusting eyelets. I try and exercise in the shoes for a while but then the heels start disintegrating so I show them to Valentin. He displays our mildewed footwear to Welder-man, who immediately takes off his own slippers and hands them to me, then disappears and brings back two other pairs for Jon and Valentin. I find this very moving, it's such a beautiful spontaneous act of kindness.

Having the 'moon' gives an added dimension to our mornings. We don't have to lie in bed, eyes staring into blackness, waiting for break-fast and the light bulb to be screwed in, but use the space while Valen-tin sleeps. Jon does yoga on the bed; he tells me it stops his mind going down dark and dangerous corridors like the mind of a caged animal. I use the floor space, adapting the poses so I don't touch the floor with my knees, avoiding the dampness. Then I sit on a stool with my back leaning against the bed and focus inwards doing a breathing practice to clear my mind. Or I do the smile meditation, smiling into my blood and imagin-ing the healing energy being carried to every cell in my body, each cell containing a clear crystal and within that crystal a small flame, a flame of love. The first time I practised this, I lost awareness of conscious reality. The scrape of the manhole cover brought me back. It was a shock to find myself sitting on that little stool in a small hot concrete box, but there was also a feeling of freshness, of being renewed.

One of the greatest joys of this time is having our clothes and sheets washed, aired and ironed. I bury my face in the pile of fresh, neatly folded clothes drinking in the scent of hot summer breezes that still cling to them, a heavenly smell in our airless swampish atmosphere. During the times of my menstruation the muslin strips come back bleached and spotless; Welderman's daughter must boil them for hours. Every few days we try to send out our mattresses that have become very compressed and soggy with condensation and sweat. It's quite an effort for Mole to drag the rolled up mattresses through the manhole and underground passage so he is often reluctant and very happy to say no when it's raining. But when the sun is shining and the mattresses are passed to us in the evening, dry and still warm from the solar heat, the bliss is indescribable.

With the change in temperature our room starts attracting visitors of the rodent and pond variety. First we hear the scurry of mouse feet sniffing around the table legs in the semi-darkness. Unfortunately Valentin hears them and throws a hard-hitting slipper that just misses squashing one of them. We quickly chase them back down the hole. At our request Mole now leaves the manhole open to help air intake. We rarely feel any wisp of a breeze coming up but it helps to lessen the feeling of claustrophobia and suffocation. Next comes the leap of little frogs; again Valentin is on the warpath and Jon drops them down the hole, hoping they survive. Valentin attacks anything that moves: flies and spiders and the occasional wasp have no chance, swatted and wacked with books and paper. I can't be too judgemental; if we were infested with mosquitoes I'd be out there swatting as well. Thankfully they only appear on rare occasions and we know there's a fair few out there from our experience of bitten nights in Grozny. One night I wake up hearing scrabbling noises coming from the manhole, interspersed with falling pebbles, then a little 'thud' and silence followed by more scrabblings, more pebbles falling and another 'thud'. I eventually fall asleep wondering what tiny creature is trying to reach us. The next morning I hear crackling from our plastic rubbish bag and watch, open mouthed, as the bag begins to move across the floor. Underneath we find an enormous, black cockroach. We are fascinated by its tough armour plating and tenacity. We persuade Valentin not to squash it and place it in an empty jar, handing it to Mole to take outside. The saddest experience we have in our contact with other creatures is when a young bird falls into the drain and cannot find a way out. It manages to fly to our end of the drain, probably following the light reflected from the bulb, and comes up against the metal grating. Freedom so near yet so far – how well we know this feeling! Another bird chirps frantically at the other end, probably its mother, but gives up after a few hours. The pathetic flapping of his wings goes on for about four days, growing weaker and weaker. It is as much a torment for us as for the fledgling and Valentin asks Mole whether he can do anything to free the bird but he says the design of the drain makes it impossible. The stench of death filters up through the grating and we put paper over it, blessing the bird spirit now free of its mortal coil. The fact that so few creatures find their way into our 'King's Chamber' shows how inaccessible we are.

The static in the atmosphere becomes more intense with the increased heat and some days there are thunderstorms. We hear the rumbles of thunder through the drain and all leap towards it, taking it in turns to lean over, waiting for gusts of fresh air that smell of rain-soaked hot earth, scorched grass and cow dung. Sometimes with a strong wind, the air rises a foot above the drain before it merges into the soup. These are the good days and the absurdity of having to resort to sniffing a drain for fresh air doesn't escape us. But the amusement is edged with sadness.

Valentin decides it's time for a spring clean; he asks Mole for a dust-pan and brush and sets to work. We take it in turns to use the brush and pan to clean under the beds as well as around the table. We are amazed at the amount of hair that has gathered in the corners; Valentin's convinced it's all ours and not his! Well, he could be right: I'm shedding a lot more in this heat. I'm feeling a little on edge with the heat and premenstrual tension, and when I see him taking one of my precious cloths, a ripped square from the blue towel that got burnt blocking one of the hot air holes in the sauna, I'm on the alert. He uses it to clean the condensation lake around the churn and I'm thinking 'Well, that's OK we can wash it afterwards' but then he puts it in the churn and my fuse blows. 'How dare you, that is one of my special cloths, it's as precious as gold to me.' I point out the gold sweet wrapper on the wall to emphasize my point. Valentin replies

218

(roughly translated) 'Why make such a fuss when we can ask for some more cloth?' I try to explain that sometimes we have had nothing and had to make use of any little scrap that came our way. In the future it might happen again, who knows? We are both rather wild-eyed and angry but Valentin gets my point and lifts the lid of the churn and is about to put his hand in, to fish the cloth out, I am horrified and screech in a loud whisper 'Niet, niet, niet, not necessary.' We both calm down and end up by shaking hands. Jon remains the pillar of calmness throughout.

The argument acts like a thunderstorm, clearing any oppressive grumbling thought energy out of the room. I feel more compassionate and understanding towards Valentin; maybe he feels the same or maybe not, I don't know. However, afterwards we all three sit on our stools discussing the fact that we come from different cultures, have different belief systems but now we live in the same, small, concrete world. This is our state and we all run it together. Valentin grins, proposing that Jon should be the mayor, I grin back and agree as Jon has certainly managed to control his emotions more than us, and is the best arbiter. There have been other times when I have wanted to point out to Valentin some things that I find irritating and disrespectful and Jon has talked me out of it. Also he tells me when I'm being 'pigheaded' and using too much space (usually in retaliation, very childish). Later I have a little giggle to myself about the madness of having an argument about a ragged square piece of blue cloth, but it is also a symbol of our plight, the way our values have changed to help us survive in our captive world.

During our discussion with Valentin about our free, independent state he makes the comment that 'freedom is a state of mind'. I couldn't agree with him more. I feel that on several levels of my being I have achieved a state of freedom, yet on many others I have not. I'm aware of the mental and emotional constructs I have within myself that were formed at a very early age and have determined my future decisions and thoughts. Then I ask 'Why, what is real?' and confusion enters my mind and I am shaken to the core of my being. Maybe these construct foundations aren't as real and sound as they have appeared to be. It seems that I need to build my mind's foundations in a fluid state not set in concrete ideas based on past conditioning. I laugh to myself and wonder whether I will ask myself these questions when I am on the other side of these concrete walls. I hope so, over and over again until the questions cease to exist.

The renewed communication gives me the confidence to ask Valentin if it would bother him if I go topless. I have already seen that nakedness does not carry the same meaning as it does to all the Muslims surrounding us. He is a practical man. Why wear clothes when the temperature is approaching 40 degrees? They only induce suffocating stress and ill health. He takes his flannel off the line, sews open ended pockets on two sides and threads through a string creating a 'G' string pair of pants, thereby still maintaining a sense of privacy whilst leaving most of his body free to breathe. Jon follows suit. I am wearing my sarong as a halter-neck dress, but still find it very restrictive in the heat. Having got to know Valentin a little better, I felt more confident that me being semi-naked will not arouse any sexual fantasies or frustrations and so I take the plunge. His response is a dismissive 'Niet probliem,' and there's no leering or lewd comments. Obviously Russians are used to seeing more naked flesh and do not immediately associate it with loose sexual morals, which makes their attitude more healthy in my opinion. The bizarre nature of our attire, Tweedledum and Tweedledee with their matching flannelettes and me in a scarf miniskirt, do bring a twinkle to my eye. Also the mad panic when we hear the noise of someone coming, trying not to bump into each other, legs and arms akimbo, pulling on clothing more suitable for the morals of our Chechen friends. I think Welderman is a bit perturbed when he sees me using my 'platok' (scarf) as a halterneck dress (it's a time when my white shirt and pink skirt are in the wash), and he shouts something to his daughter hidden in the passage below. A few minutes later a cotton yellow and red spotted nightie with short frilly sleeves and a long grey dress with white spots and star buttons all down the front are handed to me. Precious gifts.

The compassionate and forgiving nature of Welderman became evident in the latter part of May. He appears one day, maskless, and settles himself on the floor on the other side of the bars. Wearing his white skullcap and slippers he leisurely lights a cigarette and looks at us and smiles. Then he begins talking to Valentin about the plight of Chechnya and the history of Chechnya under Russian rule. He speaks about the immense suffering when the whole population were deported to Kazakhstan in 1944. Welderman was born in the early years in Khazakstan; some of his siblings had died in the cattle trucks on the way there. He doesn't speak with a vitriolic and accusatory tone, just calmly stating how things appear from a Chechen point of view, and he allows Valentin to voice his views. He also points out how the Russians always seem to want to control the states that practised Islam rather than Christianity and not allow them independence. 'Was religion the main reason for the Russians bombing Chechnya?' he asks Valentin. Valentin shakes his head, looking Welderman directly in the eye and says 'Niet, dengi (money).' I can see that Welderman is impressed by his honesty and he nods his head in agreement. After this initial meeting Welderman comes in periodically for chats with Valentin. Camilla and I are very excited about these meetings; two men from very different cultural and social backgrounds, supposedly enemies, both in their early fifties, are managing to talk and listen to each other without getting uptight or angry. They begin forming a friendship, sharing ideas and jokes. On one occasion Welderman comes into our room and plays a game of chess with Valentin, the chessboard balanced on the bed between them. I can see that neither of them is trying to win, and the game ends in a draw – how tactful! I wish all conflicts could end like this, with mutual understanding and respect. I actually believe Valentin is being sincere in his friendship, although there were times earlier on when he quite obviously put on the diplomat's charm, trying to negotiate a deal for freedom with Welderman who just smiled knowingly. After one of their talks Welderman turns to us and, pointing at Valentin says 'Haroshi moushina (good man)'. He means it.

One evening Jon and I are lying on the bed and Valentin is sitting on his stool combing his hair when the manhole cover slides open and Welderman's head pops up; he was so quiet none of us heard him approaching above the sound of the fan. Welderman's eyes open wide on seeing Valentin sitting naked except for the flannel loincloth, for Valentin hadn't had a chance to dress. He tut-tuts and mumbles something about a video and disappears again. Later that night Mole and Welderman bring in a video camera and this time it's Valentin's turn to talk. He sits, very erect, on the stool, staring into the lens and speaks at great length in a loud confident voice, showing no fear. The next day a new pair of pale blue and white stripey pyjamas are presented to Valentin.

Messages from home

As we continue to hold prayer circles a few times a week we notice the energy flowing through us becoming more and more powerful. Camilla often feels

*and 'sees' a shaft of purple light shining down through her, and purple keeps
coming into my dreams. We feel it gives us strength to overcome obstacles on
our path, a ray of healing and forgiveness.*

*We sense a lot of people are praying for us. There are times when I can't
get to sleep at night because there is so much energy piling in. I'm almost
making prayers to say 'Ease off with your prayers, you're keeping me awake!'
Then I remember we are in a pyramid of light and can radiate these prayers
out to our captors and other suffering people and into the land. We plant
seeds of light wherever we are held.*

1 June. We are woken quite suddenly before the usual breakfast time.
I'm still trying to wipe the sleep from my eyes as Mole, in a fluster, un-
does the two padlocks. There's an air of excitement about him as he comes
over to us with a pale yellow envelope. 'Letters, read and reply, you have
ten minutes then I take them away,' and he thrusts some squared paper
and a blue biro into Jon's hand, sternly holding up ten fingers, then leaves
the room while we open the envelope. It is addressed to us in Mum's
handwriting – the first correspondence we have had from our families.

Jon carefully takes out the contents. There's a letter from his father,
one from his mother, one from my sister and one from my mother with
a few photos. As I read I try and absorb every word, but I don't think
I'll have time to memorize them. I look at the photos: Ashok gazes up
at me in his school uniform, a big grin on his face, then there's Ben in
the garden at Lydney and one of Jon's mum with a glass of white wine
in her hand and finally a group photo taken at our farewell party a few
days before we left for Chechnya. We quickly scribble a note each, trying to sound as positive as possible and letting them know we are coping
and managing to heal ourselves. Jon writes about dreaming purple then
we reluctantly hand them back to Mole, asking why we can't keep them.
Valentin pleads for us too, Mole looks flustered and unsure of himself;
avoiding eye contact he says nothing and disappears down the hole.

We feel elated yet very tearful at the same time. The letters were dated
from the end of December, six months ago, so we still have no idea of how
our families are in the present, how they are coping being held captive
in their thoughts and actions by our continued absence. We had so little
time to feel them through their letters, or to remember their words and
their faces. We retell the news to each other throughout the day, trying to
remember all the details. The minds of the hierachy of the gang must be

so unbalanced and so full of paranoia to believe that letting us keep a few letters and photos of our families will harm them. Their fear is so great. Welderman brings our supper and I see the pale yellow envelope peeping out of his breast pocket, my spirits soar, can it be possible? Yes, it can! Oh how I love him! He hands us the envelope, followed by a small plastic bottle of arnica pills that must have been sent by Mum. 'Do you want these?' He asks. 'Yes please, it's good medicine,' we reply. We explain to Valentin that arnica is very good for stress and we all take some.

How great it is to receive news from home! It's really weird how time erodes the memory and you can start to forget how people look, but when you see a photograph you are reminded and it all comes flooding back. There's a great photo of Ben in my parents' garden with the flowers all around; he's leaning forward with his cheeky little grin and wearing his school tie akimbo. It's great to get these photos but in many ways it twangs the heart-strings and reminds me of the people I love and I am not with. I do not have any freedom of access. I am not like a normal prisoner where they can come and visit me and talk with me. I have had no contact since we sent e-mails back in Moscow many months ago. I look at them now and then and read the letters, just to keep me alive and connected to them in a different way, a way other than just thought.

In the following weeks, almost every day during my private morning coffee ritual when Jon and Valentin are sleeping, I prop up the photos, read the letters and think of all the family, sending them love and strength to hold on. Mum's last words, 'All is well,' give me peace. I think of Ashok and some of the precious moments I spent with him. Our deepest conversations happened when we were driving together, just the two of us. He would fly over from the Netherlands or France and we would roam the country, visiting friends or family. On these long journeys we would reintegrate with each other, talking of happenings on the outside and feelings on the inside. He would sing a little made-up ditty, I would join in and he would get angry so I would shut up or we'd make a ludicrous song together, a mixture of rap and operatic, letting it swell hugely to end in a vast discordant crescendo. Sometimes we would converse in nonsense language full of drama and hard-bitten silences, always ending in laughter, so liberating for the mind. It's very hard, thinking back to these times, not to get washed away with strong emotions. I always pull myself up on the bank, knowing that I must keep stable and strong for Ashok but if the current is too strong I reach out a hand for Jon's support and he always responds. I would like to light a candle at these times and calm myself by meditating on the warmth and beauty of the flame but they are too precious, needed for the times of darkness.

The power cuts become more frequent as the summer goes on. I find these times very hard, sitting on the bed hearing the whirr of the fan dying down, my spirits decelerating at the same pace and being in complete blackness until someone manages to grope their way to the table and unwrap the plastic bag that holds the matchbox, strike a match and light the candle. We have become wiser after spending one day in darkness when the matches were damp. The oppressive humid heat envelops us like a suffocating blanket. 'I'm feeling a bit panicky, Jon, there's not enough air, I can't breathe properly.' 'Remember, you only need 2% oxygen to survive,' he replies; and I calm down, breathing more deeply. I imagine the Amazonian forest and the tribes of Indians who live there convincing my body and mind to adapt to our hot wet climate as they have done to theirs. Sometimes I imagine myself as a tropical frog, growing a froggy skin, basking in the hot dampness with a wide froggy grin on my face.

Four days of darkness, nights of perspiring semi-consciousness, various limbs flung against walls or hung in the air away from the damp heat of the bed. One leg hits the deck as I fall asleep, pulling a muscle in my groin. Day comes and at first I manage to concentrate on some sewing, sitting close to the single candle flame. I'm sewing a flower picture to give as a present to Welderman's daughter when we leave; her washing and ironing and good cooking help to make life bearable in this stinking oven. It is a rose head with overlapping petals as a centrepiece and four sprays of smaller flowers in the corners – a challenge because I have no pencil to draw the design but must sew directly from the design in my head. It keeps me absorbed for many hours despite the eye strain. As the dark days continue I cannot even concentrate on the sewing, for the sweltering humidity is dulling our senses. I take a stool and sit next to the bars looking down through the manhole; I see a faint glimmer of grey light and can hear the birds chirping merrily and it helps give me the illusion of breathing fresher air. I can imagine myself sitting in the shade of a tree, the sunlight dancing across my skin, my mind full of the sweet birdsong. It's not easy. Valentin lies limp on the metal base of his bed having handed out his wet mattress to be dried; Jon sits cross-legged meditating on our bed. Sometimes I test out my balance in the near darkness, swinging heavy slow limbs through the fetid air in a tai chi form of wobbly grace and I sing out to the damp walls a soft yearning lament that opens my heart and lifts my spirit. As the days go on I'm feeling more desperate and I discuss with Jon ways of sleeping nearer the floor. Perhaps they can take our bedstead away and bring some bricks and boards instead. There is probably only a degree or two difference in the temperature near the ceiling and the floor, but anything for a few extra minutes of sleep at night. I'm clutching at straws.

Valentin has become our spokesman and he explains to Welderman our difficulties. On the fifth day Welderman finally consents to opening up the round hole he had blocked with cement just before Valentin's arrival. We hear lots of banging from the outside as the cement is chipped out then Mole appears with a mallet and starts swiping at the piece of wood wedged in the hole. The problem is, it's far nearer the inside of the wall than the outside, and the wall is very thick; he only succeeds in wedging it in more tightly. I'm dying to give him some advice and lend a hand but decide Mole would not appreciate it. He's just having a taster of the hot steam bath we live in and with the added exertion he's swimming in sweat and frustration. Despite their good intentions the room stays as airless as ever. Late afternoon arrives and the diversion of this morning's activity has worn off. I'm back to my snail-like movement – any faster and my head aches, shrouded in a dizzy haze. Suddenly our room is illuminated, air blows through the fan blades – the wonder of electricity, our saving grace!

The conditions we live in are perfect for the growth of fungi. I'm surprised we're not covered in mushrooms! As it is we do suffer small irritations: Valentin has conjunctivitis in both eyes, and Jon and I have difficulty closing our eyes at night because of stabbing pains, a form of arc eye caused by the single harsh light from the bulb in combination with the heat and humidity. In the morning a layer of sticky grit glues our eyelids together, 'How's your eye cement this morning, darling?' I joke to Jon. I have thrush, but the infection that concerns me the most is my suppurating belly button. The virus has a rhythm, weeping fluid and crusting over in a seven-day cycle. I spend hours lying on my back holding my hand over my belly button sending it healing. Sometimes I visualize myself in a sunlit hospital room with a motherly nurse in her crisp, white starched uniform plumping up my pillows. Jon does some hands-off healing as well. It may not cure the virus – the humid conditions make that difficult – but it certainly calms the mind.

We are having problems with the food. Not too little but too much, and too rich for us to digest properly in this heat; we're all suffering from constipation. Valentin asks for pills and we decide to go on a four-day fast. We explain to Valentin why we are doing it and ask him to put our case to Welderman as we know the Chechens won't approve. We manage one day fasting before Welderman comes to visit us in a very agitated mood. 'Why don't you eat? You must eat, it's good food, it's not good you not eat.' He stares at me, a pleading look in his eyes. I try to explain that we are grateful for the food but we're not doing a great job of labour in here, sitting around doing nothing all day except using our minds, which doesn't burn up huge amounts of calories. I try to explain that we could do with some lighter food. Valentin translates this as salads and fruit to keep us healthy in this heat. Welderman promises to bring some.

True to his word a variety of chopped carrot, beetroot, cabbage and onion salads follow and we enter the melon season. Vast watermelons appear in glistening, pink crimson slices arranged on a tray, also smaller yellow melons which we are allowed to cut up with a blunt knife. We can't keep pace with the melon supply and soon have a pyramid of small football-size melons hiding under our bed.

Despite the good food our nerves feel thin and frayed, worn down by the constant humid heat. A period of 'fan wars' begins involving endless discussions between Valentin and me on the best possible positioning of the fan to give us the most effective relief. Valentin talks from a theoretical basis. 'I studied and taught physics in St Petersburg for many years so I should know best,' he says, while I argue from my 'hands on' experience using fans in confined dusty spaces on building sites. I give up and let Valentin have his way but we notice a couple of days later Valentin has moved the fan to the position that I had suggested in the first place! We say nothing.

Illness and healing

Valentin is ill, he has pain in his kidneys. He walks to the bars, bent over, perspiration beading on his forehead, and taps them for attention. It is a while before anyone hears and we feel so helpless in the face of his agony. Eventually Welderman appears and is very sympathetic, he says he'll send someone to get some medicine. Valentin curls up on his bed gasping; we mentally send him love and healing – we can't see what else we can do. Welderman returns with boxes of phials containing penicillin, antibiotic powder and liquid Novocain, a strong painkiller, and some throw-away syringes.

Valentin says 'How am I going to inject myself?' Welderman replies 'This is what I have, I can't do it, I've never done it before.' So I step in, saying 'I'll do it'; they both look surprised. I explain that I've done a first aid course and have a certificate. I ask Welderman and Valentin a few questions to prove I know something about it, 'Do I inject into the muscle, the vein or just below the skin?' Luckily it needs to be injected subcutaneously, something I think anyone can do. What I don't tell them is that I have never injected a person before – on the course we only practised on balloons!

For the next seven days I am nurse, twice a day injecting this cocktail of pain killer and penicillin into Valentin's buttocks, being careful to alternate to avoid excessive bruising. My only concern is the difficulty of smashing the tops of the glass phials without getting glass into the mixture, even though I guess the broken glass will never be small enough to be sucked up the hypodermic needle. I find it highly amusing and ironic after Valentin's previous attitude towards me that now I am his nurse. Camilla turns away in respect of Valentin's dignity. I have studied some Chinese medicine and know that apple juice is very good for cleansing the kidneys and so I tell Valentin and he passes on the information to Welderman. The next day two litres of apple juice arrive and continue to come at intervals over the next couple of weeks. On occasions we even get peach juice.

I offer to do some healing on Valentin's kidneys and he accepts. He stands in the middle of the room in his loincloth and I massage his back, then lift my hands away, keeping the palms facing towards his back, feeling the change in temperature as I move my hands. His right kidney is distinctly cooler than his left. I remember from a massage course many years before that the cold spots are the places that need more attention. I allow my body to be an open channel for the healing energies to flow through and give Valentin some relief from the pain. He asks for a daily healing session so I know it gives him comfort and helps him to relax. The course of injections lasts a week and after another week Valentin seems to be completely recovered. I certainly notice the difference in temperature of his kidneys; the energy is much warmer and his skin colour healthier.

Welderman decides to give Valentin a treat. They have a long conversation through the bars and afterwards Valentin tells us he is going out for the evening. Going out? We wonder if we have understood him properly. There is no electricity, the sodden grey walls glint in the candlelight, rumbles of distant thunder echo up the drain. Supper arrives brought by Welderman, he winks at Valentin then disappears again. Valentin dons his striped pyjamas and sits and waits. Two or three hours later we hear the grating slide of metal on concrete and Welderman's impish face appears with a blindfold and a chair. He unpadlocks the door and beckons to Valentin. Blindfolded Valentin steps down onto the chair then disappears through the dark tunnel. Expansive silence – this is the first time we have had the space to ourselves for about three months. I do a little celebratory dance, swinging my arms in the extra space; then I make two ceremonial cups of coffee laced with cream that by some miracle has not yet soured from the morning milking, with a sprinkling of damp sugar on the top. We listen to the rain hurtling down, sweet music to our ears, and the resounding booms and crackle of overhead thunder, the blinding glare of lightning only to be imagined. A car comes and goes and we wonder if they are taking Valentin for a drive. Chatting away, we allow ourselves to speak above a whisper, for no one can hear us over the storm. Then we have a little cuddle, such a rarity as very early on we decided not to be affectionate in front of Valentin, knowing it would make the situation much harder for him. Sounds of giggling come from the tunnel, and I'm sure I hear someone saying 'baby', perhaps they think we have been making babies in Valentin's absence. Hands to their mouths they try and muffle their giggles, whiffs of alcoholic breath escape through their fingers. It sounds like Valentin has had a good night out and I'm glad.

The next morning he is quite dismissive of the whole affair, saying they had talked on the veranda for hours and they would not allow him to take his blindfold off. Disappointingly he doesn't give us any information, perhaps feeling we wouldn't understand.

Valentin takes a razor to his pyjamas, cutting off the legs to make shorts, more suitable for our climate. Jon manages to make a pair of shorts for himself out of the leg tubes that Valentin has cut off. I am so impressed by his ability to visualize how and where to cut up the material, which is a fairly complex task when you have a gusset to include. Now we sew side by side, Jon sewing up his shorts with tiny yellow stitches and me sewing leaping kangaroos on to his purple and black chequered shirt. Valentin has been given a book all about the movement of various animals with lots of clear line drawings which I transpose on to the material with a needle and thread. It is extremely satisfying but gives me eye strain. Sometimes when Valentin is having a snooze I borrow the glasses he has been given by Welderman; the extra magnification keeps the aches at bay.

My shorts finished, I turn to house building with matchsticks. I have always wanted to build my own home and now I have the time to give it some thought. The house must feel good to be in with lots of natural light, as well as being highly energy efficient, using active and passive solar power and underfloor heating. So with my pile of matches I form an octagon, a much more interesting shape than a box, with no acute angles to gather clutter. Over the next few weeks I build and rebuild the model house, relocating rooms and fireplace, adding a subterranean utility and boiler room and a softwater well. Perhaps I'll build the walls out of rammed earth and rubber tyres. One day when I'm out of this small sunless place the house may become a full-size reality.

English literature

19 July is a red-letter day. Welderman proudly hands a fat magazine to Jon through the bars. I peer over his shoulder and see the title *Car*. Oh no, my spirits drop, a *car* magazine. Well, it's one up on toothpaste tubes. We scan the cover and I flick through it. There seem to be a fair number of articles amongst the photos of shiny, metal machines. Things are looking up. It also happens to be the third anniversary of Jon and I being together. What a good present! I glance down the contents. There's an article about Colin Dutton designing a car to drive across water and his first attempt at crossing the Channel; this looks more exciting than car performance test results. Colin and the *Car* reporter set off from Folkestone harbour in a choppy August dawn; the reporter looks rather green and is having trouble keeping his breakfast down. Eventually he begins to enjoy himself and the startled looks of passing boats. About five miles from the coast of France they smell burning in the engine: some wires have caught fire and they have to be rescued; shoulders hunched, sombre faces, what

disappointment. Maybe they'll try again next year. We learn all about MGF's and my favourite, the Italian sports car Barchetta. The Vauxall Vectra has just come off the production line, designed for the use of the long distance salesman. A reporter takes it on a test drive through Germany. Good at handling corners, comfy reclining seat for catnaps, plenty of space for hanging jackets but, oh dear, the cup holder isn't big enough to hold a Coke! I laugh at the account of a reporter who, while testing a car out in Italy, was stung in the bottom by a scorpion and had an uncomfortable ride home. There is an advert for a French tour of the châteaux of the Loire valley; we imagine ourselves surrounded by Louis XIV furniture delicately nibbling the mouth-watering French cuisine, our little white Lada parked amongst all the Rolls Royces and Bentleys in the courtyard. Sometimes I practise my tai chi form using car terminology for all the movements; it made me chuckle – anything for a bit of humour.

Wow, some English literature, albeit a car magazine, a feast for the eyes. it gives me a strange sense of home. I devour the articles one by one, regardless of content. I'm fascinated by the use of computer-aided design and laser technology to build a car out of plastic that can be rejigged over and over on the screen before the final shape is formed. I even read all the ads in my hunger for written English. Do I want a super-chip in my car? Are there that many people who want a radar detector? Are there that many who continually break the speed limits? Looks like it. I read about the performance test of some new sports cars cruising around the Cotswold lanes ending at a small country pub to compare notes and drink some good beer – I'm almost there!

The magazine keeps us amused throughout the rest of our time in Welderman's abode although by the end of August every word has been sucked dry of meaning and reason by our thirsty eyes.

Valentin has had enough of the stream of diverse books passed through the bars, none of which particularly interests him, and he has asked for newspapers so he can do the crosswords. Welderman not only supplies him with newspapers but also with a crossword puzzle magazine and a Biro. Before he sends the books back we retrieve a small atlas and the book about animal movement – at the moment I'm sewing a nice plump frog on to Jon's shirt copied from it. The atlas we use as a springboard for imaginary and future journeys around the globe and to trigger memories of past journeys. Valentin shows us the routes of his travels. When he was still in his teens he joined the merchant navy and sailed through many oceans, primarily the Arctic, Black Sea, White Sea and North Sea. He eventually became a navigation officer before leaving to further his career on dry land. He did very well because he ended up as mayor of Archangel, his home city, and could afford holidays in Greece. On one break he travelled for a month, driving all the way from Russia to the southernmost tip of Spain and back. I wonder what his impressions had been of the different countries but our limited vocabulary doesn't stretch to conversations of any depth. We ask if he ever visited the British Isles, he shrugs his shoulders and shakes his head and I get the impression he thinks it a small, cold, wet island not worth visiting.

Valentin's hair is beginning to flop over his eyes which is irritating him greatly, so he asks Welderman if he can have a haircut and Welderman says, with a face-splitting grin and a twinkle in his eye, he will arrange it. Later that day Mole appears in a white coat with a large pair of shiny, professional looking hair-cutting scissors and a comb. The scene is wonderfully surreal with Valentin sitting on a stool in the middle of the room and Mole deftly snipping away in his barber's coat and black mask. Locks of blond hair fall to the floor and Valentin emerges with a very stylish haircut. Mole taps on the bars, signalling for someone to let him out. He has been locked in with us, presumably to prevent us from overcoming him and escaping, but unfortunately for him no one is out there listening. He taps again, and again, then resigns himself to a wait, sitting with his back to us, shoulders hunched in despondency. A little taste of his own medicine, tee hee. It is outrageously hot, the sweat pouring off us in our skimpy clothing, I can't imagine what it must be like for him in long trousers, tee shirt and long-sleeved overall topped with a woollen black mask. The minutes tick by; Valentin offers him some grapes which Mole brushes away curtly, not deigning to look Valentin in the eye. We begin to feel quite sorry for him and try to open up communication by offering some water, again he refuses to take any and remains silent. At last we hear movement and Welderman appears with a jangling key to release his son from his unexpected sweat-drenched confinement. I don't think Mole will be offering to do any more haircuts.

Valentin makes the same request every day: 'aftershave please'. And after a while his request is granted. That evening when Jon and I lie on our bed attempting to sleep Valentin sits on a stool, the little glass bottle of luminous green liquid on the table by his side. Slowly he unscrews the top and takes a sniff, then shakes a few drops onto the palm of his hand and pats his cheeks. I think I'm going to die. I have an aversion to after-shave in general and this is particularly foul smelling to me. It's a struggle to hold my tongue because I can see how much this gift means to him and what a boost it gives to his self-esteem yet I'm finding it hard to breathe. I turn to the wall, keeping my nose covered by the sheet, away from the direct stream of fan blasted aftershave air. The next night it gets worse, my lungs contract, I begin to cough and feel an explosion of angry words about to erupt. I leap out of bed and turn the fan away from the table and our bed and attempt to explain to Valentin the trouble I am having breathing his coveted aftershave fumes. Poor man, he screws the top back on, relinquishing his pleasure for my sake. He does not use it again.

Our stomachs are bearing up well, although I have a couple of bouts of belladonna poisoning as we enter the aubergine season. Mole's sister pro-duces a tantalizing new dish: baked aubergine halves in olive oil sprin-kled with garlic. Twice the aubergines aren't cooked well enough and I spend what seems like hours bent double with sharp stomach gripes over in 'milk churn corner' emptying my bowels and producing poisonous smelling fumes. When I re-emerge Valentin has his face smothered by his jumper. Rather unreasonably, I feel irritated. I can't help it, can I? He and Jon manage to escape the indignity of these 'sick as a dog' occasions, but I manage to escape the 'ear de-waxing' ceremonies that Jon and Valentin have to perform more and more frequently as the summer progresses. They are both getting increasingly deaf and Valentin complains about it to Welderman who is at a loss as to know how to help. Jon asks for some oil and a teaspoon and I pour warm oil, heated over a candle flame, into Jon's ears and he offers to do the same for Valentin. But the process isn't having much effect so they start sculpting warm candle-wax plugs to stick in their ears to draw out the earwax. This works better and I enjoy watching them sit at opposite ends of the table, their faces highlighted in the soft warm glow of the candle, absorbed in their task. The light and the atmosphere of quiet concentration remind me of a Rembrandt painting.

Jon's shout

Jon is beginning to find the heat unbearable; red spotty rashes are appear-ing all over his body. His head pounds and aches most days. We find

232

some relief by dousing our flannels in water and draping them over our heads. When they become too warm we wet them again and hold them in front of the fan to cool down.

We've been living in these hot and humid temperatures for two months now. This evening I can feel this almost unbearable tension; my body is covered in a heat rash and I have two red bumps on my forehead like horns trying to break forth and a wacking headache. This heat is the last straw after over a year living in a constant state of tension. I can't hold on any more and I tell Camilla I'm going to shout. I feel in total control yet one part of me is out of control and after the warning I start screaming as high as my strained voice can muster, 'I can't take any more of this, I've had fucking enough, how much more of this fucking heat? Let us go you bastards, let us out.' Valentin tries to calm me, but is condescending. So I swear at him, releasing all this venom from my being. After a few minutes we hear Welderman bombing along the underground tunnel as fast as his little being will take him. His head pops up through the hole and he asks 'Jon, Jon, what's the trouble, what is the problem?' I carry on ranting in English saying 'It's OK for you, you can go outside, you can breathe fresh air, you get to move around. I'm stuck in here, day after day, night after night, not knowing my fate at all.' I'm kneeling on the floor, still snivelling, my eyes streaming, my nose running and my voice totally croaky. 'Jon, you're a man, you're a man, stop crying.' I feel relief inside but I carry on, acting a little now. He does not know my mind, only I do. He starts suggesting things to make my small world nicer, more tolerable. 'Fruit juice?' 'No, freedom,' I reply. Then he says ' To hear home, London, the BBC?' 'Da, Da (yes, yes),' I reply. I'm not really sure what he means but I think he means a radio. Eventually I calm down and he praises me saying I'm a good man even though in some way I feel he still mocks me a little because it is not the male Chechen way to cry or to be seen crying. I have failed their test.

I am crying now as well, even though I know Jon is half play-acting. Welderman and Valentin have a surreptitious giggle and I know they are thinking how 'unmanly' it is of Jon; they do not know the pain he is in or the act of bravery he has just performed. Jon knows he could never have behaved in such a way with our 'fab four' but he knows the compassionate nature of Welderman and took the gamble that somehow this outcry would work in our favour rather than against it. He is proved right. The next day, 6 August, Mole produces a little black 'worldwide' radio with our breakfast.

A window on the world

What an amazing gift, worth a few moments of madness. We switch it on, it works, it even looks new. We're touched by Welderman's sincerity and the fact that he actually went out and bought a radio for us. Another more dismal thought passes through my mind: 'OK, so how long does it mean we are going to be here?' Anyway, we tune in and after half a day of search- ing the air waves we find the BBC World Service. It's as if this small black box has blown a massive hole in one of our concrete walls, giving us a win- dow on the world. The reception is not very clear so I ask for something to make an antenna. Mole brings an aluminium coat hanger, the worst kind of metal to conduct radio waves, but I wedge it up our so-called ventilation hole and move the radio around in an attempt to get a better signal. It's pretty hopeless so we end up holding the radio close to our ears, taking it in turns to listen, Valentin to the Russian programmes and us to the English ones. Shortwave radio is an amazing invention; the low energy signal is being bounced off the ionospheric layer of gas in the atmosphere back to us in our concrete bunker, half below ground in the middle of Chechnya. I wonder where the nearest booster station is?

Welderman comes to visit us quite often after my shout and asks Valentin 'How is he? How is he?' It really irritates me that he asks Valentin instead of me. Then one day he asks me if I am all right and to remember that I'm a man. I look him straight in the eye, calm, composed, projecting love and compassion and nod. Welderman turns to Camilla and says 'Jon, haroshi moushina (Jon's a good man).' 'I know,' she replies.

Early morning, the radio hugged to my ear, I'm in the Mongolian des- ert looking for wild camels; one has been sighted, lying in a ditch. Com- ing up closer, we see we have hit the jackpot – not only a wild camel but a female wild camel giving birth. I feel the hot breeze and the stony ground beneath my feet, I hear the groans of the camel and the shouts of delight from my companions as the baby camel slithers out of its mother's womb, all wet and sparkling in the bright sun. The image begins to fade and the hot solar breeze becomes the musty recycled breath of the fan and the stony desert the cement floor of our cell.

It's the Proms season and the World Service is transmitting some of the performances. The sweet sounds of Puccini's 'La Bohème' ring in my head, followed by the grating sounds of a contemporary piece composed by a Finnish man, which I don't find inspiring at all. I usually like discordant pieces, but not this one. In our magazine there is a photogragh of a Chrysler car taken outside the Albert Hall so when we know there is going to be a transmission we look at the photograph, imagining the excited audience streaming in and the sounds of the orchestras tuning up, then hold up the radio between our heads, close our eyes and merge with the music.

There's movement in the underground passage. Jon nudges me and I prise open my gritty eyelids, gathering my sleep-mushed dream thoughts into focus. The manhole cover scrapes open and a video camera rises up majestically, followed by Mole and the Welderman. They open the padlocked metal door and enter our concrete boudoir. Valentin sits up but Welderman tells him to lie down and face the wall. Jon and I sit on the edge of our bed and Welderman tells us to talk into the camera; he doesn't instruct us, or command us to read a script, just gestures wildly with his hands saying 'Talk, talk'. After the last video in May we realize that Welderman doesn't care what we say. He has given us this small freedom and we are determined to use it to speak out our feelings. I peer into the lens; the 150-watt light bulb is blinding my right eye and I must look like a stricken albino mole. I start speaking.

'It's the middle of August and your letters, the ones from the end of December, still give us joy to read. Love to have more and some photos, if you are allowed to send them.' Jon continues: *'This is the first time I have spoken in a normal voice, told to whisper for the past year so if I sound different it is because I am not used to speaking at this volume. Eating well, pretty hot, no windows.'* 'But we have a fan.' *'And we'd like some more letters, a newspaper and a book.'* 'And much love to all, especially Ashok and Ben; maybe they could write too, that'd be good.' *'Please don't make it too much longer; I don't know how much longer I'll remain sane.'* Help! I'm thinking, I don't want our parents to worry that we are going mad, so I add 'But we will.' *'And we have a shortwave radio now.'* 'We listen to the World Service . . . keeps us sane.' *'I hope this video reaches you in good condition because somebody has forgotten to switch the video light on! That's all for now, can't think of anything else to say.'* 'Lots of love and we pray, pray that it's soon. Remember to smile, it keeps you healthy.'

I am very tired of being held in this place of limbo, doing nothing, waiting, waiting for my life to continue. I wanted to speak my truth, my feelings of this place of despair. Not holding back, painting in words the stark

235

truth about our environment, hoping some governmental conscience will be moved enough to get us out of here. I am angry.

A couple of months ago I had asked Valentin when was his birthday – 23 August, he told me. As the day gets nearer I start sewing him a birthday 'cloth card'. Whenever he has a nap I take the cloth from under my pillow and painstakingly hem the borders and sew 'Happy Birthday Valentin. Love Jon and Camilla.' I think he is a little embarrassed when I present it to him; maybe his birthday isn't 23 August after all!

Valentin has a midnight treat – it's his turn to be videoed. He sits on a stool in his black and white striped jumper looking very upright and spruce and speaks for what seems like hours. They also take a photo of him. Then Welderman turns to us as we are sitting watching the show and asks if we want a souvenir. Jon shakes his head but Welderman ignores him and clicks away with the Polaroid. We are handed a photograph – Jon with beard, looking bored, and me peering at the camera (that 150-watt bulb is really affecting my eyesight), attempting to smile, looking thin, white, and at least 90 in my patterned, frilly nightie.

In the early morning when Valentin is still asleep and Jon is doing his meditation I have the radio clutched to my ear. The 'abridged book' programme lets me escape into other lives and worlds, *Anna Karenina* or the compelling web spun in *Human Croquet*. Then there is the News, mostly rather grim but we feel more in touch with the rest of the world by listening to it.

Another kidnapping, this time in the Congo. A group of tourists went on a trip into the jungle to see gorillas and were captured by some Congolese rebels. One of the party was Douglas Kear, a distant cousin of my father's; that was a bit strange. We also hear about the bombing of the American Embassy in Nairobi and a few days later as we are listening to Voice of America *the programme is interrupted by breaking news – we hear the voice of President Clinton announcing that in retaliation America is going to bomb rebel targets in the Sudan and in Afghanistan. Valentin doesn't believe us until he hears it on the Russian news 24 hours later.*

There's a great programme on the World Service about kung fu. It's about a teacher and his journey through the spiritual aspect of the martial art. I trained in the art of 'Hand of the Wind' kung fu. Towards the end of my training I was working with a partner and had my eyes closed while he attempted to hit me with ten strikes and kicks. I managed to sense all of them and deflect them before my body was hit, it was spooky. I learnt through the art of kung fu how precious life is. I realize it has helped me understand and control my feelings of revenge towards the 'fab four'.

Freedom?

Welderman visits us and says we will be released by 5 September. That's only ten days away. Can it be true? I don't doubt Welderman's integrity but he may not have the whole story. The days pass, 5 September arrives and is lived through without any great hope and then it's another day. I feel depressed and listen to the radio as much as possible. The batteries run out after only one week. It usually takes two before we get new ones from Mole.

I have the feeling Welderman and his family are getting a bit fed up with having to look after us – it is over four months now. The body language of Mole is desultory and begrudging, Welderman doesn't visit so often, and I'm sure his daughter must be getting weary of all the extra cooking and washing. As the summer is waning the days are getting cooler and unwanted little thoughts start popping into my head about how we will cope in the coming autumn and winter. After 5 September Welderman starts hinting that we may be on the move soon, but this time there is no mention of release or 'going home'. This news jangles our nerves. 'Please can we stay? We are happy here and appreciate your hospitality.' His shoulders slump and he doesn't smile. 'We cannot look after you any more,' he replies.

On 9 September, listening to the BBC evening news bulletin. 'Hey Jon, they're talking about us!' Jon puts his ear to the radio and we hear our own voices, our messages to our families from the last video. Valentin comes closer to listen too. How strange and what a boost to our morale! I feel so light and warm inside. Now we know our families know we are still alive, and, just maybe, this publicity exposure will help our release happen. But the commentator also mentioned that a close friend hopes there would now be renewed talks implying a break in negotiations for our release. How many more months or years will it be?

17

The Cricket Cellar

The night of Monday the 14th arrives and Welderman brings us supper with the message that we will be moving tonight. Even though my stomach has started to churn with anxiety, I feel I ought to eat a little, for we never know when we are going to be fed again. And guess what, I've just started my menstruation, fantastic timing!

We all have a 'last ditch' attempt at changing Welderman's mind by telling him once again how we are happy with his family, but to no avail. He says we are going to a 'good place (haroshi miassa)' but he doesn't look very convinced or happy about it himself. So we start packing up our plastic bags and go to the loo, always important in these harrowing times. I find the piece of cloth on which I had embroidered flowers, a present for his daughter who had made our time here in this airless concrete box bearable. Then the wonderful 'waiting game' begins. I'm feeling shaky and start doing some qigong and breathing exercises to calm myself. Valentin joins in. Finally there are muffled noises in the underground passage and Welderman and Mole appear, carrying some strips of cloth to tie around our eyes. I hand the embroidered cloth to Welderman, looking him straight in the eye and saying 'Podarok tua dochka,' roughly translated as 'a present for your daughter'; then I added in halting Russian, 'A "thank you" for all the good cooking and clean clothes.' He nods and takes the cloth from me.

They have placed a chair below the manhole so we can step down with a guiding hand. They take our plastic bags and say they will bring them later. I go first and Mole puts on my blindfold; thankfully it's only a strip of cloth and he makes sure I can breathe. The underground passage is smaller than I remember – we have to crouch. As I reach the other end I'm hauled up by the armpits through another manhole. They lead us out and into the back of a vehicle like a Land Rover. Jon and I sit on metal seats along the sides and they guide our hands to a grab rail and throw a cloth over us. There's a smell of straw and sheep. We hear Welderman telling Valentin to lie down on the floor behind the front seats. There are a few whispered grunts and the vehicle shudders; it sounds like it's a bit of a squeeze. The journey is bumpy and there are some hills to climb. Eventually we are guided out into a building, down some steps leading to a room; luckily I can see the ground below the blindfold so I don't stumble. I look down as we enter the new cellar, I've definitely got the best footwear – Valentin's heels are sticking out beyond his slippers, which are too small, and Jon's wearing mildew-green and rusty trainers; I've got Welderman's slippers, two sizes too big, but comfortable.

We're in a cellar, concrete and brick, with a steel door, no windows but three times the size of Welderman's and at least two metres high. Wow, the space, space for our auras to expand, room to walk more than three paces, room to stretch our arms up without hitting the ceiling, room for more air and certainly cooler than our King's Chamber oven. There are two beds and a table with three chairs. In the corner is a milk churn with an enamel bowl, a plastic jug and a tablet of soap on the ground beside it. On the table is a pile of books. Welderman points these out to Valentin so I'm pretty certain he must have brought them. Our new host stands in the doorway silently watching us. There is a single light bulb in the middle of the ceiling giving a dim yellowish glow to the room. Thankfully there are sheets, blankets, pillows and towels, although all pretty threadbare and worn. Our new hosts are not as wealthy as Welderman's family. Welderman leaves and the steel door clangs shut with the scraping sound of a key turning in a padlock. We are all pretty bushed and so go straight to our beds. Camilla and I 'top and tail' for greater comfort.

In the King's Chamber I made up a bedtime prayer which Camilla and I have whispered every night for some time. I remind her tonight; it's good to keep up the practice. So we lie down and raise a palm to the ceiling saying:

We give thanks for this day,
For the food we have eaten,
For the water we have drunk,
For the air that we breathe
And for the love and the light we have received
We give thanks this day.

Morning and the steel door opens, a masked figure comes in with a tray of bread, fried eggs, a plate of small green apples and three glasses of tea. I see a pair of slippers and wrinkly socks in the gloom below the door as it swings back – it must be his wife. Jon asks for some material so he can construct a screen around the churn and washing area. The man nods but says nothing. After breakfast I sort through the plastic bags and realize they have forgotten to bring the one with the radio in it. This is a big blow to our morale. Luckily I still have the plastic 'Rama' margarine pots in which I can soak my precious muslin menstruation cloths. I feel sick and my stomach's making all kinds of weird gurgling sounds. Luckily Valentin decides to have a nap because I have to squat over the churn for what seems like hours, in full view of the whole room. It's a bad bout of diarrhoea. As the cramps recede I realize that I have missed the churn altogether and decorated the wall behind it. Oh my God, I hate this! I appeal to Jon to clear it up and he retorts 'I'm not going to have a wife who can't clear up her own shit!!' and I know he's right. Why should I expect him to do all the smelly jobs? I feel just like Gandhi's wife when he told her to clean the latrines, usually the work of the untouchables. So I find one of the bits of cloth we've collected and use water out of the jug. Once I got down to it it wasn't so bad, even without hot water and bleach.

I lay on the bed for most of the day, still in pain, my nerves feeling raw, and the tears flow. Jon massages my feet which helps me relax. That evening the door opens and in walks Welderman with the errant plastic bag. I could hug him! He sits down with Valentin and has a long intense discussion. Valentin gives him two phone numbers of people who might be able to help in his release. Thank God Welderman has stayed in contact with us, a ray of hope. When breakfast arrives the next day our host also brings us a large swathe of material and some binding twine; Jon is delighted. Valentin asks for some cushions to make the chairs more comfortable and, although our host makes a few disgruntled noises, he reappears with three squares of foam that are decorated with a young child's drawings – figures with oblong bodies, round heads and thin, stick-insect arms and legs. This explains the swift light footfalls above our heads and the occasional high-pitched voice.

We have noticed over the past few weeks that Valentin is having difficulty peeing. Jon is convinced that he has a prostate problem. Today he's in a lot more pain, probably brought about by the stress of moving. The pain gets worse and he starts knocking on the door. No reply. His knocking gets louder and more urgent. Still no reply. He retreats to his bed curled up in agony. There is nothing we can do except send him healing with our thoughts. Jon begins to knock for him and eventually, a few hours later the grumpy host appears. Valentin tells him his problem and what medicine he needs. The man starts arguing that Valentin is not telling the truth – he is lying, trying to get attention, making big problems. He goes away and Jon starts knocking again. I'm lying on the bed, still weak with diarrhoea. The man returns looking more grumpy saying he hasn't got any money for medicines so Valentin asks him to contact the Welderman. Miraculously we hear a car engine rev up and disappear. A few hours later Welderman comes in with the medicine that Valentin needs.

Valentin and Welderman sit and talk. It sounds as though Welderman has had no luck with the phone numbers that Valentin gave him but he has some news for us. When Welderman has gone Valentin tells us we shall be released in two days. 'What, all three of us?' 'No,' he replies, 'just you two.' This must be so hard for him. But we have heard these words so many times before and nothing has happened, so we try not to believe or hope too much.

Valentin and I sleep much sounder that night while Jon spends most of it bending bits of wire and sewing, creating a screen wall for our bathroom.

We now have a piece of material for a curtain screen but no attachments so I scout around our new abode looking for resources. Luckily for us the builder of the house was not too concerned with tidying up after the wooden shutterings used for the concrete were removed so there are lots of bits of rusty wire protruding from the concrete walls. I work my way around the room twisting off all of the longer pieces and then bend them into curtain rings, about two dozen. Now down to some sewing; it takes about two hours to sew all the rings on to the cloth. Then I thread the baling twine through the new curtain rings and hang the material from the ceiling using more wire and twine. It hangs about a metre from the floor and 'voilà' we have a curtain screen offering us some privacy and an 'en suite' bedroom!

Jon is so fantastic at this kind of thing and we wake up to a beautifully screened off bathroom. Valentin and I are the main users of our new 'bathroom' – he because of his overactive prostate and me because of my menstruation. Between the three of us we are filling up the 25-litre churn very quickly. My intuition tells me that it would not be a good idea to ask Mr Grumpy if his wife will do our washing. We hear them arguing through the ceiling; I don't think they are very happy about looking after us. Our only heat source is the dim light bulb in the centre of the ceiling. Jon uses some of the binding twine left over from the bath curtain to make a line near the light bulb. This is where I hang my muslin strips. Valentin washes a cloth back support that Welderman gave to him to keep his kidneys warm. He has been wearing it for days, so it must be quite sweaty, but I'm a bit sceptical about it drying properly especially as the weather has got cooler.

Jon's found another project. The knitted socks that GA had given me to wear when we were stripped of all our clothing have started rotting so Jon cuts up one of our golden masks and uses the golden material to mend them and make thick cloth soles so they will be useful as the weather gets colder. I try them on, I cannot get my foot into one of them because the ankle hole has been mended with cotton and is less giving than the wool. Unpicking to be done and more sewing, but we have time – enormous reels of time.

Supper arrives: a watery soup with bits of mutton floating in it, no gourmet food here. Then the crickets start singing, signalling the fading of the day and the onset of dusk. They are our only timepiece and I look forward to their nightly song. They are also our only connection with the natural world carrying on with its daily tasks and its daily rhythms through the seasons.

Friday morning, no electric light. Streaking through the blackest shade of black there are faint gleams of light coming through the wall, high above our bed. Jon and I stand on the bed craning our necks at all sorts of weird and wonderful angles, trying to see a glimpse of the outside world. But the light is refracting through badly cemented bricks and there is no direct view to the outside. Breakfast arrives and with it Mr Grumpy brings a small stub of candle. We only use it while we are eating, then blow it out to save it for a later time when we may not be so lucky. We lie on our beds waiting for light. One, two, maybe three hours pass before the bulb flickers with electric life and our room is, once again, dimly illuminated. Rising from our creaking beds we all begin our separate exercise routines, Valentin with his skiing exercises, Jon and I doing some qigong, revelling in the extra space. Valentin and I are feeling much better and I offer him some healing. He stands up and I stand behind him, placing my hands over his kidneys. Gently I lift my hands off and pass my hands over the whole of his back a few inches above his skin. 'Luche (better),' he says. Later that night Jon gives him a foot massage to help him relax and have a good night's sleep.

The churn is getting very full and when Grumpy brings our supper Valentin asks him to empty it. Grumpy doesn't believe him and goes to the churn and lifts it up. 'How can it be full so quickly in so few days? You must be using too much water!' Valentin explains that I have my period and it will last all week, so we need extra water. 'That's impossible, my wife only has it for three days.' 'Well, Camilla has it for seven days and that's a fact!' Valentin replies. I can't help smiling because I am amazed that Valentin is standing up for me so valiantly and arguing about the length of my menstruation period. Bless the man! Amid much grumbling and, I'm sure, a bit of Chechen swearing, Grumpy asks Valentin and Jon to bring the full churn to the door, then he lugs it away to be emptied.

This is the night we have been told we will be freed so, once again, we pack our plastic bags in readiness for the midnight knock. We stay on the alert for a couple of hours then tell our minds and our bodies to rest, it is not going to happen tonight.

Saturday 19 September. We have such a sweet surprise this morning: a green and brown mottled frog comes to visit us. It appears from out of the corner by Valentin's bed and proceeds to hop across the floor. Jon and I are praying Valentin won't see it and try to kill it; he's lying on his bed reading. We know we can't shield the frog as it hops towards the open space beyond the table and chairs. Come on, keep going, keep going, it's not far now to reach the protective shadows of the opposite wall. We will it to hop faster. It veers to the left, making a beeline towards the closed metal door. Big hop, up one step and another to reach the base of the door. It's determined to find a way out. There are two vertical metal ridges on either side of the door; in between the ridges is just enough space for the frog to straddle its body, its webbed feet pressed against the ridges so it can climb upwards, like a freestyle climber just using hands and feet to climb up between two vertical rock faces. Up it goes, higher and higher, until near the top it loses strength and falls back to the ground. I let out a yelp, thinking the frog has hurt itself, but it's fine. My yelp rouses Valentin's curiosity and he comes over to see what we're looking at. I'm getting prepared to defend the frog, but Valentin makes no attempt to obstruct it or hurt it in any way, he just watches alongside us. This is the first time that we have seen him show respect for another creature apart from a human. It feels so good. The frog doesn't give up, off it goes again on its upward journey until again its strength gives out and it falls to the ground, miraculously landing on his feet every time. After its fifth or sixth attempt, having tried both sides of the door it tries another, wiser strategy, sitting patiently on its haunches, facing the door and waiting until someone opens it.

All through the day it waits while we play 'Fool' together for the millionth time, the cards so well used now that the printed suits are fading away, and we have to re-draw the numbers and suits in biro. Our interest in the game wanes and Valentin retreats to his bed while Jon and I decide to go for a stroll down the promenade at Lyme Regis. It's very sunny today, the sea sparkly and inviting. Droves of seagulls soar and screech above us. 'Oops!' Jon does a quick side-step. 'Those damn dogs again fouling the pavement.' Valentin understands our little charade and laughs heartily. Then it's his turn to use the floor space and do his daily marathon walk, up and down and round, up and down and round, mile after mile.

'Are you planning to walk back to Moscow?' I ask Valentin. *'It's only 2,000 kilometres.'* He smiles.

As we hear footsteps bringing our supper we all turn to watch the frog. The door opens and the frog hops deftly through the space between the bottom of the door and the floor avoiding the large, heavy treaded feet of Mr Grumpy. Hooray for the frog and its newfound freedom! I smile inside with a wistful thought – if only I could shrink myself to frog size. We end the evening with a light greasy soup and a foot massage for Valentin given by Jon. And so to bed for a night of sweet dreams.

18

Freedom! Cveboda!

I hear a muffled knock in my dreams. Jon nudges me and my mind floats up through layers of subconscious to wake into the darkened room. The knocking continues, loud thumps against a wall, followed by a few Chechen stage whispers. Valentin screws in the light bulb and we hear footsteps approaching our door. In walks Welderman with Mr Grumpy hanging back in the doorway. 'Demoi, demoi!' he says, beckoning to me and Jon. I think he's saying 'Let's go' but in fact he's saying 'Home, home!' and we start dressing while he has a few words with Valentin. I put on the long grey dress with gold star plastic buttons that belonged to Welderman's daughter, over the knickers Jon designed for me, with the pink jacket of the unknown Russian woman on top and Welderman's slippers on my feet.

I'm wondering why Welderman is here. It's unusual for anyone from a previous holding place to be connected with a new one. For security reasons the changeover happens on the journey. Is this a sign? I think back to early June when I looked at the 15 scratches made by the previous prisoner on the wall of the King's Chamber and decided to start scratching days myself. I began counting down from a hundred, that's an easy number to work with, one scratch per day. It's about the hundredth day now. Could we be free tomorrow, or will it be starting all over again? I feel shaky with that thought.

We start packing the rest of our possessions into two plastic bags. 'Niet! Niet!' Welderman takes the bag from my hand and puts it on the floor. 'Demoi!' he repeats forcibly. Now I understand, he's saying we're going home and we won't need these things. I pray that he's right and it's not another 'Luche miassa (better place)'. Just in case, we take out our photos, apple seeds, Jon's birthday card and the prints of paintings and gesture that we want to take them. 'OK, OK,' he replies. Valentin is standing by his bed in his pyjamas and slippers staring at us without expression. Dear, dear Valentin, it is hard to leave you here, alone with the Grumpies. I give him a big hug and he pats me on the back. I'm thinking strength, courage and love but cannot say a thing, hoping he can absorb my feelings through osmosis. Jon gives him a big hug with the same 'pat, pat' in return.

Welderman points to the strips of cloth torn off the leg of a pinstriped suit, hanging over the iron bedstead that they had used as our blindfolds on our last journey. He ties them over our eyes. I feel a great sense of calm and for once am less shaky than Jon. We are guided up the steps and into the back seat of a car; no one gets in beside us. Welderman's voice comes from the front seat . . .

'Jon, demoi!' For some reason I am very nervous of moving so soon. I guess my nerves are noticeable for Welderman to direct his words so strongly at me. He reassures me with just two words, my name and 'home', and I allow myself a faint glimmer of hope that this is the beginning of our journey out of captivity.

We drive for about ten minutes along a bumpy track then onto a smoother road before pulling into what feels like a lay-by. Welderman and the other man in the front, who may be his son, get out and speak rapidly in Chechen to someone else. Then they open our doors and we climb out and are guided to another car. Again it is just us in the back and two people in the front. One of them turns round and says in a very cheerful voice 'Demoi, demoi!' The voice sounds familiar and the way he speaks makes me think he knows us, so I suspect he's one of the younger soldiers we had met at the Base. The driver speaks sharply to him in Chechen and he shuts up. About 15 minutes later we stop and they get out leaving us in the back. We can hear muffled whispers and then the engine of another car stopping nearby.

Someone opens our door so we get out and a deep voice says 'I am your friend!' in English. Oh yes, I think, rather cynically. The voice proceeds to ask 'What are your names?'

'Jon James,' 'Camilla Carr,' we reply.

'What time were you born?'

'Er, Er, Er' I reply, not knowing if he wants the exact time or just the date.

'Please, quickly, we have little time!'

246

'2.35 in the morning.'

'What date?'

'The 31st of January 1958.'

'Jon, were you born in 1966?'

'No, the 9th of May 1960. I don't know the time I was born.'

'OK, come on, there's not much time.' He leads us by the elbow to another vehicle. Jon is pushed into the back first, then I follow.

A body gets into the car sitting close to me, probably a guard. We move off, travelling swiftly. The surface of the road is tarmacked, with potholes that we swerve around or bump over. No one speaks for about ten minutes. I feel my blindfold being untied. The camouflage-clad guard next to me winds down the window and gestures to throw the blindfold out. I nod and he tosses it out. He then points to Camilla, gesturing that I remove hers; I whisper to her 'I'm going to take your blindfold off.' I still feel a little nervous. Are we really being given our freedom? Or just a taste of freedom and a glimpse of the stars?

Jon unties my blindfold. I don't throw it out but keep it as a souvenir. I look up at the sky – still there, dark and velvety, studded with hundreds of twinkling stars. We haven't seen even a hairbreadth of sky for over six months. We drive past a series of rounded hills with beacons of fire lighting them up, the fire of burning oil or gas from punctured pipes. It's a very surreal landscape. There is a black BMW in front of us with no number plate, only a BMW badge in the centre of the boot lid; it looks like the same car that we had seen in the Base, but we cannot be sure.

We see a little hut coming towards us on the right with a fire burning in an iron brazier in front of the door. It's a police checkpoint and a very young looking bearded man, with a gun slung over his shoulder, ambles out of the door when he hears the vehicles and flags us down. He looks a little stunned as the black BMW slows down next to him and someone talks to him through the window. As we slow down two vehicles rush up from behind, stopping on either side of us, I look over my shoulder and see another one in the rear. We are part of a five-vehicle entourage. One of the vehicles alongside us is another BMW and the other a light brown four-wheel drive Jeep which looks suspiciously like the one in which we drove to the Sauna from Grozny. The policeman scuttles back into his hut and we speed off.

The man beside the driver turns round to face us; he has a broad face and a gingery moustache. 'My name is Badri, I am a Georgian business-man working for Boris Berezovsky.' 'You have heard of Berezovsky?' 'No,' we reply. 'He is a friend of Prince Michael of Kent.' We know that Badri is the man who said 'I am your friend' with his deep voice and rich Russian accent. 'Did you have to pay money for us?' I ask. 'They always want money,' he grumbles under his breath. Then, a little louder 'Later. We will be in Ingushetia in one hour, then six hours later you will be on a plane to Moscow.'

We travel the rest of the journey to the border in silence. Jon and I are relaxed and enjoying the starlit scenery, while the other three men are alert and tense, their job not yet completed. We see a barrier ahead blocking the road, and a concrete building, the border between Chechnya and Ingushetia. The black BMW pulls over in front of the building and we pull up behind them. All four doors of the BMW open simultaneously and out jump four men, two in suits and ties and two in open neck shirts; one of the suited men is quite small and has silver hair – I wonder if it's Welderman. I like the idea of him coming to see us off as I have a feeling he helped in our release. His respect for us had grown after his initial response of how stupid it was for us to come to Chechnya in the first place. But the retreating figures moving towards the control building out of the glare of our headlights are too far away for positive identification. The soldier sitting next to me gets out and goes to join them. So strange to be alone, unguarded, just Camilla and me, Badri and the driver.

Our driver pulls alongside the BMW in front of the barrier and a young man in camouflage comes out of the control building and pushes the barrier open. We slowly drive through. The other side there are about 20 or 30 men in suits and in camouflage, some carrying guns, standing on both sides of the road. We don't stop but drive slowly past them and Badri turns to us, saying 'You will be pleased to know you have now left Chechen territory.' I have felt the bitter twang of disappointment more than once in the last 14 months and Badri's words send me into a whirl. I dare not believe these words until I sniff the air and walk the walk of freedom. I am curious about the time – the clock in the car says just after three but I'm sure it's not work-ing so I ask Badri. 'Five o'clock Moscow time,' he replies. So it must be 2 a.m. in England.

After half an hour we come to a roundabout and Badri asks the driver to stop. It seems to be in the middle of nowhere – no streetlights, just black landscape – and although I think we are safe, there is still a niggling feeling that something might happen to deflect our escape. Then he gets out and pulls a mobile telephone from his pocket and makes a call in Russian, probably phoning Boris Berezovsky to say the mission is completed. As he returns to the car I let out a sigh, letting go of the tension in my neck and shoulders. We drive fast along the straight roads – no shell holes here – and after 20 minutes or so we arrive at the most expensive hotel in Nazran, the Hotel Assa. I recognize it as the hotel I had passed with Madina and Anya in the spring of last year. There is a welcoming party of suited and camouflaged men, all armed, by the door. We are ushered straight inside and into a lift with Badri and another tall, big-bellied man. I turn to Badri and say, with deep sincerity, 'Spaseba Bolshoi (a big thank you).' He turns to his friend and they both burst out laughing. One part of me feels a bit affronted, but the wiser part knows that they are just releasing all the stress and tension built up during the operation. Badri was in a lot of danger all the time he was in Chechnya; the fact that we can see a flak jacket underneath his jumper and a gun holster is testimony in itself. I can imagine he finds the simple 'Thank you' so very understated, so very English and perhaps just a little crass after all he has gone through.

They take us into a hotel room. It's full of large Russian-speaking men standing around a long table covered with plates of half-eaten food, many half-empty bottles of wine, vodka, whisky and brandy. A bacchanalian feast! All we want to do is go outside and breathe some fresh air. Jon spots the balcony and we go out into the chill pre-dawn.

Soon it will be dawn. I return to the main room and fill a glass with red wine, then walk back to the balcony. I remember when I first left school and worked in a factory. After the early shift I would walk outside and the sunlight would make my eyes sting and water. I don't care how much my eyes sting and water now, I am determined to watch this dawn from the first light.

Silently we watch the sky lighten and distant silhouetted rooftops emerge from the matt, blank space in front of us. The dark indigo sky imperceptibly changes to lighter hues; the broad rash of stars gradually disappears. As the sun rises over the lip of the distant hills in the east its rays dance and glitter on the surface of the man-made lake in front of us and highlight the snow-tipped distant peaks. The beauty is intense on this, our first uncaptive dawn. The sky is always there.

We spend some minutes bathing ourselves in the early morning sun, then decide it's about time to soak off the layers of grime in a luxurious bath. Badri gives us toothbrushes and a hairbrush. Sinking beneath the hot water I meditate on letting go all the stresses and tension in my body. A big grin spreads across my face as I realize my wish back in the pink crystal room has been granted; we have been helped to freedom by one of Russia's biggest oligarchs, Boris Berezovsky. I remember reading about him now, after the fall of communism he has created a mammoth empire spanning media, oil and car production, no wonder he has great interest in what happens in Chechnya. I'm beginning to feel drowsy, but can only manage half an hour of sleep, I'm too excited.

We are on the third floor, well above the ground – for security I guess. Some local scrawny dogs come scrounging around below our balcony. I go into the room where all the food is and pick up some meat which I throw onto the rough grass below for the dogs. It seems surreal to be in this five-star hotel with a room full of food and wine, a full-sized bed and en suite bathroom with hot and cold water running from the taps and a flushing 'western style' loo. It's only a few hours since we were asleep in our concrete cellar. I take two baths as the water in the first soon turns a dirty dark grey colour. I enjoy the luxury of all this water but my skin comes out in a rash, not being used to the perfumed soap. Again I am shocked at the amount of skin I lose.

Badri gives instructions to one of his colleagues to ask us what clothes and shoes we need and our sizes; then he is sent to the bazaar. What a joy to have new clothes! We watch a programme about tropical fish and are mesmerized by the startling colours, for we have been starved of colour. We nibble a little food, but we're not hungry for food, just hungry to go home. At 1.30 p.m. we are told to get ready. We gather the clothes we were wearing when we came out of the cellar – more souvenirs. The only things we throw away are my mouldy, rusty trainers.

We are escorted down the lift and outside into a waiting Lada. The chief of the Ingush police shakes our hands and jokes that he hopes he won't meet us again in similar circumstances; the feeling is mutual! Two young Russian soldiers who have also been freed follow us in another Lada. We travel to the airport in a cavalcade, sirens blaring, lights flashing, all heads turning to watch us pass, and drive through some high gates to enter the airfield. It's swarming with heavily armed police.

At the airport we are taken to the 'executive' lounge, a room with plastic chairs around a table covered with a flowery plastic tablecloth. There's a plastic spray of flowers on the wall and a 'cut glass' jug of plastic flowers on the table, altogether a very plastic room. We are offered a drink – water, please. The freed soldiers are wearing combat fatigues and sit silently looking down at the floor. We ask what happened to them. Fifteen months earlier they were flagged down on a road in Dagestan by a man who said he needed help to start his car engine. It was a ruse to capture them and they were taken to Chechnya where they were kept as slaves by a Chechen family, made to do building repairs in the day and manacled to a radiator at night. I thought they were in pretty good shape mentally and physically considering their ordeal.

Eventually a plane arrives carrying Boris Berezovsky. He and his entourage come bustling into the room. We shake hands and thank him. He tries to use his mobile phone to ring the British Embassy in Moscow but it doesn't work. So we are surrounded by men fiddling with mobiles, it seems to us like a scene from a comedy. Is this real or just a dream that we are having back in the cellar in Chechnya? Finally a news reporter from ORT, the television company owned by Berezovsky, gets through to the embassy and hands the phone to him. We can hear the voice of a woman saying 'I'm sorry, the ambassador is out walking his dog.' We smile broadly: so very English, out walking your dog on a Sunday afternoon. Yes, I think, here is proof this is no dream, we have left Chechnya.

Later the phone rings and Berezovsky talks to the ambassador for a few minutes then hands the phone to us. 'This is Andrew Wood.' He asks us how we are and I can hear the emotion in his voice; this moves me – here is a man who has put a lot of energy into helping gain our release, and the energy has not only come from his head but also from his heart.

We step out of the air-conditioned container onto the tarmac and are surrounded by a whole flock of men in suits flanked by soldiers with Kalashnikovs, but there doesn't seem to be any organization so I set off in the direction of a small passenger jet. After several metres I realize the ranks behind us have been given a sign to head towards a larger aircraft so Camilla and I swerve with them. I look out of the window as we peel off the runway, slowly climbing into the clouds. One step closer to home.

Jon, I and the soldiers are given seats around a table and are presented with an enormous bowl of large slices of water melon – happy memories. The reporter wants to interview and film us for Russian television. We tell him about Valentin and he is surprised that he was held with us. We send our love to Valentin hoping he will be able to hear the interview on our little radio. Later in the flight, when the reporter has spoken to Berezovsky, he says he is sorry but he will not be able to include what we have said about Valentin because it may not be helpful in his release. I am just sad that Valentin won't hear the message of our love to help him face whatever he has to face.

We go and speak with Berezovsky and ask him how much money had to be paid for us. He said 'Luckily no money was exchanged, we used a series of argument and methodology.' How very Russian! Maybe the exchange was in lives of soldiers or resources, we may never know.

Throughout the flight I have seen the TV presenter using his mobile phone so I ask him if I can use it; he says 'Yes, when we land.' So as the wheels touch the ground in Moscow he hands the phone to me and I manage to phone my parents. My mother answers and as I say 'Hello' I have great difficulty in continuing because the emotion constricts my throat. I pause, take a breath then tell her, 'We're free, in Moscow doing 100 miles an hour down the runway, see you soon.' Then I hand the phone to Camilla.

I try ringing my Mum, but she's engaged. Somehow this doesn't surprise me!

As we leave the plane Berezovsky asks us if we want to stay the night in Moscow or go back to England straightaway. Home please. It looks as if he will accompany us; then, as I ask him to do everything he can to help Valentin, he changes his mind and heads off in another direction. I sense that he'll start working for Valentin's release straight away. We are met by Andrew Wood and his assistant Barbara Woodward and are ushered into a lounge for tea and biscuits.

Finally I get through to Mum. It's so good to speak with her. 'Mum, we're free, we're in the airport in Moscow, how's Ashok?' 'Oh my love, oh my love, Ashok's fine,' she replies, half laughing and half crying to the click of many cameras crowding her kitchen. She was walking up Solsbury Hill thinking of us when the news came through of our release and the local Bath press greeted her on her return with a bottle of champagne on the doorstep.

We are told there's a gaggle of press waiting for some words from us. Do we want to speak? Of course, we have got to let the world know we are OK. So we step outside in front of a mass of photographers and reporters. The questions come thick and fast but we are prepared; we knew this would happen and we had discussed with each other how we would respond. One thing we are keen to get across is that we feel no bitterness towards our captors, for we know their actions are the result of war trauma. The words come tumbling out of my mouth and Jon hardly gets a word in edgeways!

It's strange being confronted by 50 faces when we've seen so few over the last year. Somewhere in the sea of voices I hear a vaguely familiar one. I scan across the faces all vying for our attention but can't pick out one I know. Later I discover it was Jeremy Cook, a school friend now working for the BBC.

Andrew Wood sees that we are tiring and closes the press conference. We start recounting our story to Andrew and Barbara. Barbara asks if we want to travel alone or with her. She is a lovely woman, very direct and honest. We ask her to come. The embassy issues us with a temporary passport that has a photo of us used in the campaign. We give Andrew Wood a big hug and say goodbye, then are escorted to a small aircraft. It's Boris Berezovsky's private jet that he is lending us for the last leg of our journey home. Inside there are large, comfy cloth seats facing two tables. After a gin and tonic Barbara Woodward has to put up with three hours of verbal diarrhoea from me. Being with a woman, talking with a woman, after living in an all-male environment for 14 months and 20 days, feels wonderful!

After the delicious meal I'm invited to sit in the cockpit with the British pilot and navigator, a small boy's dream. What a beautifully compact flight deck with hundreds of illuminated dials and gauges. We are heading towards London and will make a new course once we are in British air space. After confirmation from the ground we turn towards the Royal Air Force base at Brize Norton in Oxfordshire, less than two hours from my home in Gloucestershire. We're nearly there!

By the time we're flying over London I am somewhat hoarse. I go into the cockpit, strap myself into a seat behind the two pilots and watch the preparation for landing, loads of checking dials, pressing switches, it all appears quite hectic to me and the airstrip looks so small. How are we going to land on that? I feel a twinge of anxiety, then the undercarriage is lowered and we circle round and make a perfect landing. The steps are brought to the door of the plane but before we can see our families there are dignitaries who want to see us, including the commander of the Air Force base, Baroness Symons from the Foreign Office and the Air Force psychiatrist. All I want to do is brush my teeth, so I head for the loo with its gold-plated taps.

At last we are given the go-ahead to walk down the steps onto British tarmac. There is a swathe of photographers behind a barricade to our left, but we only have eyes for the building in front of us as we try to distinguish family members from the silhouetted head-blobs peering through the windows. I raise my arm in a wave thinking, 'We've got to let them know we're OK.' Camilla raises her arms as well and we both wave. The tarmac seems to stretch out for ever.

We arrive at the porch and my brother Raj leaps out and gives us a shaky hug. Then we're inside. I notice the smiles, eyes bright with tears, the quivering nerves, the taut skin and weight loss of my mother and sister. I feel the strength of the families' love and courage and also the trauma they have been through over the last 14½ months. At this particular moment both Jon and I feel very calm and grounded; we know we are basically OK, they don't.

There's one person missing, Ashok. He and his father didn't get the message of where we were landing early enough to drive from Devon. I swallow my disappointment (I've had good training). I talk to him on a mobile phone. His voice sounds the same as I remember (puberty hasn't kicked in); the strangeness is in how normal it feels to talk to him as though we had only spoken yesterday, not over a year ago.

I hold my mum, who is bursting with highly charged emotional energy, and then my dad who carries a more pragmatic energy. Within a few moments all that time of separation dissolves even though we have missed over a year of each other's lives. I give Ben a really good hug; he's now a man – he was a boy when I left. Is it possible to make up lost time? To re-establish those connections? To get to know each other again? We shall find out. Then I see my sister with a baby in her arms who has popped into this world, not even conceived before we left. That feels extraordinary; it gives a concrete measure to the amount of time we have been apart.

After the hugging of families, there are our colleagues Chris Hunter and Patricia Cockrell. 'How's Little Star? Is it still going? and is Anya all right?' I ask Chris. He tells me that Little Star is flourishing and Anya didn't go back to Moscow after the kidnapping but stayed working in Grozny for another three months. I am amazed. Then I whisper to Chris that I was raped. I want to tell someone, maybe to begin exorcising it out of my psyche; Chris is the right person – he doesn't show any surprise or emotion. There are hordes of journalists and photographers waiting for us to speak, so we give a press conference. Many people are amazed that we say we have no bitterness against those who have held us – we're not going to play the revenge game.

We retire to the officers' bar and order a Guinness to toast Valentin, who is very much in our hearts and thoughts. Also we announce our intention to get married, we think it's important for the families to know our relationship hasn't suffered by our time together in captivity. Sitting there in the officers' bar I suddenly feel the presence of my father. He would have been very familiar with these surroundings, having spent 25 years in the Air Force; it's almost as if he's arranged for us to be nurtured and protected by the RAF for the first week of our freedom.

I start to feel tired and emotional. We have been up for more than 24 hours and I'm totally hoarse from talking non-stop. I'm missing Ashok dreadfully; the Air Force offer to send a car for him first thing in the morning, but I speak to Marcel (Ashok's dad) and he promises to drive up as soon as they wake – it's now midnight. They take us to our sleeping quarters, pointing out separate rooms and I think, are they going to separate us? Something that had been threatened so many times in captivity that the thought of it now makes me feel shaky and hollow inside. It's illogical and of course they don't mind us sharing a room, but it shows me a glimpse of the trauma inside myself that will take a while to heal.

We sleep a shallow sleep for a few hours and wake at 6 a.m. to walk outside in the fresh, moving air untainted by staleness. What a joy to walk on the green grass and pick up apples from under a tree and sniff their green appley scent!

Breakfast with our families. There is a strangeness about choosing our food and not having it thrust upon us. I am overwhelmed by the selection offered, there is so much variety in shape, colour, taste and smell. Eventually I go for the whole works – cereal, bacon, egg, mushrooms, beans, tomatoes, toast and tea.

I'm excited, nerves tingling, waiting for Ashok to arrive. I hear running feet. In he comes and leaps into my arms; he is still small enough and light enough to do that. I feel his body warmth, his vibrant energy, his 'aliveness'. No more just a memory, a vision in my mind, but a physical reality. We hug and smile, and it feels as if we have never been parted; there is no awkwardness, no shyness, no tears, just delight in our love for each other, a love that has survived undented, untainted by all our experiences.

The next week would, even in ordinary circumstances, appear to be very stressful, and it was, but somehow we coped, probably because we were now so used to dealing with stress. We were asked by Scotland Yard if we wanted to do debriefing straightaway and we felt it would be better to get it over with and useful for our own healing. So there followed four days of talking about our captivity. After a few hours my brain would start heating up and I had to have a break before it short-circuited, but it felt good to pour it out. We had some of our families around the first days, although I wasn't sure if it was good for them to hear all the details straightaway, because I didn't want them to have any more stress.

I was taken to the Radcliffe hospital in Oxford to have tests to see if I'd picked up any sexual diseases from the rape. They only found thrush but from the account of my problems in captivity guessed I also have herpes. My eyesight has suffered, particularly the occurrence of floaters in my right eye. I'm prescribed some reading glasses. Our teeth have survived well, I have one filling, Jon has none.

My mother and I take a trip to Oxford to buy some clothes and make-up. As we scoot along the road I realize I'm not used to seeing objects more than a few metres away, the rows of houses look like cardboard cut-outs against the sky. It takes me a couple of days to readjust my brain/sight connection to accommodate distant perspectives and the spacial relationship between objects. We're not used to so much visual, sound and movement input so it takes us a few weeks to come up to speed and cope with the increased sensory demands on our energy systems. In captivity we were used to a lot of silence and single focus conversations so we are amazed when people cut each other off in conversation or talk at the same time; it feels very confusing and tiring.

My sleeping pattern is a complete mess. I wake at odd times during the night and wander around. 'Hello, sir' the night watchman greets me; he must be used to flight crews working and waking at odd hours. I walk into the common room and make a hot drink, then off to the TV lounge to watch some nondescript movie, sometimes joined by a few flight crew. The debriefing is exhausting; all I want is some quiet, some peace. Time to gently reintegrate with my family. We talk to the psychiatrist and fill in questionnaires to find out the depth of our trauma. As we knew already we are not suffering from severe 'Post Traumatic Stress Disorder'. We feel confident we'll know where to turn when we need help.

Of course many newspapers want exclusive rights to our story. We need time to heal and therefore money to live on without needing to work. The *Sunday Mail* gets the deal and we spend a day talking our story. The most difficult bit is deciding whether to talk about the rape or not. I discuss it with my mother and we both come to the conclusion that it's better to talk about it now rather than later. It will help me start releasing the trauma instead of bottling it up.

An extraordinary first two weeks of freedom, experiencing a kaleidoscope of thoughts and feelings as we adapt to normal life with its wealth of sensory input. We are buoyed up by the touch, smile, love of those close to us and feeling the need to lift them up, out of 14 months of anxiety. We are unaware of the layers of trauma hidden in our psyches and our bodies – in the clenched muscles of Jon's back or my nervous system – layers waiting for the right time to peel back, revealing new, delicate green shoots of our being.

would have
liked family's
perspective

257

19

Coming Up For Air

We learn about the amazing campaign that our families had organized for us. The colour purple heralded our kidnapping, the shining ray from the crystal above our heads hours before we were taken. Can you imagine our surprise at purple ribbons being used to raise awareness after seeing purple in our meditations and dreams and the surprise of our families when they received our letters in June when I told them about dreaming the colour purple. After coming back I discover the purple ray is the ray of St Germaine, symbolizing forgiveness, compassion and the removal of negativity.

They held so many events: an open-air concert, a bicycle ride to Number 10 Downing Street, a postcard campaign, church services, an evening in the Jongleurs Comedy Club, a birthday party for Camilla's 40th in the Groucho Club, a celebrity cricket match, a pop concert and numerous interviews on television, radio and in the newspapers. John McCarthy and Terry Waite gave them a huge amount of support and attended many events.

I am keen to start writing this book but a week before meetings with five publishers, while shopping in Bath, I start crying, my head in a total fuzz. I can't cope, I just can't cope. My brain is on red alert. Stop! Stop! Stop! What am I doing, creating deadlines, creating more stress! I need to rest and stay in bed for nearly a month. I cry a lot and feel shafts of anger bubble up out of nowhere. I have no energy and don't know if I will have any again – a frightening feeling. Jon and a friend Frances look after me, and cope with my irrational outbursts and so I am able to let go until I feel peace and energy flowing back into my body. We realize we want to write for our own healing and as a story of ordinary people caught up in an extraordinary situation, not to raise a quick buck, so we cancel all the meetings with the publishers.

Being released from captivity is like the champagne cork being held under pressure, tied in by the wires, then being launched into space, flying, flying with freedom and coming back to earth, bump, bump. It is an interesting experience but not one I would want to repeat too often. Terry Waite and John McCarthy come to visit us when we are in Brize Norton. One thing that Terry talks about has stuck in my mind: he compared coming out of a traumatic situation to coming up from a deep sea dive. The amount of time coming out relates to how long you spend at a certain depth. You release some trauma and come to a plateau of understanding before rising again through another layer of trauma. When you come out of a dive you have to depressurize otherwise you get the bends. We were at this depth of emotional pressure for 14½ months, and then we came out very quickly. Now we are free from the pressure, but our bodies and emotions are still experiencing it, and it will take at least an equal amount of time to release these traumas. My physical body absorbed a lot of the shock and trauma, so I experience a lot of aches and pains. I don't know where they come from and can only put them down to that time.

Because I was deprived of information (no TV, no radio, no papers, no windows to look out from), re-emerging into the world where TV adverts are 30-second packages of huge amounts of information was quite a shock to my system. Being outside in the world was a great leap from being held captive within four grey walls, with a grey concrete sky and earth. It is hard for me to explain to people the contrast from that greyness and silence, muffled sounds and stifled air to this world of colour, movement and fresh air, too full of information for me to absorb. I remember a TV programme about some Columbian Indians. The initiates were taken into a cave as young children, given just enough light and food to keep their bodies healthy. The only information they would receive was from the wise elders and after nine years of absorbing information about the wonders of the world they would re-enter the world and see it with totally different eyes. I saw the beauty of nature with fresh eyes but as time has gone by and I am integrating back into our 'normal' world I guess I have become a little bit blind. I try to remind myself what joy it is to breathe fresh air or see a tree blowing in the wind.

We notice our lack of stamina when talking with family and friends – it's enjoyable but can be very tiring. We visit various practitioners and therapists: an acupuncturist, a cranial sacral therapist, masseurs and healers, to help keep our bodies and minds in balance and initiate the release of the trauma. A couple of psychiatrists kindly offer to help us but we feel they cannot connect with us as they do not have the same holistic point of view on life and we know we haven't got severe Post Traumatic Stress Disorder.

8 December. The four telecom workers who were kidnapped in Chechnya on 4 October are killed, beheaded. The story is gruesome and I weep a lot. My sister, Alexandra, had been helping the families with their campaign. I think the captors felt double-crossed in some way even though the ransom of millions of dollars was in Moscow, ready to go to Chechnya. I feel so sad for the men and the families and also know that our story could have ended in a similar way. Many of the group who were holding us were traumatized and unstable in their minds. We were always living on a knife edge but had the chance to escape.

Rain, rain, rain; as January 1999 comes around we feel starved of sunlight and head for the Maldives. Neither of us has been accustomed to basking for hours on beaches, turning our bodies every ten minutes like roasting chickens on a spit, but we appreciate it so much now. One night there is a barbecue on the beach and we are entertained by three moustachioed strolling players. They start singing a Gypsy King number, the very same that used to blast out of the tinny tape recorder while I was being raped. Jon and I look at each other. 'I'm going to make a new memory for this song, change the energy,' I say, leaping onto the table and dancing, barefoot and wild.

We haven't forgotten our promise to wed and we pick 5 April, which happens to be Easter Monday, the day after celebrating the resurrection of Christ. Rather appropriate, since we feel resurrected ourselves! It happens as we had planned in the carpet room massaging each other's feet in the near darkness lit only by a pencil-thin ray of natural light.

The church service takes place in St Mary's, Litton, a small village church in the Mendips, Somerset where my grandfather was vicar. My uncle conducts the service, a cousin plays the organ, Ashok gives me away, Ben is best man. Jon's dad makes the wedding cake. Another cousin makes all the food for the reception in the village hall. Old friends in the village arrange the flowers in the church and serve the food.

A 1930s ivory satin wedding dress from a secondhand shop fits me perfectly. Jon wears a cream silk suit made for my grandfather in China in 1932 by a Mr Jelly Belly. To top it all, we meet Ted who owns a fleet of vintage cars. Ted has been helping the Chernobyl children so he is very interested in our story and he lends us a 1937 Lagonda for the day with himself as chauffeur for a wedding present.

Ashok and I set off in the Lagonda and on the way through the village we see my godmother and her husband scurrying along. They stick out their thumbs and we give them a lift on the tailboard – a nice spontaneous arrival. I link arms with Ashok and walk up the aisle, holding back the tears. A beautiful service includes favourite hymns and words from the writings of Kahlil Gibran and Nelson Mandela. With a friend I sing a duet of Pie Jesu, dedicated to all our friends in Chechnya, especially the children. One of those friends is here – Adlan Adaev, whose family were so hospitable to us.

After all those hours in captivity planning sandwiches and working out who to invite, our wedding day has become a reality. It seems like a closure in many ways, a closure to our previous courting days, being chaperoned by four armed guards. The ceremony is great – there are no dry eyes. At the reception we barely get anything to eat, talking and talking to relatives and friends. After a windy journey home in the Lagonda we find we have no key to the house. (It gives me an odd feeling to be locked out rather than locked in.) So we walk to a friend's house down the street in our full wedding gear.

Reunion with Valentin, 19 May 1999

On 13 November 1998 Chris Hunter had rung us to say that Valentin was released, we danced a little jig and drank another Guinness, how fantastic!

Six months later Chris Hunter, Jon and I have a meeting at the Houses of Parliament to discuss ways of raising money for the Centre for Peacemaking and Community Development. We have invited Valentin Vlasov to London and he's staying in a Russian Embassy flat. After the meeting we have half an hour to get to Holland Park to meet Valentin; excitement mounts and the Circle Line's not working! We hail a taxi but we're still half an hour late. I'm scrabbling in my bag to pay the taxi and can see Valentin on the pavement with his bodyguard. Jon takes over the paying and I tumble out onto the pavement.

I give Valentin a big hug and his eyes shine with warmth; the deep groove in his forehead has disappeared. We walk around Holland Park, decked in all the glorious colours of spring, reminiscing on our time together in our concrete oven. While savouring the smell of the roses, the vivid greens illuminated by the sunlight, the feel of the gentle breeze on our cheeks, we remember what it was like to live in a soup of stale air. He dips a hand into his breast pocket and pulls out a carefully folded piece of cloth. As he opens it out I see it is the birthday card I had stitched for him in the King's Chamber; I am deeply moved.

It seems strange to meet Valentin in England, yet not strange, for we got to know him quite well even though we had no common language. Valentin and his bodyguard are smartly dressed; he is an important man. We spend the next days entertaining him on that small island that he didn't want to visit (too boring!). Appropriately (because of Valentin's naval history) we went on the Thames and to the Naval Museum. Here we are being tourists together in London and there we were being hostages together, in that small concrete box, our state with no name, me elected as mayor.

Chris interprets while Valentin tells us that he was Yeltsin's special envoy to the North Caucasus when he was captured and one of his jobs was to keep his eyes and ears open for news about us. Well, he found us! We ask him how he got on after we left. He was kept in the same place until he was released on 13 November. The couple got bored of feeding him a variety of food and presented him with four fried eggs in the morning with a loaf of bread and four boiled eggs at night with yet another loaf of bread. Eventually they even gave up the evening meal and wouldn't renew the radio batteries, or his candle when it had burnt out. Power failures were still common so he spent some time in the dark. The weather got a lot colder and he was thankful for the clothes we had left behind, especially the socks that Jon had so painstakingly patched, as his slippers had disintegrated and they only replaced them with a pair of undersized galoshes. His eye infection worsened and they would not give him eyedrops. After he was released the doctor told him if his eye had gone without treatment for another month the infection would have spread into his brain with fatal results. The day before his release a masked man came down and told him they were going to shoot him. Valentin had one request – to be shot in the open air. The next day they dressed him up in combat uniform and led him blindfold out of the room. He was taken to a clearing in the forest and his mask taken off. The clearing was full of men in combat uniform. He was left in the back of a car and suddenly realized there was a machine gun lying next to him. Of course the thought of suicide entered his head, but he let it pass. Eventually, without explanation, they drove him away, changed cars three times and arrived at the Ingush–Chechen border and freedom.

We go to tea with the Russian ambassador, joined by my mother and sister. Valentin stands up and says how grateful he is to Jon and me for our courage and fortitude and for helping him survive. He has come to understand the wisdom of not remonstrating with our captors and also to understand the reasons why they kidnapped us. He says the leaders who call for war have no understanding of the suffering that war brings. Laughing, he recounts how in the first weeks of captivity he used to kill all the flies and then began to understand why we did not, that every insect has a right to live and it wasn't their fault for being a noisy fly!

He asks me if I still do all the exercises and I tell him I have been rather lazy! He still practises the qigong and the breathing techniques we taught him and is teaching his colleagues. He salutes our way as peaceful warriors and we salute the courage and faith he showed and his honesty. His whole body emanates gentleness and love. I thought of the saying, 'A man who has the wisdom and power to change himself will find the strength and energy to change the world around him.'

We organize a tour around the House of Commons the next day. Chris arrives with his family and Adlan, having just received an MBE for services to the Centre for Peacemaking and Community Development. We have champagne on the terrace. Then we take Valentin and his bodyguard plus a Russian/English dictionary on a boat trip down the Thames to Greenwich. As we chug through the brown waters Valentin's phone rings; it is Stepashin, the Russian Prime Minister who helped in gaining Valentin's release. 'Priviet's (greetings)' all round.

The next day we take Valentin and his bodyguard out to a restaurant for a farewell meal. We invite Tom and Georgina de Waal. Tom was reporting in the Caucasus during our time in captivity and wrote a book with Carlotta Gall about the 1994–96 war called *Chechnya: a small victorious war*. They both speak Russian and act as interpreters for Jon, Valentin and me. They find it astonishing how much we don't know about each other's lives after living together for five months, because of the lack of language communication. We could sense each other's moods and sometimes thoughts, knew each other's body language, but didn't have enough language for abstract conversations. Also, silence was important. I think we all felt a sense of privacy was necessary for us to have some space of our own, even if only in our minds.

News of Little Star

In August 1999 we hear news that the Russians are accumulating more and more tanks and other weapons of war on the borders of Chechnya. Their government's nose was bloodied the first time and they want vengeance. The bombing starts again in September. We met the Little Star team in Norway in June. The centre was flourishing and we talked about future plans. Now we hear that the Little Star Centre had to close because it was getting too dangerous to work and many families were fleeing, including all our colleagues and friends. The situation is chaotic and so desperately sad. The Chechens were just beginning to feel they could restart their lives and believe in a peaceful future. As one of the team wrote, 'it was like living in a labyrinth of frightening uncertainty.' Then I hear an extraordinary story. Two of the team, Yakha and Natasha, were in Ingushetia looking for somewhere to shelter and were resting on a bench in a small park at the end of a hot exhausting day. They were discussing moving to Rostov when Mourad walked by and recognized them. He was a co-coordinator of the Centre for Peacemaking and Community Development in Ingushetia. He took them to the office and they managed to talk to CPCD director Chris Hunter in Moscow and discussed working with the refugees in Ingushetia. The psychologists found a house to rent and gradually all the former team came together through word of mouth.

The main focus of the project was to set up mobile groups to provide psychosocial help for children in refugee tent camps and temporary settlements. This programme could no longer be called a rehabilitation programme as there was nothing to rehabilitate to, so the name was changed to the Little Star psychosocial programme. The team met some of the children who had been at Little Star and found they were coping better than the others. One of them, Jansoor, the brilliant dancer who had had his hand blown off, said he still did the qigong exercises. Jon and I start raising funds and awareness by holding a peace concert and giving talks.

The Caucasus revisited, March 2000

Chris invites us to attend a Little Star seminar in the Caucasus. Jon is working but I decide to fly down to Sochi with two people who will be teaching techniques to release trauma. We stay in a sanatorium run on Soviet lines.

In the canteen, they play music that makes me shiver. I've heard this Russian pop before, sitting watching black mould on a blue wall, making patterns with my mind to pass the long hours in the 'Bleak House'. I can feel the effects of the recent war trauma on my friends and it touches on my own buried trauma. I start feeling pressure between my brows as I did before being raped, and the herpes erupts again. I need to cry but I don't want to create more stress for them, especially when it is obvious they all feel personally responsible for what happened to us. I teach them some of the techniques we used to survive. I don't feel any of my own trauma when I teach, it's like stepping out of my body into a different place, a place where all is well.

After the seminar I travel with Chris and Radima, the translator, on a train to Nalchik in Kabardino Bulkaria to attend a peace-building seminar. I look out at the sides of the mountains soaring above us in the twilight. As it gets darker the mountains seem to loom closer and I feel vulnerable, perhaps because we are heading towards Chechnya. We arrive in Nalchik at 4 a.m., to a smell of stale burning. I look out of the window; a train is standing next to ours, with broken windows, a scorched interior and burnt paintwork. By the reflected light from our train windows I make out the lettering on the side: 'Moscow to Grozny', a chilling reminder of the ongoing conflict. We travel in a cold, rather ancient bus with steamed-up windows. I rub away the condensation and peer into the darkness; I can just make out the outline of some hills silhouetted against the lightening sky. I'm thinking of the Chechen freedom fighters hiding in similar hills only a hundred miles away. How cold, stiff-limbed and miserable they must be feeling; maybe not even having a fire to warm themselves by in case of detection. I mention my thoughts to Radima and she tells me she is not sorry for the fighters – they are almost as much to blame for the lack of peace and stability as the Russian government. Most of the Chechen people, she says, are tired of not having homes, food or jobs, and most of all of living in a constant state of fear.

The seminar starts and a couple of young men from the 'Voice of the Mountains' youth group (Laman Az) arrive a day late having been held up at the border for two days simply because they are young Chechen men. They are unshaven and pale and have lost some of the joyous bonhomie and hope of a bright future that I'd sensed in 1997 when they thought the war was over for good. Now they collect information about the survival needs of the refugees.

I enjoy the days, learning about peace-building strategies and meeting all the young people. At night it is a different story. Listening into the dark, alert to every small sound. One night someone's knocking in the corridor, knocking and knocking, I never hear why. Another night there's gunshot in the distance and I hear a police siren. A little later a car purrs to a halt outside our building. My heart's drumming against my rib cage, armpits prickling with sweat. I'm looking for ways to escape. There's a small balcony four storeys from the ground – no chance there. In the wardrobe? Or on top curled up like a cat? Or the old favourite, under the bed? There is no escape. I breathe slow and deep, willing my heart to calm down, telling myself I am safe. I know there are two guards on duty day and night but fear has no trouble seeping in to my consciousness like damp.

On the last day we do an exercise on listening which involves thinking of a problem that's troubling us and talking about it to our partner while they listen in silence. The only problem I can think of is the stress I am feeling. As I speak I feel the tears bubbling up. I tell my partner how I felt in Sochi and about my sleepless nights here. I realize I have not been admitting the existence of my trauma, even to myself. Now I honour myself by allowing the tears to take the tension away.

Back in Moscow Chris and I have a brief meeting with Valentin Vlasov. We exchange gifts, I give him a small heart-shaped candle with a relief of a white dove flying on the top, a symbol of our joint freedom. When he is unwrapping it he jokingly asks if it's soap, remembering how important soap was to our comfort in those hot sweaty times. His eye looks much better than in the previous May. He asks about Jon and we laugh about our time in captivity together. I'm glad our friendship survived the ordeal.

Ongoing work with the Centre for Peacemaking and Community Development

From the beginnings of Little Star in Grozny, CPCD grew into a well-established international entity employing around 400 people in its range of programmes in the North Caucasus. Until recently I went out to the Crimea twice a year to take part in a teaching/retreat seminar for the 60 Little Star psychologists and counsellors. Unfortunately, by 2006 CPCD had to curtail many of its activities including those of Little Star because of financial difficulties.

At the time of writing, the situation in Chechnya remains terrible. The Russian government claims the area is reasonably peaceful and that the process of rebuilding has started in earnest. It provides some basic services such as pensions, electricity and gas and has set up a functioning education system. It has withdrawn many of its troops from the republic, ceding day-to-day running to the Kremlin-backed government made up of Chechens. But fighting, ambushes, assassinations and abductions take place on a regular basis; there is also widespread corruption and misallocation of resources.

Anna Politkovskaya, a Russian journalist who was very critical of the way the Russian government has dealt with Chechnya, was assassinated on 7 October 2006 while writing an article that started, 'After two wars of independence, the Russian-backed forces are torturing a whole generation of young Chechens to try and restore order in the troubled north Caucasus region.' The Kremlin-backed government made up of Chechens maintains a rule of fear. The abduction of innocent boys and young men as possible terrorists and the beatings and electric shock torture she described we have heard about from our Chechen friends.

One small flame of hope is the presence of 'Daimokh', a Chechen children's dance ensemble. One of the images we will always associate with Chechnya is people, especially children, dancing. Between the wars Chris met up with a Chechen dancer/choreographer, Ramzan Akhmadov, who told him how he was gathering children who had nothing to do but play in the rubble and risk being blown up by mines, and teaching them to dance. 'It gives them a purpose and they don't take up bad habits,' he said. Chris found funds to rent a rehearsal space and buy costumes and musical instruments, but then the bombing began again and the dance troupe dispersed with their families. Ramzan managed to locate a lot of them after the bombing had stopped in 2000. He found some in refugee camps, some in cellars and half-ruined tower blocks in Grozny. Now a hard core of 35 children from the age of 7 to 15 train in Grozny in the bomb-damaged rehearsal space. Ramzan named the ensemble 'Daimokh' (our land).

The children make award-winning tours around Europe. In 2001 Jon and I met them at an international conference in The Hague. We watched them rehearsing and the tears poured down our faces. It was the first time we had been in contact with any Chechen children and it reminded us of watching them dance in Grozny. The dignity, grace and ecstatic energy with which they performed was breathtaking. They gave of their whole being. After the performance the 2000-strong audience were on their feet, cheering, clapping and crying. As Ramzan had written on a smashed plaque in their ruined rehearsal room, 'A lightfooted graceful dancer is a joy to himself and others.'

Who were our captors?

We will never know for certain who our captors were but our impression was they were a group of comrades from the war, who had no form of livelihood and were looking for ways of making money, of which one was to kidnap foreign aid workers. We think they were a small group who, by chance, had learnt of the existence of Chris and the house where we all stayed. Thus the first man kicked open our bedroom door and shouted 'Chris! Chris!' I don't think they had much money and needed to turn to a bigger group for help, particularly in financing mediators and finding us 'safe' houses. We heard afterwards that our kidnapping was the forerunner of a spate of kidnappings and often hostages were sold on to different groups. Perhaps our group was absorbed by the bigger one as we did see three of the 'fab four' again in 'The One-Night Stand'.

After we were released we heard that the leader of the large group was probably Arbi Buryev, a known Chechen warlord who was killed in a battle with the Russian army a couple of years later. Seeing his photo sent a shiver down my spine and, although I don't think we met him, I feel he was involved. In the year 2000 Scotland Yard came to visit us with some photographs of capured Chechen men who may have been involved in our kidnapping and there was one that we recognized, the commander of 'The Base'. There was no mistaking his broad fresh face, blue eyes and ruddy complexion. We were asked if we wanted to go and testify at his trial. We decided not to, partly because of the added stress for ourselves and also because he had shown us kindness. Later we heard he was tortured and killed in prison.

20

Surviving in Freedom

'How did you feel having your freedom taken away from you for 14½ months?' we are often asked, and I think of Valentin's comment when we were discussing 'The King's Chamber' as our small independent state: 'Freedom is a state of mind.' So true. Yes, many freedoms were taken away, the freedom to move, to make choices, to sniff fresh air; but I still had the freedom to think and feel what I wanted, to create whole land-scapes in my mind. Captivity forced us to use our imagination, to rely on our inner resources. Even within the pressure cooker of stress I found moments of great peace. Now we have the freedom to move and make choices but where is the time to sit and smile in quiet contemplation? It takes a huge amount of discipline to create empty space, to not answer the telephone or think about the washing up!

Certainly when we were in captivity I grieved most days for the loss of that day, not being free to walk under the sky or have freedom to choose what to eat. In that place of isolation and deprivation I thought what a joy it would be to sit in a traffic jam on the motorway surrounded by fellow human beings in a rain storm. Maybe for a year or two after being released I still felt the loss of time, of contact with our families. But in some ways it brought us closer.

Prayer was the only link we had with our families; just being able to think of them and send our love and know that they would be doing the same gave us the strength to carry on. We have always had belief that energy follows thought and some of the synchronistic happenings, like the use of purple ribbons for our campaign while we were dreaming and seeing purple in our minds and the rape dreams that Mum and some other friends had, makes this belief stronger. I think our own prayers of love for our captors had the effect of changing the energy of a situation, perhaps even changing their mentality. Often when one guy had been

270

treating us badly the next guy on duty would offer us a biscuit or take off the manacles.

There was always something that gave us the edge of faith in humanity. We'd get to the point of thinking, we're not being treated like human beings, and why should it happen to us? Then the power of prayer would take us back to feeling yes, there is humanity, they are human – they're just wounded. We certainly knew that our families were praying for us, and in many ways that was the strength that kept us going. During the prayer ceremony we formalized, our awareness of the people who were praying for us grew and there were many times during the last six months of our captivity when I personally felt the power of prayer was keeping me awake. So many people were praying for us the intensity was almost palpable.

My belief system was well established before I was captured, and proved to be very helpful in keeping me sane and healthy so I don't feel I changed much in that respect. Physically my stamina was very low after coming out. At first I didn't notice because of the wave of euphoria and projected love; then, after a couple of months, I had to take a prolonged rest. In the first months I also felt fear; sometimes waking in the night, my heart pumping, imagining the 'fab four' stealthily climbing through our bedroom window, or walking down the street being aware of men watching me – what were their motives? I am sad at these reactions, which show that my trust in mankind had been betrayed just a little. Luckily I have many wonderful male friends, including Jon, and over the years I feel less vulnerable and more trusting.

Although I didn't have the freedom to write in captivity, except for a week or two in the Pink Crystal room on the little round paper badges, my desire to do so carried on. Nearly every day I would run back over the recent events in my mind, compartmentalizing them into boxes. It gave me something to focus on and had the effect of rationalizing our existence. In freedom, I use writing as a healing process. But in 2001 an itchy rash appeared over my body and the tears wouldn't stop flowing. I visited an acupuncturist friend who said 'You've been holding on, "stiff upper lip" and all that; it's time to surrender, let go and allow the trauma to come out, allow your nerves to heal.' So I did little writing, cancelled talks, and sat in silence, listening and watching the birds for five months.

After five years gently healing from living in a pressure cooker of hostage stress, another manifestation of the trauma revealed itself and I wrote . . .

I watch my breath, that breathing, that never ending in, out, in, out, expand, contract, expand, contract. My elbows touch the cold edge of the table, I place a shirt to shield them from the hard chill. Me, in my body, the clock turned upside down but I still hear the tick, like my heartbeat never ending . . . until . . . death. Death, my greatest fear? Why so? I've always prided myself on believing death is just a transition, another state of existing for us as 'energy beings' to experience. No great big deal, but the pain and suffering we feel in our physical bodies that so often heralds death, yes, I fear that, I'm just a swiss roll of spiralling anger and sadness, layer after layer.

'Unfortunately the biopsy shows it was a melanoma cancer. Do you know what that is?' The doctor continued. 'Oh shit, yes, I know what melanoma is, my father died of it,' I replied.

Cancer, that strange inner enemy, a group of renegade cells creating a discordance in the symbiotic harmony of the body. How could I trip through life so gaily and not know about this physical disturbance? I probably do have the genetic predisposition for my body to grow melanoma cells but they will only grow if they have the right manure. The manure of trauma – physical, emotional, mental.

My intuition tells me that the cause of my own melanoma arose out of my experience in Chechnya. I'm good at 'holding on', at 'surviving', but all the tension, the unsaid anger and grief imprinted in my cellular structure has to find an expression, a form of release – in this case, cancer. Now I feel I have to forgive myself for not being able to 'let go' enough to keep myself totally healthy.

I feel I am being challenged to understand the nature of my own traumas and find a way to release and let go of emotional and mental patterns that cause physical illness and dis-ease in my body. I have to examine my belief systems. During captivity I always had a sense that there was a purpose to our being there and that beneath all the daily crap heaped upon us, all was well. I felt I had some sense of control within our constrained circumstances – even with a gun pointing at us I was certain that I wouldn't die lying or without dignity. I felt if I was physically tortured to such a degree that I could take no more, I would be able to wilfully shut down and leave my body as I had managed to take my mind away while being raped.

Now I have to look in the mirror and acknowledge the anger, acknowledge that illness and death may happen when I don't feel ready. Acknowledge my resistance to surrendering, letting go of any control I thought I had. It helps me to think in the simplest terms – I am born, I live, I die. But it's my choice how I live, how I deal with joy and, this is the difficult bit, how I deal with pain. I remember choosing to look at life from the point of view of love rather than fear from an early age but it is easy to get sucked into judgement, comparison, competitiveness, feelings of betrayal, all the trappings of fear that boost the ego into believing there is a separation between me and others, my surroundings and the here and now.

Having seen at first hand the effects of war on people's psyche, how the 'fab four' had changed from being law abiding citizens to paranoid criminals, I wonder when humanity will learn that using violence never solves a conflict. We all have conflict within us, but there are many ways of dealing with it. If we had a greater understanding of the energy behind conflict and how to transform that energy in a creative, positive way rather than a violent negative way maybe the world would change and violence be a thing of the past.

In one sense I don't know how being in captivity has changed me, because I am that change. What would I have been like if I hadn't been through that captivity? What would I be doing today? How can I know? Certainly I feel more tolerant than before and can see how conflicts arise by people taking up arms rather than sitting at a table talking to each other. There are basic responses to threat, the adrenalin rises, you run or raise your fists ready to fight. In captivity there was no option to run and we chose not to fight so I feel all the adrenalin stimulated at that time stagnated in my muscle structure causing trauma and stress.

I didn't choose writing as a way of healing, so I have spoken my thoughts and Camilla has transcribed them. At first I didn't want to go back there at all – I couldn't face the anger. I'm a practical person, I need to be doing things, preferably building interesting ecological structures. But at first I found it hard to do much at all, I had little stamina and a lot of pain in my back muscles. I got so frustrated that after a year of blanking my emotions my mind erupted in confusion and turmoil. I wanted to scream for help but didn't know who to ask, so I shouted out of my bedroom window 'Help!' very loudly. The next day I left the house without telling anyone where I was going and ended up in London. I wanted to get a bus to Scotland where I had a friend who I thought could help me but the last coach had gone. So I wandered the streets all night disoriented and confused. I saw all the different forms of trauma that humanity is dealing with in the faces of the homeless, the drug and alcohol abusers. I saw the combination of escape mechanisms they were using to cope with the trauma of life. In seeing this I came to terms with the turmoil in myself and the next morning I made my way home.

I felt I couldn't ask Camilla to help me. We had relied on each other and helped each other so much in captivity that in freedom we had got to the point of saturation where we needed to take our own paths of healing. It tends to be hard to relate the 'coming-out experience' to anything that anyone can understand, apart from other ex-hostages. It is, understandably, beyond the realm of most people's comprehension as it is not part of their experience. What you need is an empathic ear, someone you can share your trauma with who will not give you a 'there, there' or a quick pat on the back, but just acknowledge it, and listen to your story without judgement.

After spending 24 hours for 14½ months in such close proximity we had to find our own space and spend time apart to stop co-dependency happening and keep our relationship healthy. The essence of our relationship is honesty, being able to communicate to each other about anything without fear of a defensive reaction. We look for the roots of any frustration, or any irritation or guilt, and talk about it. Watching Jon struggle to release his anger was very distressing but I knew I could not help; all I could do was let him know I loved him. When he disappeared without a word I just had to trust he would find a way through the pain.

One thing I found strange in our freedom was the way people treated us as special. I could not understand this. For me, we were ordinary people caught up in an extraordinary situation. We all experience trauma of one kind or other; it seems to be part of the human experience. OK, our trauma was prolonged in its intensity but no matter how small or how big you write pain it still says 'Pain'. It will always fill the conscious part that recognizes that pain. It wasn't until much later in my return to freedom that I started to discover that shock and trauma go hand in hand. If it's an extreme that the body can't cope with it'll put it on the back shelf for you to deal with later and as life goes on, if you receive more trauma, these will stack up, waiting for the day when the pressure is off, when you stop running to the office or to catch a train. I've had to deal with suppressed anger and tears to do with my divorce which happened 22 years ago. It's taken me a while to know that this is what is happening; sometimes you are just in it and can't take yourself into the observer mode. At other times I do have the clarity and ability to step back and become the observer, watching myself and everybody else.

Because of the way I dealt with my trauma, suppressing the anger and grief, feeling too afraid to express it, it became internalized and self-destructive and very exhausting. The suppression of emotions at that end of the scale dims the top end as well, so that the areas of joy, love and beauty become dulled and, at times, my spectrum of life became a bit of a mono-tone, almost as though it was in captivity. So the lesson for myself was, and is, to open up to the anger, pain and grief and let go, allowing the beauty in, the love in, letting all the colours of life flow in.

How do I release the anger? What methods do I use? It has taken several years to understand the complex mechanism of my psyche. Initially if I find things irritating I know that it is a sign that I am tired or there's some anger brewing below the surface wanting to express itself. Sometimes anger erupts when I get frustrated with my own inadequacies or those around me. I try and catch it before it erupts by saying 'Hello anger, I recognize you,' and dive in and ask what it is about.

Tears don't come easily for me, although I know they often hide beneath the anger. If I am feeling safe and secure and my subtle emotional body hasn't been whipped by somebody's words recently and there's a trigger like a film that has strong emotional imagery, I find waves of tears washing up through my body, not necessarily manifesting as tears but if they do, gently leaking, trickling down my face. I am learning ways to cry, to heal, slowly, slowly, in my own way.

Both of us were put on trial to the point of execution so we saw each other stripped to our core. This has bonded us and because it was a journey that we travelled together we helped each other to share the burdens and help each other now to peel back the layers of trauma by recognizing each other's coping mechanisms and recognizing when we are strong enough to let go and heal.

Forgiveness and healing trauma go hand in hand. In a way we forgave each day by letting go of what had gone on yesterday and greeting each day as a new beginning. It helps to understand where the person you feel has done harm to you is coming from; then you can start letting go of the anger and the underlying grief, all part of the journey of forgiving. The worst thing that happened to me was the rape. In the end Paunch apologized and that made it easier for me to start forgiving him. But I do not condone or forgive the act of rape; it is one of the grossest forms of violation of a human being, an act born out of ignorance and misdirected sexual energy. Forgiving and forgetting are not synonymous. Of course you remember what happened and you can still forgive. For me, forgiveness is the key to inner peace but some people cannot forgive and it doesn't mean they are bad people. I feel we all need to be educated in what it is to be human, how we are beings of energy inside a physical vehicle and how we all have the same basic needs and emotions. Then there might be a chance that these abusive sexual and violent acts would not occur in our human society.

Forgiveness is a very personal journey and a journey I have decided to travel. While I go through the process of letting go and working towards forgiveness, thoughts occur to me of the losses I have incurred through bad health and missing time with my family and I feel anger towards my captors, the ones that denied me that access. Yet at other times I forgive them to the point that when they come to mind I feel no emotional charge. So I'd say I have to a large extent forgiven our captors and am clearing out all the minor resentments until that vessel is empty.

21

Still Breathing

So here I am now, still tapping away, a thin white curtain shielding my cancer-scarred arm from the bright sunlight. My body is now cancer-free but this shark-bite dent is like a war wound, a reminder of those 14½ months of extreme tension and suppressed emotions. I have been forced to look at the discords in myself and the discords in the world but I have no regrets about going to Chechnya. We brought some sunlight into the lives of those children and I have learnt so much through my own suffering.

Inspired by our work with the Chechen children I am now training to be a drama therapist. Exploring trauma experientially through the use of movement, art, music, metaphor and creative role-play can put us in touch with our own creative potential to heal ourselves. We always have a choice of how to deal with whatever we are faced with.

The captivity made me so aware of the fragility of life and how my happiness is interwoven with that of my family. The unconditional love and support they gave us throughout and the suffering we shared have strengthened our bonds. Ashok is now a young man, my son, my friend, starting his own travels through life and my hope is that all the joy and fear we have experienced will help to sustain and enrich his journey.

Over the last years I feel I have been slowly making up the lost time. Ben went to Australia then university after we came out so I had very little time to catch up with him. Only in the last year or so have we really got to know each other again and have been totally honest with each other, talking our anger, crying our tears and hugging each other, knowing that our love is still there. Why does it take so long to have the courage to speak our truth, to cry the tears of grief and to let the ones we love, know? Recently at a friend's funeral I heard that she had stuck a note on her fridge that said 'There is a certain type of love called maintenance, doing the washing up, filling the car with oil, making a cup of tea for a tired friend . . .' and I guess this is the place I seem to operate the best, maybe not necessarily seen or heard for a long time but maintaining things in the background.

I've got to this place where I'm attempting to touch the joy of all things: the joy of a traffic jam, listening to music, sitting in silence, hearing the birds sing in the early spring dawn, heavy rain falling. Just living life, being grateful for the moments of interaction with fellow human beings and understanding they carry thoughts in their minds very similar to mine. We are all the same at heart so why not try and . . .

Walk and touch peace every moment,
Walk and touch happiness every moment.
Each step brings a fresh breeze.
Each step makes a flower bloom.
Bring the earth your love and happiness.

(Thich Nhat Hanh, Vietnamese Buddhist monk)